THE WAY FORWARD

THE WAY FORWARD

*Master Life's Toughest Battles
and Create Your Lasting Legacy*

ROBERT O'NEILL
AND
DAKOTA MEYER

DEY ST.
An Imprint of WILLIAM MORROW

HarperCollins books may be purchased for educational, business, or sales promotional use. For information, please email the Special Markets Department at SPsales@harpercollins.com.

FIRST EDITION

Designed by Michelle Crowe

Background texture by Kues/Shutterstock, Inc.

Photograph of Robert O'Neill by Matt Heller

Photograph of Dakota Meyer by Meagan Littlefield

Library of Congress Cataloging-in-Publication Data has been applied for.

ISBN 978-0-06-299407-3

22 23 24 25 26 LSC 10 9 8 7 6 5 4 3 2 1

"I'm just a bad guy who gets paid to fuck up worse guys."
—*Deadpool*

"There is a time to think, and a time to act.
And this, gentlemen, is no time to think."
—*John Candy,* Canadian Bacon

CONTENTS

Prologue 1

PART ONE
PREPARATION

1   *American Boys*   9

2   *Taking Aim*   29

3   *Find Your Heroes*   49

4   *Leaving*   65

PART TWO
DUTY

5   *Drilling Down*   85

6   *Open Your Eyes*   103

7   *In the Shit*   127

8   *Choose to Connect*   143

9   *Praise*   159

10   *Homecoming*   179

11   *Recuperation*   201

12   *Build Your Circle*   221

13   *Be a Firefighter of Life*   241

Acknowledgments   265
Notes   269

THE WAY FORWARD

Prologue

ROB AND DAKOTA

The M18A1 Claymore mine is a marvel of simple ingenuity. At about eight and a half inches long and almost an inch and a half wide, it rests on four thin metal legs that fold down from the bottom like upside-down scissors. On the top, there's a sight for aiming it, and two detonator wells for the blasting cap or fuse to be inserted. Inside the olive-green case, there are about seven hundred steel bearings packed on top of a one-and-a-half-pound slab of the plastic explosive C4. When a Claymore is detonated, those steel bearings spray out in a fan. That explosion of steel is most effective at 50 meters, but they can hit an enemy at 250 meters away. At some point, every infantryman learns how to use it.

Claymores became part of the U.S. arsenal after World War II. They were developed as a defensive weapon, to be deployed against fast-moving infantry attacking in waves, as U.S. troops experienced in Korea. They require deliberation and purpose to detonate. International law only allows their use with an operator to set them off; they can't be triggered automatically, with a trip wire or pressure plate, to prevent civilians and other innocents being accidentally being maimed or killed. Also unlike conventional mines, they're directional, which means they can be aimed. To facilitate this, there's a very simple instruction in easy-to-read, raised letters on the front:

FRONT TOWARD ENEMY

In case it isn't obvious, those words are there to make sure that the mine is facing the right direction. With its range of 250 meters, you do not want to be on the wrong side of the Claymore when it is detonated. And so, in very straightforward words that can't be mistaken, the Army makes it almost impossible to make a mistake. But mistakes happen. They always do. So the Claymore is foolproofed in another way. The casing is curved, so that in the dark, its user can roll it against his or her forehead to determine which side is concave and which is convex, and place it accordingly facing forward. And just in case that's not enough, the rear of the case reads:

BACK

The instructions on the Claymore are useful on the battlefield, but they're also a simple approach to life out of combat. If you follow simple instructions and don't deviate, you'll avoid injury to yourself or those you love. Your weapon will face in the right direction. You'll keep your circle safe.

Similarly, this book is not a handbook for war or a guide to the thrill of combat. It's about the other things that happen before, during, and after fighting. It's about what gets you out of conflict unharmed and alive. It's about keeping calm and staying grounded. It's about facing your enemies. Enemies that are flesh and blood, and enemies that are not. Your thoughts. Your doubts. Your boredom. Your regrets.

There's a reason that the Claymore and its front-facing instructions have a kind of cult following within the armed services and have become a credo for us and thousands of other soldiers, on and off the battlefield. Its name is part of its mythology; it's named for the two-handed Scottish Claymore sword, wielded by the inventor's Highland ancestors to carve a path through invading enemies. The mine, as it exists today, was used with lethal effectiveness in Vietnam, and Special Forces carry a mini version of it on missions. Our hope is that this book will be as simple and instructive as those raised plastic letters. That this book, like the Claymore sword, will help cleave through the obstacles that stand in front of you. We also hope that humor is just as effective a weapon, and that you can laugh along the way.

ROB

Over the years that I was with the SEAL Teams, I developed some perspectives on how to live life, which is to say, *how to avoid being killed* over the course of more than four hundred missions. They're not complicated, and they're easy to remember. *Keep it simple. Follow the rules. Don't get sloppy. Do the best you can until you're finished, and then move on and don't look back. Face your adversary. Front toward enemy.*

I was introduced to Claymores during the land warfare phase of Basic Underwater Demolition/SEAL Training (BUD/S). We read about them during classroom training, we had tests on them, and we practiced with them on San Clemente Island, using inert Claymores. The dummy Claymores had blue plastic cases, which made them easy to distinguish from the live versions, which were olive drab.

Before I got my Trident, the Teams sent me off for a thirteen-week course called SEAL Tactical Training, or STT, around April 1997. After three weeks of dive training in Puerto Rico, we spent the rest of the time at Fort A. P. Hill in Northern Virginia. This consisted of all parts of land warfare: map and compass navigation, patrolling, shooting every weapon available to SEALs, as well as explosives training. A master chief named Frank Wagner ran the whole thing. He was a Vietnam vet, and his nickname was "Pig." I have no idea why Master Chief Wagner was called "Pig," but I do know this: he ran the place exactly how he wanted it.

Early on in the explosives/demolition course—maybe on the first day—he brought us into one of the classrooms, where he had us open up Claymores. He demonstrated with a flathead screwdriver how you pry off the cover to look inside. We looked closely at the honeycomb of steel balls, the layer of C4 behind it, the detonator wells, the sight on top. Then he ordered us out to the live range.

The range was the area at the fort where live explosives were set off. Parts were wooded, other parts were open fields and brush. He gathered the forty or fifty dudes there for the course around him in one of the open areas. Then he reached into his pocket and took out a block of C4. He cut it in two, handed one lump to me and another to a second student, and gave us both lighters. Then he told us to set them on fire.

Now, I had worked with Claymores and C4 before, back in BUD/S training. One of the first things you learn about C4 is that it's completely harmless without a rapid release of energy, such as a blasting cap. It looks like white Play-Doh and has the consistency of taffy, and it's about as dangerous, as long as there's no blasting charge to ignite it. You can cut it, you can pound on it, drop it, mold it into whatever shape you choose and it won't explode. Likewise, everyone knows that if you set C4 on fire, nothing will happen.

So this other dude and I stood there with the C4 in one hand and a lighter in the other, and Pig Wagner ordered us to put the flame to the C4. So I swallowed hard, spun the strike wheel to get a flame, and after a count of three, put the flame to the C4.

Pig Wagner didn't seem like a funny guy. He was kind of a hard-ass, and he didn't mind making us do things that were probably against the rules. We didn't think he had a sense of humor. As it turned out, he very much had a sense of humor. The other thing he had was a wireless detonator in his pocket, which was linked to a receiver connected to a five-pound charge of C4 that he had put on the ground about two hundred yards away, hidden by some trees. When I put the flame to the C4, he pushed the button at the same moment.

That motherfucker blew as loud as an artillery shell. Of course, no one expected this. The more collected guys just whipped their heads toward the trees. Others bolted, thinking the explosion was at their feet. Some hit the ground. Pig Wagner, naturally, thought this was the funniest thing he'd seen since the last time he did this to a bunch of new SEAL candidates. He laughed his ass off, then gave us five minutes to go change our shit-stained shorts and get back out on the range.

DAKOTA

We have a saying in the Marine Corps, an ethos that we live by, which is "locate, close with and destroy the enemy by fire and maneuver, or repel the enemy assault by fire and close combat." It's our mission. That's just what you do with life, the way you attack everything, every issue, every problem. Everything. You lean into it. You face it.

After I completed basic training at Parris Island, my next stop after graduation was the School of Infantry–East at Camp Geiger in North Carolina. SOI is a nine-week course where every Marine— from rifleman to machine gunner to antitank missile gunners— learns the basics of combat. After weeks of live-fire training and conditioning and classroom instruction, each Marine is slotted into their specialty and ordered to report to their respective units.

Claymores were part of the curriculum at the School of Infantry. It's a device that we know a lot about. Have I held Claymores? Absolutely. Have I set them up? Absolutely. Do I know the nomenclature about Claymores? Absolutely. My class went out to the live-fire range and watched an instructor set up and detonate one. In a demonstration at SOI, the cutout silhouettes of soldiers face the Claymore, which rested on the ground with sandbags piled on three sides. "Fire in the hole!" the instructor yelled three times, and when the mine went off, a big cloud of black smoke billowed out and the seven hundred bearings peppered the silhouettes like a colander. Enemies obliterated.

Front toward enemy is the absolute epitome of the approach that

I've taken in life. It's the way I took on enemy combatants on the battlefield, and it's the same way I take on life. I'm not someone to shy away from conflict. I'm all about facing it, leaning into it, and having the mind-set that I'm going to stay squared no matter what.

Since I left the Marines, the idea of front toward enemy has taken root in another part of my life that has nothing to do with Claymores. I remember when Tim Kennedy, one of my closest friends in Austin, invited me to meet him at Gracie Humaitá, which is a jujitsu school where he trains. Tim was Special Forces and is a former MMA fighter, and he doesn't fuck around. I figured that I would just watch one of his classes, get a feel for it, and see if it was something I'd like to try. Instead, I walked in and he threw a *gi* at me. "Go ahead and put it on," he said, "because you're gonna roll today."

I put the *gi* on and joined the class. I spent the next hour or so basically trying not to get killed. Every round, I would end up pinned or in a choke hold or facedown into the mat five or six times, tapping my sparring partner over and over to be let up, only to be taken down again a minute or two later.

Now, I roll a lot of jujitsu with my friends in Austin. Some of them are MMA fighters like Tim, some just like the conditioning, but all of them know the most basic aspect of grappling and martial arts. It didn't take me long to learn the most basic rule of jujitsu pretty quickly, which is that you can only win if you're facing your enemy. I've been a fighter my whole life, and this I know: never turn your back to anything you don't trust, whether it's an animal on the farm, or a guy sporting a knife or a gun. There's a reason that someone you trust will say, "I've got your back."

The back is that most vulnerable part of every human being. The moment an adversary is behind you, your chances of failure increase exponentially. Only when there's no more hope of winning a fight, when one person has bested another, does turning your back make sense. Because at that point, the only way out is to run, and you had better be fast enough to get away safely.

PART ONE

PREPARATION

1

AMERICAN BOYS

ROB

Don't Forget Where You Come From

You can barely hear yourself inside a Chinook helicopter when the cargo door is open. A CH-47 is a beast; it's a flying school bus. It's about as comfortable, too. With the cargo door closed and the ramp up, it's quieter inside, the roar of the rotors muted to where it becomes possible to focus, to think, to have a quiet conversation, or maybe just sleep.

We used CH-47s for nighttime missions in Iraq and Afghanistan. As we flew toward the sites where we would land and hike to our targets, I would sit and go over the mission in my head. Think about who I was going to kill that night. Shut out the background noise.

On a flight in 2010 where I was jumpmaster, the door was open and I couldn't hear myself think over the thunder of the rotors. The wind howled in my ears as I knelt on the ramp, holding on to one of the hydraulic jacks and looking forward for our drop zone ten thousand feet below. Below me, it wasn't razor-sharp peaks of the Hindu Kush mountains or the noisy sprawl of Jalalabad's streets and bazaars. Instead, I saw the richest hill on earth: Butte, Montana, my hometown.

As the Chinook thundered north, I could see hills dotted with sagebrush, and stands of ponderosa pines reaching up into Highland Mountains. I spotted my high school and then the campus of Montana Tech and the boxy HPER Complex, where I once shot 105 free throws in a row and learned to swim to become a Navy SEAL.

I looked closely at the familiar grid of streets and saw my father's ranch house on Bittersweet Drive and my mother's bungalow near East Middle School to the north. The wide mouth of the Berkeley Pit and the turquoise tailing pond came into view before we banked right across the East Ridge and over Saddle Rock, where the towering white statue of the Lady of the Rockies looked down over the city.

Then the Chinook slowed as we completed the wide circuit around the city and approached the airport. A dozen guys waited behind me, ready for the signal to hurdle themselves off the ramp into the sky over Butte. Somewhere two miles below, my mother and father waited, looking for our chutes. The pilot had turned on the green *go* light. I held up my finger in the air to show one minute to jump, then my thumb and index finger for thirty seconds. When it was time, I punched the outside of my thigh like you would in a game of "Rock, Paper, Scissors" then extended a "thumbs up." *Stand by.* Then I held my hand straight out from my chest, pointing out the door: the go signal. One by one, my guys launched off the ramp, tumbling toward the ground before stabilizing at terminal velocity.

And then it was my turn.

———————————

EVERYONE'S FROM SOMEWHERE, and my somewhere is Butte. It calls itself a city, but to me, it's a town. A tough-guy, mining town, I guess. The miners who helped build Butte in the late 1800s were born hard, had hard lives, and when they weren't underground digging for coal, they drank and fought, which made life hard for everyone around them, too.

Mine shafts go everywhere around and under Butte. Marriott

built a hotel there recently. I'm betting they did underground site surveys so that it didn't collapse into a hole. There was a brothel in town called the Dumas Brothel, which had a tunnel that went right down in a mine shaft, so that the miners could conveniently come up and visit the ladies on their lunch breaks. Crazy stuff.

Butte used to be a boomtown of a hundred thousand people, the biggest city between St. Louis in the east and San Francisco in the west. Now it has fewer than forty thousand. Gold and silver mines made Butte "the richest hill on earth." Later, it was copper. And it was copper, not gold, that gave Butte one of its lasting landmarks: the old Anaconda mine in the northwest corner of town, which also happens to be one of the biggest toxic waste sites in the country. It closed in 1982, but the hole that it left behind is colossal. That son of a bitch is two thousand feet deep and a mile and a half wide.

After Anaconda shut it down, the mine filled up with toxic water. Now it's the country's biggest Superfund site. Canadian geese land there and die in the water after they splash down. It's sort of a tourist attraction, and I don't know if that says more about the site or the tourists who come to see it. When I brought my wife, Jessica, up to Big Sky Ski Resort to the east, near Bozeman, she looked at the mountains. "My God, Montana is beautiful," she said, before adding, "Nothing like Butte."

You could say the mines gave Butte another landmark, though. A more personal touchstone. Get this: Butte is the most Irish town in America, as a percentage of population. No shit. Most of the miners came over from Ireland and brought St. Patrick his holiness with them.

In 1979, an electrician named Bob O'Bill came up with the idea of building a shrine to the Virgin Mary because his wife was dying of cancer. She recovered, but he pledged to build it anyway. Instead of being a five-foot-high statuette in his backyard, it became a ninety-foot monument that now presides over the entire city. He acquired some land on the East Ridge, right on top of the Continental Divide.

I'm talking 8,500 feet above sea level. I was about three when construction began, and it wasn't finished until 1985. It's a big-ass statue. She's called the Lady of the Rockies, and she stands over the ridge with arms outstretched, palms up. She glows at night, lit up with white and green spotlights. When you're in downtown Butte, "the flats," all the east-west city streets seem to end at her feet. When I looked up and saw her, she seemed to be looking down over the city and blessing the hard-luck Irish miners with her upturned hands, always visible from the sky and the ground. As far as I was concerned, the whole world was Irish Catholic, and she was watching over all of us. Sometimes my mom would drop us off at the trailhead at the bottom of the mountain, and we'd hike up to her. She'd grow taller and bigger the closer we got, until we stood at the foot of her flowing robes and looked up at her, as majestic to us as the Statue of Liberty.

For me, Butte felt like the center of the universe. The biggest ball game was right before Christmas when Butte Central played Butte High School in basketball. If you were lucky, you got to go over the mountain to Bozeman or maybe northwest to Missoula and watch the Montana Grizzlies play the Montana State Bob Cats. That was the big time. Butte didn't have a lot to hang its hat on. It did have Evel Knievel, who was from there. No shit.

Both my mom and dad grew up in Butte. There were four kids total in my family: two sisters and me and my brother. I went to the same high school as my parents had, Butte Central, which was the private Catholic high school. It was split up into Boy's Central and Girl's Central. My dad went to the University of Montana right out of high school on a basketball scholarship, and my mom went to Montana Tech for her first two years, which is where I ended up going to college. Then she transferred to UM to be with my dad. She became a math teacher, because she enjoyed solving problems. That's where I get that from. A lot of combat is solving problems. It's slowing down, calming down, and finding solutions.

Now, some people assume I must have been a badass growing up.

I was never a badass. I didn't beat people up when I was kid; in fact, I was probably beat up more than I did the beating. My childhood wasn't packed with martial arts classes and hard-hitting football. It was filled with jokes and laughter. This originated with my dad, who let us watch *Trading Places,* John Candy's *Delirious,* and other movies like that. Totally inappropriate for kids. I held on to his sense of humor, too. I always want to make people laugh and keep morale high. That's good for families. It's also good for soldiers, and it was an essential element for my teams. You'll hear some of the funniest things in the most dire situations in the middle of combat. Like when I first arrived in Afghanistan, I assumed everything horrible that I heard on the news was true: suicide bombers everywhere, gunfights in the mountains, and land mines all over the place. As we were walking in the mountains to try to rescue Marcus Luttrell, I asked my boss, "What if we walk through a minefield?" Without missing a beat, he said with a completely straight face: "It'll be fine. Just plug your ears."

Growing up, Butte felt like the hometown of every kid in America who wants to be somewhere bigger or more exciting. You think that just because someone's from Phoenix, Arizona, they're better than you. Or because someone's from Chicago, they're better. It gives you a little bit of an inferiority complex.

I always knew there was something else out there. I had to get to Great Lakes, Illinois, to go to U.S. Navy boot camp to see other scared kids just like me and realize that everyone's pretty much the same. I recall two dudes who left Los Angeles, one from Watts and one from South Central, in order to get away from gangs. Another person from Westchester County, New York, told me he couldn't stand it. Everyone has to get out of somewhere.

I try to get home about every two months. My mom and dad are still there, although amicably divorced, and I have to go back and check to see that my dad is behaving himself. My brother, Tommy, is still there, too. He has a morning drive-time radio show. Everyone in Butte knows him because he reads the school hot lunch menu every day. It's completely ridiculous. He gets to tell the kids if they're having *beef ole'* for lunch that day, which is essentially chili and Fritos. I think he's probably better known in Butte than I am.

———■———

BACK WHEN I BROUGHT MY SQUADRON to my hometown for a training mission in 2010, my team was at the highest point for morale. Especially in ███████████—my squadron—because we hadn't lost anybody in combat since I had gotten there. We've been doing really well and we just finished a deployment.

When I was putting together training trips for my team, I thought, Man, I'd love to go home on the government's dime and bring a bunch of buddies up to show them the town. So I sold it as a high-altitude skydiving trip for about a dozen of us. Butte's already a mile above sea level, so by the time you're in the CH-47, we're about three miles up and that air is thin. When you're landing a jump at five thousand feet, your parachute is going really fast and you need to know how to do it.

I knew a former Air Force Pararescue guy who owns a company in Butte called The Peak. And I knew we could probably get an airplane up for free from the Air Force Base in Great Falls. And then I get the government to pay for our room and board, and I know the guy who owns a hotel, so I can put up with some good business. The trip was about two weeks long.

So, no shit, there we were, two miles above my hometown. High-altitude jumps can be hard if you don't take it seriously or get complacent. There is a lot going on and it's easy to get cocky or overzealous or just plain forgetful. You have to calculate exactly how to get upwind of the drop zone, get the correct altitude to start your downwind portion, and then correct your "crosswind" portion so that you can turn and go into the wind just before you slow down to land. If you screw something up and come in too hot, you burn in, and that usually means that you die. If you "auger in," you hit hard and hurt yourself badly, but you'll survive. On one of the jumps, one of my guys augered in right in front of my family. He slammed into the ground in a big cloud of dust, then jumped up and pretended he was fine because he was in front of everybody. We have a saying: "If you're going to be stupid, you better be hard." Once we got back into the CH-47, and after we got into the air far enough from the crowd, he looked at me in pain. "Oh, that fucking sucked," he groaned.

As jumpmaster, I went last. I could hear the guys all around me laughing and talking, and when it was my turn to go, I got out there on the ramp. We were hovering almost directly above the house where I grew up. I watched the guys below me, shooting nose-first toward the ground. The sky was wide and huge over me, and below Montana spread to the east and west on both sides of the Continental Divide. I got up from my knees and ducked under the aft fuselage and launched outward and down, and as the wind rushed against my face at 120 miles an hour, I looked toward the streets and buildings below, getting closer and closer as my hometown rushed up to meet me.

We'd jump during the day and at night go out to drink at Maloney's, a bar on North Main Street. It's got a big shamrock on the awning over the door, and Irish flags hanging over the bar. It boasts Jell-O shots for a dollar and nude centerfolds plaster the walls and ceiling inside the men's bathroom. Not exactly PC, but hardly a surprise, either.

When my guys and I went to Maloney's, something would happen almost every night. The regular patrons would see a bunch of new guys in their bar, and after a few drinks would talk some shit. Pretty soon everyone was on their feet, ready to go. But there's a big difference between being a tough guy and a technical fighter trained in close-quarters combat. When one of the regulars would start to get in the face of one of my guys, I would try to tell them as gently as I could, "Don't do this. You don't want to do this."

We really didn't get in fights. It went more like this: tough guys would try something, and then my guys would knock them out. Boom.

"I told you not to do that," I'd say afterward.

One of our SEALs sent a tough guy to the hospital, and he showed up at the bar the next night again with his jaw wired shut. What's great about Butte is you can knock someone out and then help them up and have a drink with them. We didn't have a drink with the guy with the broken jaw, though, after one of his buddies grumbled, "Maybe someone should pay his medical bill," and one of my guys cracked up and said, "Maybe someone should learn to fight." Don't get me wrong, guys in Butte are tough and everyone has a "puncher's chance" of landing a good one, so if you visit, don't get too cocky.

We didn't spend *all* our nights at bars. We were there to train, and not just for high-altitude skydiving. Montana was a great place to train for disappearing into the mountains. Often, during missions in Iraq and Afghanistan, we would drop several klicks (kilometers) away, hump it to the target, do the job, and then cut out. But other times, we'd camp in the mountains for days at a hide site so that we could reach a hard-to-get-to target off in the middle of fuck knows where. And one of the ways you can get around in the mountains in Afghanistan is on horseback or on mules. That's how the mujahideen drove out the Russians; they could fade into the mountains and move around on horseback. The United States even provided them with mules to do it; some of the mules that went to the muj came from farms in central Tennessee, not far from where I now live. So, in Montana we figured we'd find some cowboys to teach us how to pack a horse into the backcountry. They'd show us how to water the horses and take care of them, how to get everything strapped in tight, and spend a night or two in the mountains.

For this, we needed the right gear. I worked a line item into the budget for footwear for the training. After we arrived, we went up to Miller's Boots and Shoes, a Butte mainstay on South Arizona Avenue, around the corner from the Dumas Brothel, and outfitted everyone with cowboy boots. Before the trip, I argued with my bosses that we *needed* boots because of rattlesnakes, and the bosses rolled their eyes and said, "Yeah, okay, I know what you're doing, but go ahead and get the boots." The owner of Miller's gave me a free pair of goatskin gloves because I'd brought in so much business.

For the pack training, we found a guest ranch called the Iron Wheel about twenty miles south of Butte. We got there on the first day, had a huge meal consisting of biscuits with gravy and steak, and then spent the entire day learning how to pack mules and saddle horses. We went back to the hotel that night, then back out to the ranch first thing in the morning. This time, we packed up, rolling up our rucksacks in tarps, and then hit the trail. We probably went about twenty miles into the Highland Mountains. When we got to the campsite, we watered the horses and cooked our dinner and ate under the stars. And then we lit a big bonfire and stood around it passing bottles of whiskey that we'd strapped into the saddlebags, telling "cool-guy" stories that usually started with something like, "So there I was, no shit, knee-deep in brass and hand-grenade pins," or "Back in my class, when BUD/S was *actually* hard . . ." and so on. They always ended with us laughing about how badass we all were. And then we got into our bivvy sacks, put Nalgene bottles full of hot water at our feet to keep them warm, and went to sleep. We called those camps "TACBIVs," which is SEAL-speak for "Tactical Bivouac." I came up with that term; thank you very fucking much.

After two weeks, it was time to go. At the end of the trip, we all got together for drinks at a place called Metals Sports Bar and Grill, which is in the former Metals Bank building. In the bank, the old thirty-two-ton vault has been turned into a dining room, with the original vault door used for privacy. Where the safety deposit boxes once were, now there's a wine cellar.

It's a family restaurant, so we didn't run into any tough guys that night. But as we were getting ready to leave, a Butte cop who was in the bar came over to shake my hand and accept a truce over all the bar fights that my guys had caused over the last two weeks.

"Hey, man, you know, we're really glad you came up," the cop said, holding my hand in his. "And we're really happy to see you leaving."

DAKOTA
Don't Shoot Tinker Bell

A thin blanket of snow lay over Atlanta when my flight home landed in December 2009. It had taken days to get home from Afghanistan, waiting for connections in foreign airports and dozing on flights before my plane landed at Hartsfield-Jackson. I was exhausted, my body thrown off by eight time zones. In a daze, I made my way from the gate to the luggage claim, waited alone for my bag and went through customs, and then followed the exit signs down to the long chute to the terminal.

When I walked through the security doors at the end, I stepped into a heartwarming scene of waiting families with balloons and "Welcome Home" banners, waving American flags and looking past me to the sliding door for their sons returning home from war. Tearful wives, kids, and grandparents lined up behind security ropes, grinning with anticipation, ready with their cameras and cell phones to snap pictures of their soldiers in their uniforms. None of them were looking for me. None of the hand-made signs had my name. I walked past the crowds as quickly as I could into the world of duty-free Givenchy and Burger King and winking Christmas lights, wondering how the fuck I had ended up here by myself.

When I had deployed to Afghanistan six months earlier, I had flown with my entire unit to Bagram. I had always thought that when we came back, we would return together, and the terminal would be filled with families cheering for all of us. We could return to a better, safer world. The war would be behind me. Our work would be done. Instead, I had come alone, leaving behind the rest of my unit. I had lost almost everything that I cared about in the

Ganjgal Valley. My whole world was upside down, and I had no idea what the future held.

I went quickly past the family reunions to check on my connecting flight to Kentucky. At least I would be home soon, back with my dad, Big Mike. Atlanta was supposed to be nothing more than a layover, a final stop before I got back to Louisville. But when I reached the departure monitors, I saw that the connecting flight to Louisville had been canceled because of the snow. *Un-fucking-believable.* Stranded in Atlanta.

I could have waited out the snow and gotten on the next flight. Instead, I called my dad and asked him to come get me. The drive from Kentucky takes at least five hours, but he got right in the Trailblazer and headed south to pick me up at the airport.

It was still snowing when he pulled up to the curb in my Trailblazer. I told him I'd drive home to Columbia. He said okay. I got behind the wheel and started driving north on the snowy highways.

I hauled ass up to Kentucky in the snow. I'd been driving in Afghanistan for the last six months, and I couldn't have told you the last time I had driven a civilian vehicle on an American road. I drove in the middle of the highway as fast as the truck could go, like I was still outrunning mortars in the Ganjgal Valley, while Big Mike held on to anything he could get his hands on.

Big Mike isn't easy to shake. But as we ripped north through Georgia and Tennessee, he finally said something like, *Ko, you're not in Afghanistan anymore,* trying to get me to slow down. He wasn't wrong. I wasn't in Afghanistan. But he wasn't completely right, either.

———————— • ————————

IF THERE WAS ANYONE that I could count on to pick me up when I came back from Afghanistan, it was Big Mike. If it weren't for him, I don't know that I would be here today. He has always stood up for me when everything around me was falling down, and he took me in to live with him on his farm. He gave meaning to my life, he gave me structure that came from working hard from sunrise to sundown, making sure the animals were fed and bedded, that the gates were locked and everything in its place.

I never knew my biological father. I don't know what happened to him, or even who he was. After he split from my mom, she married Big Mike, and even though I wasn't his boy, he adopted me when I was a baby. Big Mike and my mom didn't last long and were divorced before I can remember. When I was little, I mostly lived with my mom and my stepdad, who was crazy and barely ever in town. I don't remember much about what my stepdad's relationship with my mother was like, but I know it wasn't good. Fighting, cops showing up at the door, drunken fights, sober fights. It was always something. I would tell my grandfather what was going on at our house, and he would come intervene, which only made my mother angrier. But I was glad when my grandfather did show up. One of my earliest memories wasn't of Christmas or a birthday or my first puppy; it was a memory of a man in our apartment with a gun. I barely remember it; I was probably four years old. My stepfather was out of town for a construction job, and that night it was just my mom and me when someone broke a window and climbed into the apartment.

I don't recall much, but I do remember that it scared my mom to death. After that, she slept on the sofa every night with a gun on the floor in easy reach.

I have to give my mom credit. My mom couldn't hold a job and didn't know how to parent, but she worked to make sure I was provided for. We never missed a meal. We always had a roof over our head. She was only sixteen or seventeen when she had me. Maybe if she had a few more years to grow up and focus on herself a little bit more, she wouldn't have continued to make terrible life decisions the way she did. I guess you could say I'm to blame for all of it, in a way. I don't say that because I feel guilty. I say it because it's the thread of empathy that connects us.

My escape from the chaos came when I went to Big Mike's. Because he had joint custody from the adoption, he brought me to the farm every Wednesday, every other weekend, and for part of every summer, which was the best part of my year. When Big Mike would pull up and I'd hop into his truck, I think he could tell how tough of a time it was for me at home, because I'd always plead to come live with him. He never said one negative thing about my mother, but he always reassured me that if that's what I wanted to do, he would make it happen when I was thirteen, which was the legal age in Kentucky to decide which parent I wanted to be with.

During the summer that I turned eleven, I was at my grandparents' kitchen table when the phone rang. My Pepaw, Dwight, was at one end of the table, and my Memaw, Jean, at the other end, with the TV behind her. The TV was on—it was probably Chris Allen on the Channel 13 news. Pepaw answered the phone. "It's Lisa," he said. My mom. Big Mike took the phone into the other room, which he never did.

When Big Mike came back in, he said: "So that was your mom."

"What'd she want?" I asked.

"How would you like to just live with me from now on?" he said.

I couldn't believe it. "Are you for real? I would love that!" I shouted.

He left it up to me, and I said yes. An emphatic yes. And that was it. That was the last conversation about it. I didn't see my mom again for over a year. I didn't know the circumstances that had led her to leave and I truly didn't care.

———————•———————

I'VE BEEN MAKING DECISIONS about life and death since I was ten years old. When I went to live with Big Mike, everything changed. Before that it was just a blur of different homes, different beds, different confusion. I had no control over anything. But after that night in the dining room, everything had order. And I had responsibility for maintaining that order.

Big Mike's farm was about sixty miles north of the Tennessee border, located on a road that goes along a forest and empties out on tobacco fields that sit on bottomland in a big crook of the Russell Creek. The farm has about 350 acres. Around five or ten of those were used for tobacco, until Philip Morris bought us out. We also had 120 head of beef cattle. I built my own house there around 2012, just up the road from where I grew up. I built a workshop for Big Mike, whom I'd call my dad, right next to it.

Everyone in my family farms, and all within a few miles of each other on Highway 532. If you turn off my dad's road and go west on 532, after about a mile you come to Myers Road. You turn there and it ends at Memaw and Pepaw's farm. I would walk there from Dad's, following the creek around to where it came out in their fields. If you keep going on Highway 532 about a mile more, it curves and there's my aunt and uncle's farm. I'd ride back and forth on our ATV. Sometimes I'd take Dad's truck.

Big Mike worked eighty, maybe ninety hours a week. He worked at Southern States, a farm co-op, and after work he would come home and tend to the farm. Before I went to school every day, I had chores to do. That was the way it was: take care of the cattle and give bottles to the calves. And my work had to be done before my bus got there at 6:30 A.M. I could wake up a little early, do my chores, and take a shower before going to school, or I could sleep in, miss my shower, and smell like shit at school all day.

Here's the thing about farms. There's a systematic order to it because all of the animals rely on you. They depend on you showing up in the morning with a bucket of feed. They depend on you keeping the barn door closed so they stay warm and healthy. And if you fail, or if you falter, they will die. On the farm is where I learned to do what I do best—take care of things.

There are two sides to that equation. There's the part in which you step up and take care of these animals. I call that the *living* part, like every farm is fucking *Charlotte's Web*. But the other side—the one nobody wants to hear about—is the one in which you have to make hard decisions about when and if animals live. Beef cattle have to be slaughtered. Animals have to be put down sometimes. Life and death. That might seem like a heavy thing to put on a ten-year-old, but it was a package deal for me. Anyone who's grown up on a farm understands this.

There's something else that kids who were raised on a farm know about: 4-H. Even though we owned a tobacco and beef farm, we had a couple of Holsteins, and I would show them at the 4-H youth programs. Being awarded a ribbon meant that one had the best calf in town, and I *wanted* that ribbon. 4-H is where I first learned responsibility and discipline.

My prize was a beauty named Tinker Bell. I took care of her all year long, every day, just so that I could bring her in front of the judges and get those ribbons once a year. It wasn't only that. I loved that cow. Every morning when I did my chores, I talked to her so that she knew my voice. I fed her peaches and Dr Pepper as a reward for maintaining a good disposition. Sometimes I would ride her like she were a horse.

I stopped showing her when I was about fifteen, and we turned her out to pasture. She wasn't old, but I just didn't have the time or the desire to show her off anymore, so she just became a regular old cow. My folks joked about how easy retirement was for her—no more shows, no more performing, just endless green pastures, like she was in cow heaven. When she got pregnant, we waited for her to calve. It was going to be her first.

One day when I came home from school, I knew something was wrong. Cows are creatures of habit, and she wasn't where she usually was. It was springtime, before it got unbearably hot. I'll never forget how hard it was raining when I went out to look for her.

I found her lying in the field behind the barn, rolled on her side. She was in labor, and the calf wasn't making it out. It had turned inside her, and she was really weak and struggling. I knew that I had to call the vet. He knew us well and he came out right away. He took one look at her and knew there was no way that calf was coming out alive.

The only question was whether there was any way to save Tinker. She had been in that position with the calf for so long that she was basically paralyzed. The vet gave it to me straight: there's no way she's gonna to make it; you're gonna have to put her down. My dad agreed.

But I was hell-bent on trying to save her. Sitting there in that fucking muddy field with the rain pouring down on me and Tinker just lying there, I knew what I wanted to do. Maybe it was self-pity that flashed over me in that moment, remembering all the times I'd spent with her and all the ribbons we had won, but I decided there was no way I was going to let her die.

Right there in the soaking rain, my dad made a deal with me. He'd agreed that we'd try to save her, but that her life would depend on me and only me. My dad was very clear. This was my responsibility.

"This is going to be your undertaking," he said.

"Of course, of course," I said. "I'll do whatever for my cow."

There's something called "hip huggers" for cows like Tinker Bell. It's a metal brace that slides down and cups the cow's hip bones. You screw it tight and it supports the weight of the cow so that she can stand up. It was like she was in traction in a hospital bed. She wouldn't be able to stand on her own, or move, or graze.

It would take a few days to get the hip huggers, and in the meantime, there was no way to get her out of the field. I built supports on either side of her out of hay bales to keep her from toppling over. I drove fence posts into the ground and stretched tarps over her like a tent to protect her from the weather.

Rain poured for about three days straight. It was fucking miserable. Every time I went out into the field, I slid down in the mud up to my shins. I'd have to go out every morning before school to feed and water her. And then I'd have to clean up and run for the school bus, and then come home and do it all over again.

After a couple of days, we got the hip huggers. We clamped her into them and used a chain to hoist her up using the tractor. With the front loader holding up her back legs, we could walk her slowly into the barn, staggering along behind the tractor. In the beginning, she couldn't stand at all. Every morning and every evening I would lift her using the tractor and stand her up.

This went on for probably two months. All kinds of other problems developed: She got mastitis, which is an infection of the udders, because we couldn't milk her. She would topple over, and we'd have to get her back up again. She began to walk short distances, but then she would fall and couldn't get up. It was a nightmare. I started to ponder whether shooting her would've been the easier way for all of us.

One day I came home from school pissed over who knows what. Instead of blowing off steam like other kids my age, I had to tend to Tinker. She'd wandered out of the barn and of course had fallen down again. She wasn't getting up.

"I'm done. I'm done with this," I said. I called my dad and told him that I was tired of dealing with it. No sympathy from him; he told me this was on me. But it had gotten to the point where I knew he was right. I couldn't do this for the rest of her life.

I grabbed my rifle, got on my four-wheeler with my .30-30 across my lap, and opened up the throttle and tore over to her where she had fallen, about two hundred yards from the barn. I was thinking about how I put all this time into this cow and how I cared about her and, at the end of the day, I had fucking failed.

I was going to end it. I was going to put a bullet in her head, hook her up to the tractor, and drag Tinker Bell into the woods and leave her there to rot.

As I hauled ass on the four-wheeler, with the wheels bumping over the field and my gun bouncing against my legs, I drove right up to her and slammed on my brakes as hard as I could before sliding to a stop just inches from her.

Now, this is the part of the story where, as you're reading, you cover your eyes and say, *That motherfucker is going to kill his pet cow Tinker Bell. What a cold-blooded asshole. After all that. Jesus Christ, what a dick.*

Well, not exactly. I told you how I tore up to Tinker Bell on the ATV and braked so hard that I slid right up next to her. What I didn't tell you was that I freaked that damn cow out so bad that she jumped up and took off running across the pasture like there was nothing wrong with her. I sat there with the gun in my lap, my mouth open, and watched her stupid, muddy ass run across the field. I'd like to say that I had healed her, that my gentle ministrations had nursed her back to health, but you know what I think? I think she was fucking with me the whole time.

I never did have to use that .30-30. After that, Tinker had another calf—maybe a couple of them—and died of old age years later. I was relieved more than anything that I didn't have to kill my favorite cow.

I still have those 4-H ribbons; they're in my dad's house, the same place they've been ever since Tinker won them at the fair. It's a part of who I am. I didn't spend two months of my life trying to save that cow because it would make me a better person. It was because my biggest fear in life was not being able to be what someone needed me to be when they needed me to be it. It's still my biggest fear. To this day, I carry a med kit everywhere I go in my truck, so that if someone needs help, I won't let them down. Because I couldn't live with myself if I did.

I still see my mom sometimes. We don't spend a lot of time together, but every once in a while, when I go back to Kentucky, I'll be in a restaurant having dinner with a friend, and I'll realize that she's in the restaurant, too, in a different booth.

She's had a hard life, and it's changed her. In 2019, I had a big Easter dinner at the house for my relatives and friends. There were probably about fifteen of us. And I had invited my mom. Everyone was drinking and socializing, and my mom was playing with my daughters, Sailor Grace and Atlee. My dad was there with his best friend, a guy named Mike Allen, having a drink.

After my mom left, Mike Allen asked my dad, "Who was that woman playing with the kids?"

And my dad said, "Hell, I don't have a clue who that was." Everyone in the room busted out laughing, letting my dad have it: "You don't even know who your ex-wife was?" they cried.

The thing is, my dad has a great memory—believe me, I know, because he remembers all the dumb shit I did—but he truly didn't recognize her. I don't blame him. I don't blame her, either. My mom brought me into this life and will always be a part of my world, even if sometimes I don't even realize that she's there.

————

2

TAKING AIM

ROB

Never Shoot out of a Moving Car

It was still dark when my uncle Jack and cousin Cory pulled into the driveway of my dad's house, and Dad stashed his brother's .30-06 rifle in the trunk of Jack's beat-up old Datsun. It was an early Sunday morning in October 1988, and it was the first day of antelope season in Montana. My sisters and my brother Tom had groaned at the idea of going hunting, and were sound asleep down the street at my mother's when we left my dad's house about 5:30 A.M. I squeezed beside Cory into the backseat of the two-door sedan. After Dad flipped the passenger seat back into place and got in, Jack turned the car out onto Butte's deserted streets.

I could feel the excitement pumping through my twelve-year-old body as I stared, wide awake, out the window. I had never gone hunting before, and going out for the first time with my dad felt like an adventure. I wasn't actually going to do any hunting—at twelve, I was too young. I didn't have a hunting tag. I didn't have a gun. I was just barely old enough to take a firearm safety course. But even though I couldn't shoot a gun, I wanted to come along and find out what it was like.

In Montana, hunting runs through the state like a vein of silver ore. It's part of who we are. When hunting season opens, it's like Christmas and the start of summer vacation rolled into one for a lot of Montanans. That October morning, all I could think about was standing next to my dad when he took down a buck.

We pulled off Harrison Avenue into Town Pump, one of the gas stations owned by our family friends the Kenneallys, to fill up. The Pump sold decent coffee and premade sandwiches, and we packed the cooler with crucial provisions like Twinkies, Zingers, and Coke. When we had all the supplies we needed for the tough morning ahead, Cory and I climbed into the backseat again and we turned back out onto Harrison to the ramp onto Interstate 90 west, before turning off and heading south on I-15 toward Dillon.

When I got older and went hunting with dad, I would doze in the car as we sped through the darkness, but this time I was too pumped up on adrenaline. We drove to Dillon, where we met up with a family friend, John Dunn, his daughter, Linda and son John Jr., along with other friends of John's packed into John's Bronco for the trip. My dad followed John as he turned onto Blacktail Road out of Dillon. It was slow going for the Datsun as the pavement turned to gravel and we did our best to keep up with the glowing taillights of the Bronco. The Matador Ranch sprawled on both sides of the road all the way to Yellowstone to the southeast. Up ahead, I could see the ridgeline of the Blacktail Mountains against the brightening sky. We were only about thirty miles from the Idaho line, and Yellowstone Park was about forty miles to the east. The road continued south through the rolling grassland, so endless I thought it must end somewhere in Mexico.

As the Datsun bumped along the wide gravel road, I realized quickly that this was not going to be an intimate bonding experience with my dad. We weren't alone as we headed toward antelope habitat; there were trucks all around us, heading in the same direction. We could see the glow of headlights and brake lights in front of us and behind us. It was a vast, wide-open area, but antelope run fast and a long gun like a .30-06 has a range of one thousand yards. There were a lot of hunters out there with us for opening day, and they were all looking for the best spots. We passed trucks that were pulled over onto the shoulder, with hunters pointing their spotting scopes and binoculars out the windows, scanning the hills for their first quarry of the season.

The sun rose red over the mountains, and the gunfire began almost as soon as there was enough daylight for shooting. And in that moment, as the sound of shots echoed all around me, I realized, with a mix of twelve-year-old panic and exhilaration, *This was going to be fucking chaos.*

MY DAD HADN'T TAKEN UP HUNTING because he was a sportsman; he took it up because he needed a hobby. Dad hadn't hunted since he was a kid, and he didn't even own a rifle; he had borrowed the .30-06 from his brother, Brian. He had never really been that excited about it. As far as he was concerned, hunting usually meant trekking off into the mountains without a plan, and returning home after a day of boredom or soaking rain without ever firing a shot or seeing a single deer or elk. Dad was competitive—he was a stockbroker and a monster on the basketball court—but it wasn't his appetite for shooting animals that sent us out on that Sunday morning. It was because he was in a funk.

He had just gone through his second divorce. After his marriage to my mom had broken up, he'd remarried. My stepmom was a much younger woman named Suzanne. Sort of a trophy wife. They got married in the living room of his house after a short engagement. I would go over to his house every other weekend and play Nintendo with her son, my stepbrother, but even when we were all under the same roof, I didn't see much of her.

It didn't last long. When their marriage broke up, my dad fell into a rut. Maybe you could call it a midlife crisis. My uncle Jack, who was a serious hunter, prodded him to go out with him to get his mind off the painful divorce. As far as Jack was concerned, firearms, bullets, and camouflage were the perfect antidote for marital blues. My dad was skeptical, but finally he agreed to get off the couch and turn off the soaps, and promised to take me with him.

For our first outing, we were on our way to hunt pronghorn antelope. Hunting pronghorn is no joke. Here's a fact for the un-initiated: pronghorn antelope are the fastest land animals in North America, and the second fastest in the world, after cheetahs. They can run 60 miles an hour for three to four minutes, and 30 miles an hour for about five miles. During hunting season, they basically don't stop running. They don't jump fences, either; they either go under, or they'll just turn on a dime and run parallel to the fence line, or they run straight into the fence, which doesn't end well. It's probably because they've been running on the open plains for a long time—20 million years. They're a living link to the Ice Age, and they don't have any relatives; every other related species died off long ago. I'd have a tough time adapting after that long, too.

After we got to the Matador Ranch, Dad and I climbed into John Dunn's Bronco to hunt. The ranchland in the foothills of the Black-tails is crisscrossed with fences, but there are built-in access gates so that vehicles can cross a fence line without going to a cattle gate, which could be miles away. The access gates are usually two posts slack-wired together, with only one of the fence posts buried. One person unhitches the loose post, drags the post and the barbed wire out of the way until the vehicle goes through, and then drags the post back and closes the fence up again.

Here's the hitch: the Matador Ranch allowed hunting on its land, but hunters could only enter their property on foot or on horseback. Except for our friend John Dunn, who had special permission to enter the Matador land in his vehicle. Now, Montana law doesn't permit shooting from vehicles, but John could, because he was a paraplegic from an accident when he was eighteen. What that meant on that

Sunday morning was that one of us popped out of the Bronco to open the gate, John drove through, and after we closed the gate behind us, John tore across the prairie at 30, 40 miles per hour in pursuit of antelope. The Bronco bounced and bucked over every rock and rut, and sent us flying around inside the car. I don't know if John pointed his rifle out the window and shot at an antelope with one hand as he drove, but if he did, I wouldn't be surprised at all.

As the sun came up, I could hear gunfire all around us, as hunters took aim at pronghorn fleeing for their lives. All around, hunters five hundred, one thousand yards away were firing at antelope streaking across the grassland, the sound of the guns bouncing off the foothills of the mountains, while John drove like a wild man in his Bronco. It was like the Indy 500, but with firearms. It was probably the most unsafe thing on the planet short of a firefight in a war zone, which is what it sounded like. Every single one of those yahoos out there probably considered themselves to be the best hunter in Montana, and every single one of them was doing the craziest shit imaginable. I watched one guy go up to a buck trapped in a corner where two fences met, and shoot the trembling animal point blank. Not exactly sporting.

Eventually, John turned onto a dirt road that led to a ravine. Dad and I got out and hiked for a short distance. After we reached an elevated spot, we looked down and saw three or four antelope coming up the draw. My dad raised his brother's rifle, took aim, and shot the lead doe. John was waiting down below us with the Bronco, so Dad and I had to drag the doe all the way down so that we could load her up and bring her back to the road.

Back at the road, we regrouped and got lunch. I remember my uncle Jack announcing that he was going back out in the truck to hunt some more and telling us, "Get something else to eat. It'd be a shame to leave this buffet hungry." From then on, lunch while we were hunting was referred to as a "buffet."

Unlike most of the boneheads out there on the Blacktail, John got a buck, and his son showed us how to dress it with a gut knife. I watched as he slit the belly all the way from the neck to the tail. I won't lie; it was gross watching the heart and lungs and stomach come sliding out onto the ground. To me, meat was something that was neatly packaged and arranged next to the premade pizzas in the coolers at Safeway. *No way I'm going to do that without gloves,* I thought, feeling kind of queasy.

Afterward, we went back to Butte. Along with other hunters, we stopped at the Flying J on the outskirts of town to use the restroom and wash up. It was as much a part of the ritual as the hunting itself. The trucks lined up outside the convenience store, some with antelope secured with ropes in the back, others with empty payloads, but everyone full of stories to tell about the day, about the one they got or the one that bounded off. There was cigarettes and beer and laughter, and hunters compared notes on the gun they used or the bullet that took the antelope down, and then bragged about how it was bagged. Bragging, but not too much, because that might reveal the secret spot where the hunter found his prize. Later in the day, before going home, we did the "parade," driving through Butte with the prize in the back, doing slow circles through downtown so that everyone could see that we had bagged an antelope.

When we got home, I couldn't stop talking about what an exciting day it was. I hadn't touched a gun or fired a shot the whole day, but I think I had more fun than I had ever had in my life. Even after I was back at home that night, I could still remember the anticipation and the excitement and a taste of danger from all the rifles firing around me, watching the animals flying over the sagebrush faster than any animal I'd ever seen. Everything about it was still crisp and clear in my mind. I loved joking and laughing with my cousin and uncle. I loved the shitty sandwiches and the Zingers and all the other junk food from our Flying J buffet. I loved the parade afterward. The hunting bug had bitten me hard.

Here's the thing, though. What I didn't realize right away was that there were other parts that I would come to love, which would turn hunting into a lifelong passion that would one day make me into a SEAL Team ███ operator. I didn't know it that day in 1988, but that crazy shooting gallery on the Blacktail Road was the start of something that would stay with me for my whole life. Sure, it was fun, a day of pure chaos that was ridiculous and dangerous and left me with an aching stomach from laughing so hard. But it also gave me a hint, even as a naïve twelve-year-old, that there was another way to be a hunter.

In time, I would learn to love the solitude of sitting on a ridgeline, listening and watching, the smell of sagebrush in my nose. The stillness in the air when the nearest road is five miles away. My breath condensing into clouds of steam in the crisp, clear morning air, sipping a thermos of hot coffee that would be cold long before I fired a shot. How time stops when a beautiful elk or mule deer steps from the brush and stands quietly, looking and listening. And of course, the thrill of a successful hunt when I came home with a dressed animal in the back of a truck and had to tell the story of how I got it. How I loved to tell the stories.

As soon as I was old enough, I took the required state hunter safety class and learned the basics of handling a firearm. These were the ABCs of hunting. *Never point a gun—loaded or unloaded—at another person. Never discharge a firearm when you don't know what's behind the target.* These were good rules. These were rules. But over time, I learned other, unwritten rules that they don't teach you in safety class, things learned over years of experience. The way animals react in their natural habitats, how they flee and how fast, their behavior at rest and in flight. How to read the wind. How altitude and weather and terrain affect ballistics. How to be patient. How to be silent. How to wait and be tactical. How to respect your quarry, in life and in death. The kind of rules that meant that most of the lazy hunters lining Blacktail Road wouldn't bag any pronghorn that first day, or any other day. Rules that one day would make me want to become a sniper.

Two years later, I went hunting with my dad again. I was fourteen by then, and I had started high school. I remember that trip as clearly as the one on Blacktail Road. Just as on the first day of antelope season, my dad and I stopped for gas at Town Pump. Dad had graduated from the crappy Datsun to a sporty, midsize black Chevy pickup. To keep the heat running, he left the keys in the ignition with the engine on while we went inside for our sandwiches and Zingers for the cooler. When we got back to the truck, Dad realized that he had locked the door of the truck. It took about an hour and a half, but we finally poked open one of the rear side windows and used a broom handle to get the doors open and finally get inside. It was so hot in the truck from the heat blasting that we had to drive with the windows open to cool down. By the time we got back on the road, the sun was long up, the prime morning hunting hours gone. We were resigned to feeling like the day was a bust. Still, better late than never.

By then, I had been hunting for two years, and had never returned home with a deer. I had begun to think that taking big game was something others could do, but I couldn't. Maybe it was insecurity, maybe it was just inexperience that made me believe that, but it had begun to take root in my head, a seed of doubt that maybe I wasn't cut out for this after all. We drove in the same direction as the antelope hunt—south toward Dillon and off onto Blacktail Road toward the Matador Ranch. This time, though, we took a left on a side road, heading east. The road climbed until it came to a ranch house. We got out and knocked on the door to ask permission to hunt. I remember the man who answered said two things: that his name was Buster Brown, and that he was fine with us hunting on his land. We continued on.

The road went up and up, growing narrower and bumpier. We drove through a series of gates, each one progressively crappier, until the road ended in a canyon on the banks of Timber Creek. We got out, and I shouldered the one rifle we had for the two of us, my dad's .30-06. Years later, I would purchase my own rifle, a .300 Winchester Magnum, the same gun I would use as a SEAL sniper.

We hiked up the bank to the right and passed through some trees. The canyon opened into a wide, golden bowl. Up there, the mule deer could be anywhere. Often, they would hear us coming and move farther up the canyon ahead of us. Sometimes they would stop, completely motionless, and watch. When they spooked, they thumped their hooves on the ground to warn other deer before bounding away. I always thought that was incredible.

We spent the day up there without seeing anything. Around lunchtime, we went back down to the truck for our midday buffet before returning up to the bowl. As the hours stretched into afternoon, we still didn't see anything. The sun was beginning to set when we finally started back to the truck for the day. The light drained, turning the grass golden and the canyon walls copper. We were crossing through a stand of trees and into a clearing when my dad spotted the buck.

He stepped from the trees right in front of us and stood still, staring at us. He was a young mule deer buck. I slowly lowered the rifle from my shoulder, while my dad dropped to the ground in front of me. I carefully raised the barrel, held my breath as I aimed, and pulled the trigger. It was high, a terrible shot, but lucky for me it went through the deer's spine and dropped him right there. He felt nothing. I, on the other hand, felt ecstatic. It was almost an out-of-body experience, because I was finally a member of the club. As I walked up to the buck, I was taken by the beauty of this creature that had been living and breathing just seconds earlier. It was the first time that I felt the gravity of what it means to take a life. I always wanted a clean shot to ensure that the animal didn't feel pain. That's the reason that to this day, I have never hunted with a bow. It takes them too long to die. As a hunter, I have the ultimate respect for the animals, and never take the life of one lightly.

We dressed the deer right there in the clearing, trying to remember how John Dunn had done it two years before out on the Blacktail. It took about an hour, maybe longer, and the sun had set long before we began dragging the carcass down the hillside to the truck. On the way back to the highway, we pulled into Buster Brown's to show him the deer and thank him.

And then after we reached I-90 in Butte, we pulled off to stop at the Flying J to wash off the blood in the restroom and wolf down a skillet of eggs and bacon and gravy. And of course, to sit by the window with a view of the truck with the deer in the back, so that we could watch everyone who came over to admire the deer while we enjoyed our buffet. This time, I was the one who could boast about my kill.

That was the start of my confidence and fascination, I guess, out there on Buster Brown's property. Getting my first kill made me believe in myself as a hunter. Once I got a kill, I wanted to get another. Soon my dad and I were hunting bull elk every year. Bull elk are the biggest prize in Montana hunting, and I know guys who have hunted for decades and never gotten one. At the end of my senior year in high school, I not only expected to get a bull elk, I got one. Eventually, we hunted grizzly and caribou in Alaska. I would pass up animals that I had in my scope because they weren't big enough, because I knew I could get a better one. If we got a moose on a hunt, we'd go to a different diner, 4 Bs, which also had skillets and cinnamon rolls and window seats to watch the truck.

One day I would walk into the recruitment office because I knew how to shoot, and Marines knew how to shoot, and the recruiter would convince me to join the Navy, because they too knew how to shoot. It would become the reason I enlisted. It was the ability to walk into the mountains lightly and silently, to melt into the trees at night, to know the terrain enough so well that I didn't worry about anything. It was the ability to be steady and aim true, and to only need one bullet to take a target without causing suffering, and to respect the life that I'd taken, even if it was an enemy. And someday far in the future, I'd be standing around with members of SEAL Team ▮, laughing about the shit we'd see that night when we were out hunting al Qaeda in Baqubah or in Baghdad. Sometimes when I was walking in the mountains of Afghanistan with a different kind of rifle over my shoulder, and the light was just right and the air was crisp and quiet, I would swear I was back in the foothills of the Blacktails, looking forward to the day, even if I came home empty-handed and had nothing to show for it but a cooler full of Zingers and Coke, as long as I had stories to go with it.

DAKOTA

Know Your Rock from Your Axe

Nothing's quieter than woods at night. Every tiny noise, every minute movement is amplified. The breeze roars like a tornado; breath is thunder. If there's moonlight, the world is lit by silver. If it's cloudy or a new moon, the dark is so thick that you can reach out, take a handful, and stick it in your pocket.

When I was little and went hunting with my dad, I'd practically sleepwalk out of the house to one of our deer stands around the farm, trying to keep our feet from crunching on the leaves. I'd carry my sleeping bag, and when he would climb the tree with his rifle, I'd stay at the bottom, unroll my sleeping bag, and crawl inside. I'd sleep while he stayed awake above me, waiting silently for the deer to come out of the trees, until the sound of the rifle shot woke me.

When I got a little older, around ten, I'd hunt with him, too. I had compound bows for archery season, which began in early fall, and a rifle for gun season, in autumn. When I was kid, I was a terrible shot. With everything. A bow, a gun; I couldn't hit a thing.

One time during bow hunting season, my dad and I used climber stands, which required a slow, painstaking process for getting up and down from the tree. We each chose our trees, and then began to shimmy our way upward inch by inch, dragging our foot stands and the seat up the tree with us, all while tethered to the trunk to keep from falling. When I finally got about fifteen or twenty feet off the ground, we sat down on the tiny platform. My weight locked it in and kept it secure. Then I had to get my bow. My dad and I had left them at the foot of the tree, tied to the end of a rope. I grabbed the rope and hauled the bow up to where I sat. And then I waited, with an arrow notched for the deer that I knew were coming.

I sat up there with my compound bow, and as deer passed by me, I shot arrow after arrow and missed every one. I missed so many times that I ran out of arrows. I had to ratchet my way slow back down to the bottom, gather up as many arrows as I could find, and climb back up the tree. I probably scared away every deer within a mile radius.

One morning, Dad brought me out to a stand. I had on an orange hunting vest over a camo sweatshirt and camo pants. When we reached the tree we were going to sit next to, he used his foot to carefully push the leaves to the side, so we didn't accidentally step on them and spook a deer. We sat at the base of the tree, him on one side, me on the other, when a big eight-point buck came out of the trees near us.

Neither of us said a word. My dad tapped my shoulder. I lowered my shotgun and fired. This time, for some reason, my aim was good and the stag fell right there. We dressed him on the spot, dragged him back to my dad's red Dodge, and loaded him up.

I was so excited to get home with the deer, and get it carved up and put away in the freezer. But we didn't go home—not yet— because there was something we had to do first. I had to show him off to my grandma and grandpa. That was the first thing we did after a hunt—go to Memaw and Pepaw's house to show them what we killed.

When we pulled up to the farmhouse, my grandparents were already up; they were always up early. My grandpa wasn't the most expressive guy. In fact, he's the hardest man I'd ever met. But that morning, he took picture after picture of me sitting on the tailgate of the Dodge next to my dad, holding up the buck's head by the antlers, with big, silly grins on both our faces. I think my grandpa might have been even more excited than I was. I'm not sure if I was grinning so hard because I was proud of my deer, or because my grandpa and grandma were proud of me.

———————

BIG MIKE, MY GRANDMA JEAN, and my grandpa Dwight were like three legs of a stool that propped up my life. Don't get me wrong: they were tough, and Dwight could be mean. My grandpa was by far the loudest man I've ever met. He could shout at me across a field from two hundred yards away and I'd hear his voice over the motor of the tractor as clear as if he were shouting in my ear. The drill instructors in the Marines had nothing on my grandpa. My dad is the same way. Our family is just very, very loud. I've been yelled at my whole damn life. If you yell at me, you're not going to scare me.

Memaw and Pepaw were cut from the same cloth, born two months apart in 1930. I call them the rock and the axe. My grandma Jean was a tough woman. She was the rock. She was a registered nurse for forty-three years and has helped more sick people in her life than I could ever count. She was up every morning before my grandfather, to make his coffee, and she cooked dinner for them both every single night. She also worked out in the tobacco fields with us, alongside the hired workers and me. She was the foundation of everything in our family, the cornerstone.

My grandpa, Dwight, was the axe. I called him that because he was a force of nature. He was sharp and he was resolute, and he was effective. When he came down, he came down hard with blunt force, and he knocked apart what stood in his way through sheer force of will. He grew up in a different time, before Americans got soft with all the convenience we take for granted now. Before most people had cars. Before electricity reached rural parts of the country. Before there was a safety net outside of your family and your church. He was from that generation that saw the world change in front of his eyes. Born in the Great Depression, eleven years old when the Japanese bombed Pearl Harbor, he saw one president assassinated and another resign, he saw the twin towers fall, and he endured the tragedies and milestones of the twentieth century.

My grandpa was a lot harder on me than my dad—astronomically harder. There was no bullshit with my grandpa. He didn't show much emotion. I can't ever remember him saying "I love you" to me, even though I know he must have. He just didn't feel the need to express it. When I was young, I didn't understand him, but when I was older, he made more sense to me. Some of what I learned about him came from men who worked for him. After the Corps, he became a civil engineer, and he had a construction company for years before he retired. His company built the Corvette plant in Bowling Green. He sold the company when he retired, though sometimes he would go back and do construction on the side in his later years.

After I served in the Marines, I had a construction company, too, and I had guys who worked for me who used to work for Pepaw. *You know, your grandpa was the hardest man I've ever had on me in my entire life,* they told me. *But the one thing he always did to every single one of us every afternoon after working for him was he always thanked us for our work.* And everybody remembers that. Some people hated him, but everyone respected him.

He wasn't much of a talker about himself. Until I enlisted in high school, I never even knew he was in the Corps. "Well, you know, your grandfather was a Marine," my dad told me after I signed up, kind of matter-of-factly. You could have knocked me over with a feather. I had seen Marine Corps stuff around their house, but I had never heard him talk about it.

He opened up to me only after I signed up. He told me he was a navigator on Marine aircraft, usually on long-distance transports during the Korean War. He didn't fly the planes, but he got them where they needed to go. He did it by navigating by the stars, mapping the course of the plane using the constellations overhead. He was like the flesh-and-blood GPS, charting the route using the heavens as his guide to bring those big transports thousands of miles between Asia and the United States.

Eventually, he told me that he wasn't just guiding any old cargo planes; he was on transports returning the bodies of American servicemen home who had been killed in Korea. I don't know how many of the 36,914 American servicemen killed in the war got home because of him, but he brought some of them back, at least. He told me a story once that made me wonder if those missions were part of the reason he was so hard. As he told it, he was in the cockpit of one of those flights, with the cargo hold loaded with bodies. And midflight, he glanced back into the cargo bay, and as he looked, one of those dead bodies sat up. The reason was rigor mortis, but if it were me in the cockpit, that would have been the last thing on my mind, because I probably would have jumped out of the fucking plane. Like with everything else, he didn't say much more about it than that, but I'm betting that he just turned back around, and kept that plane right on course as if nothing had happened.

My grandpa took a fall in 2015. We checked him into rehab so that he could regain his strength. The nursing home was in Louisville, and it took about an hour and a half to get there from home. But I was flying out of Louisville a lot by that point, so I would swing by and see him at least once a week. I'd sit on his bed or in a chair on the side, and we'd bullshit and get caught up on stuff.

I'll never forget this. I was in New York for the marathon, on November 1, when I received a call saying that he'd fallen again. He'd gone to Baptist East Hospital in Louisville and wasn't responding well to the medication, I was told. *That can't be true,* I said. *I just talked to him.*

I flew back to Kentucky as soon I could. When I got to the hospital, the doctors told me his kidneys were shutting down because they couldn't process the morphine he was receiving for the pain. I convinced the doctors to let up on the morphine. They agreed to do that long enough to bring him out of his morphine-induced stupor for a time so that he could see that the whole family was there. My aunt and uncle and my cousin. My dad. And Memaw, of course, in a wheelchair. She barely knew where she was, but she wasn't going to leave his side. She sat next to him, holding his hand. Eventually the pain was too much, and the doctors boosted the morphine back up. Then it was just a matter of time.

Like I said, he was stubborn, and he hung on longer than any of us thought possible. The doctor would tell us that he wouldn't make it through the night, and then morning would come and he would still be with us. This went on for days.

Finally, just before 8 A.M. on Friday, November 6, my grandma announced that she wanted to go home and get a shower. *Who knows how long this is going to go on. I'm going to get some clothes and come right back.* She kept saying that. *I'll be right back.* And Big Mike started wheeling her out the door.

The minute the wheels on her chair crossed the threshold of the room, my grandpa gasped for air. My aunt ran out of the room to stop my dad—they were just outside the room in the hallway—but by then it was too late. Grandpa had died. I think he was holding on because he didn't want her to see him die. Because he was that stubborn. Because he knew what dignity was.

My grandma loved to tell me the story about how they met. He was stationed in Jacksonville, Florida, where she lived. He'd seen her at a party and gotten her number from her. Afterward, he told his buddy, "I'm gonna marry that girl." Well, he kept trying to call her and she wouldn't go on a date with him. She finally agreed to go on a date with him. She always told me, "Well, I decided to go on a date with him just so I could get him to leave me alone."

When they went on that date, he told her, "I'm gonna marry you." Vintage Pepaw. She told me that that was the craziest thing she'd ever heard. She thought he had lost his mind. And then three months later, they got married, and they stayed married for sixty-two years.

There's a reason I know that story so well. Toward the end of her life, my memaw developed dementia and would tell the same stories over and over again. She only had about five stories, and she told me that one every time I came into the house. I must have heard it a hundred times. I always tell people that you'd better make a bunch of good memories, because you're only going to get about five of them if you get dementia. They'd better be funny or they'd better be sweet or maybe a combination of the two; otherwise, it's going to be no fun for anybody.

My grandma got to a point to where she couldn't drive anymore, but you couldn't tell her that. She had this big Lincoln Town Car that was big as a boat. Before she got dementia, she and my grandpa would drive this thing into town, and they drove *slowly*. I'm talking 35 miles an hour on a 55-mile-an-hour road. It was like driving behind a fucking tank.

When the dementia kicked in and she couldn't drive anymore, we told her the car had broken down. She would go out and try to start it, but we had taken out the battery or unhooked it. Eventually we just took the Lincoln away altogether. There's this garage called Don Franklin's that used to work on the car, so we parked the car at my aunt and uncle's but told her that it was at Don Franklin's, getting worked on. I'd come in and she'd be sitting at the kitchen counter smoking Kools.

"Hey Memaw, where's your car?" I'd say.

"Well, you know, I just took it to Don Franklin's a week ago," she said. "I don't know what they're doing."

One day, she wanted to call them to check on the car, so my dad got on the phone and they made up this story that the parts had to come from New York and China and all these other places. They told her that it would be ready in another week. I think the car had been there for at least a year by that point.

Memaw passed away in 2016, about ten months after Dwight. Like I said, she was the rock—unpolished and rough and cut from hard generations. Their marriage wasn't perfect, but it was unconditional. Unconditional love doesn't ask for anything in return. It seems like everything these days is conditional. Friendships. *He'd be my best friend if it weren't for*—fill in the blank. Marriage. *We'd get married except for*—fill in the blank. Patriotism. *I love my country, but*. But-but-but. There's always a but. What I loved about my grandparents' marriage is that there were no buts. There was no asterisk. There was no fine print. There were no goddamn filters.

I like to think of them as a frontier couple from two centuries ago, with only a few tools to build a life for themselves, clearing away the wilderness without complaining, for those like me who came later. Memaw was the foundation, and Pepaw hewed the logs laid upon that foundation. That's how a house was built back then—rocks and axes.

When I was kid, I didn't really understand why Grandpa was so hard. I just lived with it. But after I enlisted, a funny thing happened. When I made it successfully through boot camp at Parris Island and came home on leave, everything was completely different with my grandpa. He and Grandma were in declining health, so they couldn't make it down to South Carolina for graduation day and watch me march in formation in my uniform. I know that burned them up, because they wanted to be there at every milestone in my life. I saw them when Dad brought me home for a couple of days before the start of the School of Infantry. It was September 2006 when my dad's truck pulled up in front of their farmhouse. When they came outside, he wasn't any less loud, and he wasn't any less proud than the day I rolled up with that deer. But something had changed. I had passed a test, in his eyes. He didn't need to be so hard on me anymore. He knew what it took to become a Marine, and I had gone and done it. I was part of the brotherhood.

He and I had something else in common that we never talked about. I flew home from Afghanistan wanting to kill myself. The plane was filled with living, breathing passengers in the seats around me, yet I had never felt so lonely, because my team had come home dead before me. I did the only thing I could in Afghanistan, which was to carry their lifeless bodies out of the firefight and load them on a plane back to America with the dignity that they deserved. My grandpa, he didn't know those dead soldiers he flew home from Korea, but he got them back to their families, even though he was just a terrified navigator barely out of his teens, in charge of returning a plane full of dead heroes.

I don't hunt anymore, period. It's not exciting for me. But I would have liked to have hunted with my grandpa. In my entire life, I never did, even after I became a sniper. I would have liked to have walked with him through the darkness, listening to the world moving around us, to all the things we can hear but can't see. I would have liked to have looked up at the night sky with him, and known which way to go with only the stars to show us the way.

3

FIND YOUR HEROES

ROB

Aim, Shoot, Repeat

When I was twelve, the driveway at my cousin Mike Regan's house was a kid-sized version of a bigger world beyond Butte. Mike lived a few blocks away from my mother with his seven brothers and sisters. Their house was a magnet for play. Bikes lay scattered across the lawn where they'd been dropped and forgotten. His parents picked their way through a maze of scattered toys. Kids ran up and down the stairs, bounced off the walls, screamed their heads off, sprinted around the house. Total mayhem.

We usually ended up playing in the rear of his driveway, where his dad had hung a basketball hoop for him, and we used the pavement as a court when there wasn't a car parked in it. We had dunking contests for hours, running up and slamming the ball into the net. The backboard was the furthest thing from regulation you could imagine. I think the hoop couldn't have been more than eight feet off the ground, way short of the standard ten-foot height. Mike's ball wasn't regulation, either; it was one of those novelty varieties, the kind that fill up discount bins in the drugstore. The ball was small enough for a twelve-year-old to palm, but every time we dunked it, we felt like Dr. J or Larry Bird.

This was 1989. Throughout the decade, the raging Celtics and Lakers rivalry was the stuff of legend, with Magic Johnson and Kareem Abdul-Jabbar matched up against Larry Bird, Kevin McHale, and Robert Parish. Mike and my brother were huge Boston fans, and as an Irish kid in Butte, the shamrocks everywhere screamed "Celtics" to me. When we watched the games in distant cities on TV, with fans yelling loud enough to raise the roof, we had a glimpse of a wider world, of celebrity sports, of heroes with skills beyond our measure. So when we played out on the driveway, we pretended to be Bird, streaking toward the basket in the boiling hot Boston Garden, as make-believe fans thundered "Beat LA! Beat LA!" in our ears.

One day in early 1989, I wandered over to the Regans', and as usual, Mike and I went out back and started dunking. Mike was a funny kid, verging on dorky. In high school, he would become a stud who would badger members of the Butte High School girls' soccer team for dates, and get them. But when he was eleven and I was twelve, we were just awkward kids with seriously shitty layups and dunks. While Mike and I messed around, missing basket after basket, he asked if I'd seen this new movie called *Come Fly with Me*, about Michael Jordan, the Chicago Bulls phenom. The movie had come out in January and Mike had a copy on VHS.

I hadn't seen it, so we decided to go watch it right then. We put down the ball and went up the back steps to the deck, through the sliding glass doors into the house, and down the stairs to the basement playroom. Mike popped the tape into the VHS and pressed play, and we plopped down on the sofa to watch.

I had heard of Michael Jordan and seen him in TV ads, but to me, he wasn't yet the hoops folk hero that he had already become to the rest of the country. He had led the NBA in scoring in the previous NBA season and gotten league MVP, and the Bulls even made it out of the first round of the 1988 playoffs before Isiah Thomas and the Detroit Pistons finished them in round two. But to me, in Butte, Montana, he wasn't yet *Michael Jordan*.

With the screen still dark, I heard the sound of a single basketball smacking against a court floor. Then the darkness faded and we saw Jordan's lone figure in an empty school gymnasium, dribbling and shooting, dribbling and shooting. His deep voice spilled out of the TV. "I can never stop working hard. Each day I feel I have to improve. Hard work, determination—I've got to keep pushing myself." And when the eighties-tastic title screen appeared, the sound of rushing wind spilled from the TV, like I was soaring above the clouds.

We were mesmerized. For forty-two minutes, we watched his story unfold, from losing to his brother on the court behind the family house in North Carolina to being cut from his high school varsity team to blowing past Larry Bird and Kevin McHale when the Bulls played the Celtics in 1986. When the movie was over, we went back out to the driveway with a piece of chalk and drew a fake free-throw line. And then we began launching ourselves from that line and slamming the ball into the net like we had seen on the tape. This time, as I flew through the air, I didn't pretend I was Larry Bird. Now I was Michael Jordan.

———————

I WAS SPELLBOUND watching that movie. As I watched him soar across the court as if he had wings, something clicked in me that made me look at basketball as a discipline rather than just a game. There was a purity to Jordan's style and skill, an elegance. But it wasn't just the sheer beauty and grace of his presence on the court that riveted me as I sat in the Regans' basement; it was the idea that perfection comes from practice. Mastering the basics. Repeating something a hundred times, a thousand times, until you have it perfect. Being the first one in the gym and the last one when the lights go out.

I couldn't wait to follow Jordan's advice, and I didn't waste any time turning that concept into practice. Not long after I watched the movie, I asked my mom for a regulation-sized basketball, a real one. Mike and I abandoned his backyard kid's court and started going over to Greeley Elementary School. I would dribble the three blocks from my mom's house to the court, go in through the gate, and start practicing a drill called the Mikan Drill—layups over and over, first on the left, then the right, over and over and over.

About five days into my new regimen, my dad pulled up in his truck. He had left work and swung by my mom's house looking for me, and my sister said I was over at Greeley shooting baskets. That surprised him, because he didn't know I had such an intense interest in basketball.

So he rolled up next to the court in his truck, still wearing his tie, and yelled to me out the window.

Can I join you? he shouted to me.

Okay, I told him.

Let's start working out together, he said. *I can help you. And you can help me and we can make this a lot of fun.* And that's kind of how it all started for us.

I knew that my dad had played basketball in the past, but I didn't know how intensely he had played until I started playing myself. I definitely hadn't known he had been a standout in high school and had gone on to play college ball at the University of Montana, and what an achievement that was. Before that, I just figured that everyone's dad had a scrapbook with long-ago pictures of playing basketball. I had seen the still photo of him, as a senior in high school, doing a one-hand dunk barefoot. That seemed normal to me, because I thought everyone could do that at eighteen. It wasn't until I started playing that I realized that if you're not really tall, dunking takes serious athletic skills, even with shoes on. Another picture in my dad's scrapbook was a picture of him and my older brother Tom at a Clippers game. I didn't even know what that meant, and my takeaway—for some reason—was that my dad played for the Clippers, which I probably bragged about at school without realizing how ridiculous that sounded.

Dad and I began playing together pretty much every day after he finished work. We moved from the hoop at Greeley to a community center called "the Courtrooms," which eventually turned into a YMCA. It was just the two of us in the gym, running drills, doing jump shots, repeating ball-handling fundamentals, practicing drop steps and pivots. When he eventually bought a house in the Butte Country Club, he brought his hoop from his old house, and I started practicing on that. The only thing we didn't focus on was nutrition and conditioning, which was a mistake, since basically everything in Butte arrives at your table with gravy on it.

The thing about my dad was that he was incredibly competitive. I think the only time we ever fought was on the basketball court, arguing over fouls or mechanics of some skill. Take free throws. Watch the ball or keep your eyes on the rim when you shoot. Larry Bird looked up at the ball. Michael Jordan looked at the rim. My dad insisted on watching the ball. I always kept my eyes on the rim.

Here's why it mattered. One of our rules was this: one of us had to sink twenty free throws in a row before we could break up and go home for the night. Let me be clear: this is very fucking difficult. As the minutes go by, you get more and more tired, and that means you hit fewer and fewer baskets. And if no one hit that mark, we would just play and play through dinner, through exhaustion, as the night got later and later. Another incentive: if one of us got twenty-five in a row, they got a dinner at the Derby, a steak house up on Harrison Avenue.

We kept moving the goalpost, upping the necessary streak, drawing out every game and raising the stakes. Eventually my dad sank 91 in a row, which set a family record. That stood for about six days, until I got 105 in a row. We had a ton of fun on the court, but that was only a part of it, and not the most important part. The important part was the repetition, taking the shot over and over and over. That's just the basics of basketball mechanics.

My dad liked to say that the only way to have success in the future is to have failures in the present. I didn't feel that way when my 106th shot bounced off the rim. My dad remembers that I was pissed at myself when I missed that free throw, as if the 105 baskets before it had never happened. But at least I could look forward to steak for dinner afterward.

At the Courtrooms, there were pickup games every night—usually five-on-five—after we used the courts to practice. I wasn't big enough to play in the adult games, but my dad would jump in. Sometimes he'd be playing against guys he had gone to high school with, all in their thirties at the time. It was very physical—a lot of contact, a lot of fouls. They were so intense, I remember thinking, there's going to be a *fight*.

My obsession with basketball went everywhere with me. In 1991, when I was fifteen, my dad took all of us down to Orlando to go to Disney World. The Bulls were in the NBA Finals for the first time, and we missed game one against the Lakers because we were on that damn flight to Florida. When we got on the plane, I was wearing Bulls gear from head to foot—Bulls T-shirt, Bulls hat, Bulls shorts, even Bulls socks. Back then, there was no Internet or TV on the plane, so I just gnawed my fingernail until the plane landed in Florida. The game was just ending when we got into the terminal in Orlando just in time to see Sam Perkins sink a three-pointer that put the Lakers ahead. I almost never forgave my dad for making me miss that game.

In fact, I was so angry that I ditched Disney World and spent the vacation in the hotel, playing the basketball arcade game Arch Rivals and waiting for game two. Dad pulled the whole family out of Disney World for that one so that we could gather around the TV and watch. Chicago wiped out the Lakers 107–86 in that game and went on to win the championship three games later. I idolized Michael

Jordan, but I also loved the fierce competition, the team rivalries and what they stood for. I couldn't have been prouder to wear my Bulls gear when they got the win.

Dakota and I did different sports, and for different reasons. I don't think it matters what sport you play, or really even if you play a sport at all. The crucial thing is mastering what you like with discipline and hard work. Success doesn't happen spontaneously; it happens through grinding repetition. Doing the same thing over and over again until it becomes second nature.

Don't be fooled: I didn't harbor any views that this six-foot-one white kid from Montana was going to the NBA. I wasn't going to be a Spud Webb, bouncing out of nowhere to become some insanely improbable all-star on the court. When I reached a little bit of maturity, though, I realized that I could probably get college out of this. So that was what I did: I went on to Montana Tech, my mother's alma mater, and plied my trade. In this case, my trade was something that I just loved to do.

The Montana Tech campus is up in the northwest corner of Butte, a couple of miles from my mom and dad's houses. It's a beautiful, spacious campus. A big iron archway spans West Park Street, the main road that runs into campus, with crossed picks and axes on each side, the school symbol representing its century-old history as a mining school.

Past the statue of the school's founder, Marcus Daly, near the entrance, the Orediggers football and baseball fields unfurl on your left and eventually lead into the HPER Center, which stood for Health, Physical Education and Recreation Center. That's where I practiced and played. And directly to the north of the HPER Center, there's a rounded mountain dotted with scrub brush. That mountain is what's left of an old volcano that last erupted 50 million years ago. It's called Big Butte, and it's where the city gets its name. At the very top of the mountain, facing east, there's a giant white letter *M*.

"The Big M" is what we called it, and when it lights up at night, it's visible for miles around. It was built in 1910 as a kind of beacon for the school and the town. I'm mentioning this not because of sentimentality over my alma mater or a secret passion for geology, but because that fucking mountain kicked my ass.

On the first day of practice, Coach Dessing had us doing sprints and suicides and line drills. We were already drenched in sweat and exhausted when he gave us the kicker: *Go run up to the Big M and back,* he told us. *Then you can hit the showers.*

The Big M wasn't far—probably three-quarters of a mile—but it rose almost a thousand feet in elevation. *You've got to be shitting me,* I thought. But off we went, up the switchback trail that threaded between volcanic rock and granite, winding our way up to the pine-studded ridgeline above the city, and then across the ridge to the Big M, up to 6,299 feet. Then we turned back around and returned to the HPER Center, our hearts pounding and five pounds lighter from sweating, where we finally washed off our stench in those showers.

I wasn't angry afterward, just exhausted. And I also remember thinking: Why haven't I been doing this since eighth grade? And it also made me wonder why I would scarf down a quarter pounder with cheese and Chicken McNuggets right before a game. All those liter jugs of Mountain Dew. Eating pork chops sandwiches at the Freeway or at John's. Not that those sandwiches aren't delicious to the last bite, but you just won't see Olympians scarfing them down every day. Not wise.

And then I think there's another way to look at it: that if you're striving for perfection at every moment, you can begin to lose perspective. I mean, kids now look at their lives through the filters of Instagram and TikTok, and there's nothing wrong with that. But when I was growing up, I didn't have much to compare myself to, and as a result I didn't have much to feel bad about. I couldn't look at YouTube workout videos of kids my age and feel like I should give up, because I'd never be that good. I only had myself to look at. Well, and Michael Jordan.

I must have watched that Michael Jordan movie at least once a day for years, probably twice a day. I know it seems kind of comical, that a fat, redheaded kid from Butte, Montana, idolized Michael Jordan to the point of obsession. And it is funny—I mean I'm certainly laughing.

On the other hand, it's completely serious. When I speak publicly these days and get asked how to sum up the secret of success, or how to have a good marriage, or how to master a skill, people are always looking for the golden answer, something that quickly summarizes how to get the help they need. "Why are you such a good shot? Why are you such a good sniper?" I'm asked. Shit like that. My answer for them?

"Free throws." Plain and simple as that.

I know how ridiculous that sounds, which is precisely why I say it. It catches people off guard. It has the intended consequence of making them ask a follow-up question: What do you mean?

And here is what I say: I'm a big believer in the basics. If you want to be great—hell, if you want to be good—master the basics. It's like shooting a free throw. Dribble, dribble, dribble, spin the ball back, bend your knees up, and then release. Watch the rim, or watch your fingers, but do it the same every time. Front-sight, focus. Over and over and over. You want to get good at something? Do it a hundred times. If you want to be the best at something, do it a thousand times, and then a thousand more. Even if that means starting out with a piece of chalk and a line on a driveway.

DAKOTA
Three Mikes, One Way Forward

When I wanted to take my life into my hands, I went to my buddy Michael Keltner's house. He lived on the same road as I did, on a farm that was walking distance from ours. Mike was one of my best friends growing up. Still is. I'd ride the lawn mower over to his house or drive my dad's truck when I was older. Like Rob's cousin Mike Regan, I would sometimes hang out with Mike Keltner all day when I wasn't in school or had chores at the farm. He was a smart kid, he knew all about computers, and he was always the adult one in our crew.

That didn't mean we didn't do some seriously dumb shit together. When the MTV show *Jackass* aired for the first time in 2000, we took the show as a challenge, not as a warning. For those that don't remember it, the show was just a series of stupid, dangerous pranks, like snorting wasabi in a sushi restaurant, launching a porta-potty into the air with a guy strapped inside, cutting down a fifty-foot tree with two guys in Santa suits at the top, or trying to capture adult anacondas in a ball pit meant for kids.

God knows why, but Mike had a shopping cart at his farm. Like on the show, it provided endless entertainment. We'd take it to the road, I'd strap on a helmet and climb into the cart, and Mike would push me down the hill. He'd film me as I screamed like a crazy person as the cart whipped down the hill before it spilled and threw me out. Afterward, we'd watch the clip over and over again and laugh our asses off at how fucking ridiculous we were.

One summer, we found an old car hood lying around. If there had been snow on the ground, we'd have hitched it up to the four-wheeler and taken a spin, like a big metal version of Flexible Flyers, the plastic saucer sleds. But it was summer, so we came up with a better idea. We took the seats out of an old car on one of our properties and welded one of the seats onto the hood. Then we ran a rope to a four-wheeler and he dragged me across the fields while I was strapped onto the hood, like I was tubing on dry land. That wasn't fast enough, so we found a truck hood that was bigger, and welded a couple of seats onto that one, then used a chain to hook that up to my truck. We pulled that fucking truck hood so fast that it became airborne like some kind of demented, Mad Max, X Game event. Mike sent me a video of it the other day. I watched it and laughed all over again, thinking, *Oh, man, we're so lucky we're not dead.*

There was another Mike in my life, a high school friend named

Mike Staten. He was always positive, even though he came from nothing and his home life was so rough that he basically raised himself, living at friends' houses. I got to know him when we were on the football team together, even though I was a freshman and he was a senior. We both played running back and linebacker, and he was #20 while I was #21. I really looked up to him, and I can honestly say that he was probably the first person in my life that I really wanted to be like.

During my freshman year, my dad took Mike and me to the Florida–University of Kentucky game. Mike Staten was a big Gators fan, and the trash talk was pretty heavy, especially when Kentucky was winning. Florida came back toward the end, and when we went to Hooters to eat afterward, things got pretty rough. I kept pushing him and needling him, and finally my dad told me I'd better back up my words. So I challenged Mike. *We're gonna box,* I said. *You and I are going to box.* I had never taken classes or trained, but I had the gloves and a bag.

No, I'm not going to do that, he said, but I kept riding him, and finally he gave in. *All right.*

So we went back to Big Mike's and gathered in the front yard. It was long after dark by then, but there was a streetlight overhead, and we faced off on the grass between the driveway and the front door. Big Mike acted as the referee, and we went at it, circling around, while a couple of the guys from the team watched. Mike and I were about the same height, five eleven, and he probably had twenty, thirty pounds on me. He was bowlegged but fast. He went easy on me, and after I landed a few on him, I started to get confident. Too confident. I started swinging for the fences, and that was when he clubbed me with a roundhouse to the jaw that dropped me on the ground.

I'm not sure if it was the punch or my head hitting the ground that knocked me out, but I woke up with my dad bending over me, slapping me awake. The impact gave me a concussion and I had to go to the hospital. This was on a Saturday, and when I tried to play football on Monday, the coach benched me because I was still dazed and couldn't remember the plays. Mike felt terrible about it, but I thought it was funny as hell once I recovered. I looked up to him so much that after he graduated and left the team, I asked to take his jersey number. I became #20.

———•———

YOU DON'T START FIGHTING for no reason. You don't start fighting because everything in your life's good. I was lucky that I had Big Mike to take me in when things in my life were going downhill, but I had a lot of pain that built up. Fighting was the way I handled it. It wasn't anything profound or an embodiment of a warrior ethos for me. Fighting just became a part of who I was. Sometimes I'd start swinging because I was mad, sometimes because I was bored. It was usually over something stupid. But here's the thing I haven't told you: I *liked* to fight. It wasn't something that I saw as a character flaw or a problem; it was just a part of the way I made my way through the world. It was part of how boys became men where I lived, and it was part of how men related to other men. Through force. Through strength. There was something ritualistic about it. I'm not saying it's right—that was my mind-set at the time. And that was the mind-set of the people around me.

It's probably no coincidence that I started fighting and playing football around the same time. I know for sure why I fought in middle school, because I still remember the names of the assholes who bullied me. At school, there was a guy and his dumb-ass sidekick. I can still see them smirking at me. You never forget the faces of people who torment you. I don't know why these guys decided to pick on me. Maybe because I didn't have the money that they did or own nice clothes and shoes that were the talk around school. The *why* doesn't matter so much as the *what*, however. And the *what* is that I was getting beaten up in the bathroom, and being harassed in the hallways, and always watching and waiting for the next time it would happen. So that was when I got the boxing gloves, and started using them as often as I could so that I could eventually fight without them when I needed to.

I wouldn't describe myself as a small kid back then. I shot up to five-foot eleven inches in middle school, and have stayed at that height ever since. And farm work makes you strong; all of that time stacking hay bales, driving fence posts, even harvesting tobacco builds you up. But size has nothing to do with it: I've learned this lesson in the military, too. If you have the will to fight—if you have the *why*— that's what you do.

That's why I started playing football, too. I first signed up in seventh grade. I didn't have anything to prove, and the football team wasn't that good. It was just what you did when you were a boy of a certain age in Columbia, Kentucky. I'd like to say that it was about creating a better mind-set. Discovering strategy and teamwork. But that's bullshit: I started playing football because it was badass, and because it was fun, and because you can tear someone up on the field and everyone in the stands will get on their feet and cheer for you.

Here's the thing, though: I learned to appreciate things about the game that weren't obvious to me at the start. For example, football is a game of inches. You have to earn every yard. You have to fight your way forward through shrewd tactics and skill. You have to probe your adversary's weak spots and exploit them. You have to find the hole that no one else sees or learn to expect where one's going to appear. And yet, sometimes, football is just brute force. That's what's so appealing about it. Sure, there's strategy and game play and skill, but sometimes winning comes down to hitting someone as hard and purposefully as possible. I played hard, so hard that in practice games, I would disrupt the play. *I've got Dakota,* Mike Staten would say, and then I'd face him across the line of scrimmage as the game continued.

My friendship with Mike started out as kind of a mentor relationship, but it turned into something so much more. He taught me a lot on the football field, and he also taught me about overcoming adversity. Rob had Michael Jordan as his role model, but Mike Staten was mine. We didn't really see it that way at the time, but with the benefit of hindsight, it's clear as day to me now that he helped make me who I am.

I remember one game during my sophomore year, after Mike graduated. I must have been playing running back, and I carried that ball twenty or twenty-five times before halftime. And I was getting slaughtered each time I had the ball in my hands. My line wasn't blocking for me or protecting me, so I was just taking hit after hit as I plowed down the field. I got beat up so much that one of my elbows swelled to the point that I could barely bend it. My coach brought me into the locker room at halftime, planning to take me out.

I was in there getting ready to sit out the rest of the game with ice on my elbow when my dad busted in and told me that that wasn't going to happen. He told me I needed to get up and get back out on the field. Coach was powerless against my dad. *Okay, get back out there,* Coach said. So I did.

My dad was ultimately right. Just because something is hard and hurts doesn't mean quitting is the right thing to do. Just because I could sit out the rest of the game doesn't mean I should. Comparing war and football is a shitty analogy, because one is a game and the other is a lethal, fucking desperate fight for your life. But the similarities remain. I was part of a team, using my mind and my muscles. And the team doesn't win if everyone doesn't face the field and work together. The biggest difference is that in football, you get to go home afterward if you lose. In war, you go home in a body bag.

Eventually my entire school year revolved around football. I played a different sport every season—football in fall, basketball in winter, track in the spring—but as far as I was concerned, winter and spring were just conditioning to keep me in shape for football. Rob's sport was basketball, and mine was football. Both of us gained discipline and determination playing. And we had fun.

It was similar to fighting. Even though it was primal, I treated it like a sport, like football. That would change, of course. One day in the future, in the middle of a bloody firefight in Afghanistan, I would look into the eyes of a dying man whom I was killing with my bare hands. And all of my love of fighting, that excitement over using my fists against another person, would leave me forever. It would never be fun for me again.

I go back home to Kentucky all the time now. I have a love-hate relationship with my hometown for sure. I love the simplicity. I love going home. I love the farm where I grew up and I love the house that I built for myself next to it. But there are also parts that I can't stand: the small-town mentality, the petty jealousies, and how everyone's in everyone's business. I've never gone back for a school reunion. Sometimes I look up people I know from school, the guys I fought with, those I argued with. I googled one of my tormentors and found his mug shot: indicted for breaking and entering. No surprise there.

That's something that Rob and I have in common: we both felt stuck in towns that we knew we needed to get out of, towns that were big when we were kids but that we outgrew as we got older. We both had to leave in order to come home.

I've stayed in touch with both Mikes, even as my life is completely different now than it was when I was teenager. One of them gave me a sense of adventure, and one of them gave me a sense of purpose. And then of course there's the most important Mike of all, my dad Big Mike, who never let me quit and drove into me the stubbornness to work hard and push through. They're my holy trinity, I guess you could say. If there's anything that those three Mikes had in common, it was this: facing forward and staring down problems and fears. Front toward enemy.

I've still got that sense of adventure from playing with Mike Keltner. We just did whatever crazy shit we wanted to—that we needed—to have fun. Today, what kid could weld together a death-trap like we did without a parent hovering around making sure they didn't kill themselves or burn down the farm? Don't get me wrong:

it's fucking crazy and I'd never let my kids do it, but I still laugh my ass off when I think about us whooping and screaming as we bounced across the pasture, looking death in the eye.

I still have that thirst for adventures. I skydive, and I own a helicopter now. Someday I want to fly it all the way from Austin up to Columbia, and I want to land it in one of those fields where Mike and I dragged the car hood behind the truck, where Mike Staten punched me out on the front yard, where Dad and I waited before dawn for deer to show themselves. I'd like to look down and watch the grass flutter in the rotor wash, and see the cows low and scatter. Then I want to fly low over the treetops and across the hill where we pushed the shopping cart, and land my bird in the front yard of Mike Keltner's house. If I time it just right, maybe I'll scare the shit out of him, and then we'll laugh our asses off.

4

LEAVING

ROB
Never Say You Can't Do It

In 1995, I had a summer job at Montana Resources, a copper and molybdenum mine on the eastern outskirts of the city near the Berkeley Pit in Butte. It was a dirty, backbreaking job that required no skills, but I took it to get some extra conditioning and money. I had already enlisted in the Navy by then, and would be going to boot camp in January of the next year. I worked at one of the conveyor belts that moved ore to the pulverizers, which extracted minerals from the crushed rock. My job was to scoop up the rock and dirt that fell to the ground and return it to the belt, and I wore a respirator to keep my lungs from filling up with dust. But at fifteen dollars an hour, I could have done worse.

My friend Brad Salvagni worked at the mine, too. When we were hired, the bosses called us "the college guys," and predicted aloud that we'd run the mine eventually if we stayed. My mom would pack turkey, cheese, and mayo sandwiches for me, and during break time, Brad and I would bring our lunches to the break room, a windowless box with safety posters and OSHA laws posted on the walls, along with a running tally of "incident free days" at the mine. When we took off our masks to eat, black dust covered our faces, except for a white circle around our mouths where our respirators had been.

During one lunch, another guy joined Brad and me at our table. Brad asked me when I was leaving. Curious, the new guy said, "Shipping out for what?"

I told him I had joined the Navy, that I was planning to become a SEAL.

He scoffed. "Oh, you're gonna become a Navy SEAL? That's fucking ridiculous," he said.

"What do you know about it?" I shot back. "You tell me. What do you know? You don't know shit."

That fucker wasn't the only one to say that. Tough guys worked in the mines, and they gave me a lot of shit about enlisting. I heard it over and over again. *Oh, you'll never be a Navy SEAL, you can't do that. No one can do that.*

That was one of the reasons I needed to leave. I loved Butte, but I was suffocating from the small-town mentality that comes from living in a bubble, from being too comfortable with what you know, and too scared to go beyond. And while I was in the mine busting my ass shoveling dirt and rocks, all I could think about were those tough guys in with me who never got out and never went anywhere. Guys who wanted to make sure that everyone around them stayed stuck in their place, too, and how if I stayed in Butte, I might be their boss one day. And I sure as shit wasn't going to let that happen to me.

———————

BEFORE I ENLISTED IN THE NAVY, I had enrolled in my hometown college, Montana Tech, to play basketball in fall of 1994. But things hadn't been going well during my freshman year. Though our team was winning games, I knew I wasn't going to the NBA. School itself didn't hold my attention; my grades were slipping, and I wasn't applying myself. I hated my second semester courses. I was starting to have a gnawing feeling that if something didn't change I might never live anywhere but Butte.

That changed one afternoon in my freshman year. I had a job delivering pizzas at a joint called the Vu-Villa, a family-owned pizza restaurant in a brick storefront on West Park Street. It had a bar in an adjoining building. The pizzas passed from the restaurant through a window to the pub side. Above the bar, a neon sign read "The Vu." A sign above that read: "Where a friend is always waiting." With lots of shamrocks, of course. So many shamrocks.

The Vu was an institution in downtown Butte. It was near the junior high, so middle school kids would hang out and get pizza after school and play video games. It was just down the hill from Montana Tech, and it had a long display case of Tech gear and memorabilia. The bar side was a big hangout for students who would come in for the beer. Also, the cheese pizza was insane.

I was delivering pizzas along with a friend I'd known since I was six, a guy named Derek Hendrickson, who lived two houses down from my mom. Derek was an obnoxious loud-mouth and a serious asshole, and adults hated his guts. But he was really funny and great to hang out with; my best friend. The bar had games—some slots, Addams Family Pinball, Tales from the Crypt, and John Elway's Team Quarterback. In between deliveries, we'd play games and dick around.

I was in there one evening around November 1994 when the door opened and in walked Ben Wlaysewski, whom I had known for years. Our mothers were great friends—they worked together at the junior high—but he was two years older than me, so I was just another annoying kid to him. Back at Butte Central, he was so athletic that he had been both an offensive and defensive lineman on the football team. He had USMC stickers on the front and back of his truck, and Marine Corps hats and shirts and tank tops. No one doubted that he was going to enlist.

And now he was the Marine that he promised to be. He had been big before, really strong, but when he came in the door of the Vu, he was huge, with bulked-up biceps and a neck like an ox. When he came in, he made an *entrance*, like a confident showman walking onto a stage. Eyes followed him around the restaurant. Male patrons were jealous, and female patrons had trouble not staring.

As I watched him moving between tables and shaking hands with people he had known all his life, I thought to myself: *What are the Marines doing to these boys to turn them into men like this?* Feeling nervous, I went up to him to say hello.

"Ben, how you doing, man?" I said.

He recognized me immediately. "Hey Robbie, how you doing?" We shot the shit for a little while before he found his friends. I won't lie: his remembering me gave a little flush of pride to my ego. I also realized something else. I didn't want to be one of the guys parked at the bar looking enviously at Ben when he came in; I wanted to *be* Ben.

Ben made an impression on me when I needed it the most, but it was one of his former classmates, Jim McBride, who really steered me toward enlisting. While I had always known Ben and his mother, I knew the McBrides better. To call his dad, Bill, a well-known guy around town would be an understatement. He was a Butte native who painted highway lines before he became a bus driver, first for the schools then for the town bus system. Anyone who took public transportation in Butte knew Bill.

He was also a big Butte Central guy who kept the stats for all the basketball games, up in the booth, as well as football games. He recorded every one of my assists, rebounds, three-pointers, and steals. I can still hear his voice when I was checking in before a game: "Go get 'em, Robbie," he'd say. He had been a Marine, too, and his son Jim followed in his footsteps.

Both Jim and Ben had been in the same Butte Central class, enlisted right out of high school, and went to boot camp together as soon as senior year ended. Jim had played on the high school football team, and he was big, too. He was tall, maybe six five. But he had characteristics other than his physical prowess that I admired. He was a joker, very funny, and very smart, with a positive, sunny disposition. He was always going to be a Marine, no doubt about it, but he wasn't the type of Marine who would rip you in half. He was the type who'd pat you on the back and tell you why today's a good day.

A couple of days after I saw Ben at the Vu, I was down by my dad's house when I saw Jim jogging past on Blacktail Lane. He was wearing green Marine Corps pants with the red "USMC," and he was shirtless and tan, with rippling muscles and abs you could ski on. He was just a fucking beast. I had the same reaction that I did to seeing Ben: *What are they feeding these guys at Parris Island?*

Seeing Jim and Ben within a few days of each other planted the seed for me. I really hadn't given much thought to enlisting before I saw the two of them. There weren't a lot of Marines in Butte, so the two of them stood out. Marines were like gods to me.

And then something happened that tipped the scale. It was a girl I had been dating since the summer of 1994, right after graduating from Butte Central. We had met at a party at my friend Scott Sullivan's house. His mom was the cool mom, the one who let everyone drink at the house as long as they didn't drive home or do anything stupid. At the party, I had eyed this gorgeous brunette with a biting sense of humor. Way out of my league. But for some reason, she talked to me that night, and we started dating.

We saw each other for about a year and a half, while I was at Montana Tech and she was still in high school. And then in the winter of 1995, I found out that she was seeing other people. And so I broke up with her. It was a mess—all bruised hearts and wailing violins and shit. I showed up angry and drunk at her house one night, and her father, instead of working me over like I probably deserved, just marched me out of the house. Not pretty, but at least no one got hurt.

Nothing seemed to be going right. School, basketball, small town rivalries and jealousies, a job that was putting me on a track to be a middling manager, all that shit. And now this thing with the girl. It wasn't like it was that serious, or the end of the world. But after it happened, seeing Ben and Jim propelled me to enlist. I got my heart broken, and I said, *Fuck it, I want to be a Marine. I want to experience that shit.* When I broke up with her, I broke up with Butte.

The day I went to the recruiter, I went up the hill to Montana Tech first to see my professors. I went from office to office to tell them that I was dropping out. When I spoke to my public speaking teacher, she shook her head and told me I'd never be a good public speaker. The joke's on her.

And then I drove down to Harrison Avenue and turned into the Butte Town Center shopping plaza, across the street from the Butte Civic Center, where I played basketball. I parked in front of the Armed Services Career Center, which was wedged between a CVS and Stokes grocery store. It was about noon when I walked in the front door, looking for the Marines Corps office.

Just my luck, it was lunchtime and the Marine recruiter had stepped out to Little Caesar's or some shit for lunch. I knew the USMC was part of the Navy, so I stepped into the Navy office to ask when he would be back. The officer behind the desk was wearing khakis, which meant he was a chief, though I didn't know that at the time. I asked him where the Marine recruiter was, and he asked, "Why do you want to be a Marine?"

"I want to be a sniper," I told him.

"We have snipers in the Navy," he said. "All you have to do is become a Navy SEAL. We'll send you right to sniper school." That was total BS, of course, because he had no control over that. He was convincing, though, and I signed up on the spot.

It was a deferred enlistment, so I was agreeing to formally enlist in six months. It was an honor system; I didn't know this, but legally I could have pulled out anytime. I went home and told my mother, and then I got on the kitchen phone and called my father to tell him. I won't lie—he was pissed. "Motherfucker!" he cursed into the phone when I told him. He wasn't cursing at me; he was just angry that I had given up on basketball, after all the work that we had put into it, day after day.

Even though I had discussed it with my mother, she wanted to know what I was getting into, so I brought her down to the recruiting office the next day to watch a video about the SEALs. I don't think it convinced her as it had me.

I had about six months before I reported to boot camp. That meant six months to get into shape. Though I had dropped out of Montana Tech, I still had my student ID, which I could use to get into the HPER Center, the campus sports and recreation complex. The center had a twenty-five-meter pool, which was half the length of a regulation Olympic-sized pool. At that age, I was so dumb that I thought, *Oh, six months in the pool. I'm good. I'll be as good as anybody. If I just went and swam, sure as shit I'd become a SEAL.* The truth was, I sucked. I just didn't know bad I sucked.

The afternoon that I enlisted, I went down to the center to start my conditioning. *I'll swim one thousand meters and see how it feels,* I thought. I don't think I had swum fifty meters before I stopped, exhausted. As I floundered, trying to catch my breath, a high school classmate named Mike Driscoll spotted me. He was about to join the swim team at Notre Dame.

"Don't take this the wrong way—it's great to see you—but I've literally never seen you in the pool before. What gives?" he said.

"I joined the Navy today and I'm going to be a Navy SEAL," I told him.

He looked at me kind of funny. "Not like that, you're not," he said. "Get back in there. I'm going to teach you a few strokes." He showed me how to do a breaststroke and a sidestroke and other swimming styles. I was lucky that I ran into him. But then I got even luckier—I ran into Jim McBride again.

Jim probably kept me from failing out of BUD/S. I was at a bar one night called Brew's Billiard Balls, another tough-guy place where somebody usually got the shit beaten out of them come closing. It was the kind of place where I would ask the bartender for two shots of Wild Turkey, and instead of carding me, he'd ask me if I wanted a chaser. I'd say, "You're right . . . Three shots of Wild Turkey." Butte tough.

I was there with friends one night to see a local cover band called Uncle Mary, a bunch of long-haired Butte dudes who would play the same KISS and Thin Lizzy songs over and over all night. We loved it. And then the door opened, and Jim McBride came in, just like Ben had made his entrance at the Vu. Of course, I had seen Jim around town, but now I had enlisted, too. This gave me the confidence to walk up to him.

"I just joined the Navy, man," I told him, trying to impress him. And then, unfortunately, I remember exactly what I said next. "I'm going to go to SEAL school," I told him.

He looked at me kind of funny, like Driscoll had when he saw me swimming. "No one says SEAL school," he said. "It's called BUD/S."

Jim told me he had just been through aircrew training for the Marines. These are the guys that ride in the helicopters: the door gunners, the rescue swimmers. He'd been through the SAR course—which is maritime search and rescue—and they swim like porpoises. "Do you know what the fuck you're getting into?" he asked me. And the fact was that I didn't.

And so he and I went up to the HPER Center together. Watching him was like watching Driscoll swim, except that McBride really showed me what he learned in the military. As opposed to being a collegiate swimmer, he was a military rescue swimmer. Driscoll showed me good form, but McBride showed me the practical elements, the strokes and conditioning that would serve me well at BUD/S.

What I liked about Jim—what I still like about him—was that he was a positive guy. He didn't beat up on me or give me a hard time or make fun of me. Which was not something that I got from other people. Everyone around me joked about how I would never make it, how I would fail out and come back. Some of my best friends were telling me I'd never make it. My mom and my brother and sisters were nice enough not to say anything, but they now privately admit they thought there was no fucking way I would make it. I had dropped out college, and things didn't go well, I might end up a regular at the Vu-Villa or Brew's, nursing a flat beer and turning around to look every time the door opened in case an old friend had come home.

I spent that whole summer and fall training, swimming, running, doing endless pull-ups, and flutter kicks. I watched *Full Metal Jacket* once a day, at least. And I took the job at Montana Resources, to build up my body for what lay ahead. As I sweated alongside the conveyor belt, my arms and back aching as I tossed shovel after shovel back onto the belt, I could hear the sneering voice of that guy in the break room. *You'll never get out. You'll never succeed. Don't even try.* It just made me shovel harder.

THE DAY BEFORE I SHIPPED OUT in January 1996, I signed the final enlistment papers, and got ready to go. The Navy puts you up in a hotel the night before you leave, and since Butte had the regional Military Entrance Processing Station, there were recruits from Anaconda, Deer Lodge, and Helena who would be flying out with me the next morning. I had my own room in the hotel uptown from the airport. I sat in my room alone with nothing to do but watch the Steelers and the Cowboys in Super Bowl XXX and stew about my early morning flight the next day.

And then I said to myself, *What the fuck am I doing here?* So I went back to my mom's and watched Pittsburgh lose to Dallas 27–17, and I spent my last night in Butte in my own bed.

The next morning around 5 A.M., my family brought me to Bert Mooney Airport. I wore a gray denim jacket with a fake sheep wool lining, and a shitty pair of jeans and a shitty pair of shoes, because I wanted the Navy to throw away my clothes when I got to boot camp instead of mailing them home. The only thing I brought with me was a copy of Stephen King's *The Eyes of the Dragon* to read on the flight.

I looked ridiculous, and worse, I felt sad and scared shitless. As I walked toward the door to the tarmac, my family watching me go, the last thing I heard was my brother Tommy yell, "Good luck, Rob!" Outside the terminal, the air was frigid, and the runways had been cleared of new-fallen snow. I could still see my family as I walked across the illuminated tarmac to the plane, a small regional jet that would take me to Salt Lake City, and from there to Chicago.

After I climbed steps and ducked into the cabin, I buckled myself in on the left side of the aircraft. I looked out the window as the plane took off to the north and gained altitude. The sun still wasn't up, and I could see the lights of Butte below me as the plane banked west before turning south, following Interstate 15 toward Utah. We flew over Montana Tech and the Big M, the Courtrooms where I learned to play basketball, and the parkland where I hunted elk. And then we flew south, and it all disappeared behind me.

Nobody does that. Nobody leaves Butte to become a SEAL. Nobody. The words echoed in my mind.

One day I would come back after killing the most wanted man on the planet in the dead of night in a fortified compound in Pakistan, and I would say, *Yes, somebody did that.*

DAKOTA
Leave the Keys on the Dresser, Your Pride at the Door

The Friday night crowd was on its feet in the gymnasium at Green County High School when I stepped down from the bleachers to cuss out my girlfriend's ex over the phone. I had been dating a cheerleader named Nikki at Green County, which was a rival of my school, Adair County High School. Her ex was a star athlete named Jared Vaughn. Even though she and I were dating, he was still calling her, and I was pissed. While Nikki was down on the court leading basketball yells, I was yelling at him to leave her the fuck alone.

Jared didn't appreciate what I had to say to him. Like with a lot of my conflicts at that age, the shit talk ended with a fight. We agreed to meet after the game at the Green County Fairgrounds, which was about a mile away. I got a ride across town with a bunch of guys who wanted to watch. It was pitch black and cold when we arrived, and the fairground was deserted as we pulled into the gravel parking lot and got out of our cars. Jared had brought a bunch of his friends, too, maybe a half dozen or so. I don't recall what we said. We probably talked some more trash to each other. And then we went at it.

At one point, I got him down on the ground. But because Jared was much bigger than I was, that was all I managed to do before he shook me off, got back on his feet, and then beat the fuck out of me. He smashed my nose so badly that I couldn't breathe, he broke my hand, and he gave me two black eyes. Just worked me over like a pro until I was a portrait of misery.

Afterward, a guy named Jake who came with me brought me back to his house, where he helped snap my broken nose back into place and clean me up before I went home. As soon as I could, I went to the doctor to get my nose looked at, and some medication for the pain.

When I got to school on Monday morning, anyone who hadn't heard about the fight over the weekend found out as soon as they saw my fucked-up face, with two swollen black eyes and my nose all messed up. I was in a world of shit, and I dropped a loose pain pill into the pocket of my Abercrombie & Fitch jacket when I left for school. Anytime you bring medication of any kind to school, you're supposed to turn it over to the school nurse at the start of the day. It doesn't matter whether it's Klonopin or Adderall or Tylenol, it belongs to the nurse until the school bell rings. But I didn't turn it in. Mistake number one.

When I got to Mr. Hammond's computer class, I took a seat near two guys named Marvin Clarkson and Justin Parr. They were the popular kids in my class, the jocks with the nice clothes and the perfect hair and the pretty girlfriends, and everyone wanted to be friends with them. Even me, I suppose.

Which is when I made mistake number two: I leaned over to those two jocks whom I barely knew, showed them the pain pill, and whispered a smart-ass joke, "I'm just gonna sell it." And then they pulled a really fucking funny joke on me: they told the teacher.

———————●———————

THE REASON I'M TELLING THIS STORY isn't that the fight was important, or that those dickheads snitched on me. It's because of what happened afterward, and because that has to do with trust, which was something I didn't have much of. For a long time, I've had a hard time trusting anybody. I haven't been very trustworthy myself at points in my life, either. I can trace that trust gap back to exactly where it started. It was when I was thirteen, and my mom told me that I was adopted. I was living with Big Mike by then, but I still went to go see her every so often. On one of those visits, she asked me to come down to the kitchen. "I need to talk to you," she told me. When I got there, papers covered the table. They were my adoption papers. When she showed them to me, I didn't recognize the name of my biological father written on the papers, the father who had given up his parenthood rights to Big Mike. Big Mike wasn't my birth father, she told me, but he had adopted me as a child.

When she told me this, my whole world crashed down around me. I felt like everything I had been told was a lie. My own dad—my biological father—hadn't wanted me and had given me up to a stranger. And Big Mike, my grandparents, my aunts and uncles and cousins, I wasn't related to any of them, and no one had told me until this minute. And my mom had chosen to tell me this without Big Mike there to explain it with her.

Naturally, I took it out on Big Mike when I got back to the farm.

He bore the brunt of my fury, and then he said calmly, "I'm still your dad," he said. "Does a piece of paper change everything?" That was what we called a Big Mike Response—measured, blunt, unemotional. And he was mostly right: it didn't change *everything*. It did change one thing, though, which is that I had a lot of trouble trusting anyone again after that.

Trust is central to everything we do. It's the reason families hold together or don't. It's the reason friendships survive or die. It's the reason marriages work or fizzle. It's what makes a winning football team, and it's what holds platoons together on the battlefield. If you don't trust your team to have your back, then you might as well have no team at all.

Which brings me back to computer class at Adair County High School. I still don't know why I thought it would be a good idea to let those two assholes in on my joke about the medication, but I did. And I shouldn't have. I think it was because of the lure of their popularity. I wanted them to like me, and I wanted to be a part of their dumb world. The joke was on me, because they turned around and told Mr. Hammond. Mr. Hammond called the principal's office. And pretty soon a school police officer was at the door of the computer lab looking for me.

While everyone in the class stared, the officer hauled me down to the vice principal's office, and they made me turn out my pockets while they grilled me about what I had said to those two clowns, like I was an oxy dealer instead of a guy with a busted nose.

Of course, I wasn't selling drugs; all I had was that one pill. But after that, everything changed for me at school. I felt like I was always being watched, like I was always on the edge of being in trouble. And I knew that nobody could trust me.

It's ironic because I wanted to be trusted, and I had taken up a new sport that depended on it. In fall of 2003, when I was a sophomore, I was playing football and hanging out with the cheerleaders. They were like sisters to me—Mary, MacKenzie, and their friends. At the same time, I'd give them shit all the time about cheerleading. "It's not a real sport, right?" I said.

One of the girls in the group dared me to come to practice and try it. "Okay, done," I said.

So after football practice one day, I got a ride with the girls. Their parents took turns driving them over to Campbellsville for practice. It was about a thirty-minute drive, and we were all packed in the car, laughing about my coming with them. When we got to the building where they practiced, I saw the mats piled up, a long tumble track, all kinds of gymnastics equipment. I figured I'd do it once, just to show them.

The coach, whom we called Mrs. G, asked me to help with a basket toss. That took four of us—two girls on the left and right lock forearms as the base, with the flyer standing on the basket that their linked arms create. The fourth person was the back spot, behind. That was me. The bases lift with their legs and shoulders and propel the flyer up with their arms, while the thrower gives the flyer an extra shove into the air. In an advanced toss, maybe she does a flip, maybe she spins, but she doesn't get very high and we catch her on the way down.

These girls weren't used to having a five-foot-eleven-inch linebacker like me doing a toss. So when this girl Keisha Matney climbed up, she was definitely not expecting to go very high. I sent her up like a rocket, so high that she had to put out her hand to stop herself from hitting the ceiling before she came back down. I think it surprised her as much as it did me.

"Oh, we want him," Mrs. G said, "because our basket tosses are going to be extra high." Next thing I knew, they're asking me to do this and that—can you do this basket toss? Can you be the bottom of this pyramid? And all of a sudden, I was part of the cheerleading team.

Cheerleading is all about trust. You have to trust that the person on your left and on your right are going to catch you, that they're going to be looking out for you. You can't hold up a pyramid without a steady person at the base holding you up. You can't be confident in your safety unless you trust the spotter behind to make sure that you're not going to fall. Trust is something that you have to learn, like a muscle that you have to exercise. It takes repetition. You get sore, and you do it again. You build that muscle up, beat it back from oblivion.

I trusted those girls, and they trusted me. I think that's why I found it so easy. They didn't just teach me about gymnastics, either. By the end, I knew how to style hair for competition, how to avoid injuries. I practiced with the cheerleaders at least once a week. I like it for the same reason I like football, and the same reason Rob liked basketball. When you're on a team, you all depend on each other. It doesn't matter whether it's relying on linebackers to your left and right to protect you as you pound your way up the field, or being confident that the girls at the bottom of a pyramid are strong enough to hold you up.

Some classmates gave me shit for cheerleading, for sure, but the cheerleaders stuck up for me. They were loyal. And plus, it helped to have a sense of humor about it. I remember seeing a T-shirt once that another cheerleader dude wore. It said something like, "You can call me gay, but my hands are on your girlfriend's butt." Stupid shit, but funny . . . and true.

I lasted through the fall, and then I dropped out of cheerleading. The reason was that I transferred to Green County High School. I switched schools because of my escort to the vice principal's office. Of course, they hadn't found any drugs on me, only my prescription painkillers, but it was humiliating. It was so humiliating that I decided to leave the school and go to Green County instead.

The thing is, you never know how one thing will lead to another. I played football at Green County, too. I had taken the ACT and looked at Western Kentucky for college, with a goal of playing sports. I knew I wouldn't make it on academics alone—I needed something to keep me there other than the books. But by senior year of high school, football was no longer the glide path to college that I had expected. I messed up my knee, and it was questionable whether I was good enough to play college football even without injuries.

Maybe that's the reason that I walked up to the Marine recruiter in the lunchroom my senior year at Green County. I remember the day I came into the room and saw his table at the front of the lunchroom, displaying a bunch of glossy pamphlets. I'd seen him in there before, but I'd never talked to him. I went up to him and started asking a bunch of smart-ass questions, mostly about guns, trying to show how much I knew, which was not much. And then, after we shot the shit for a while, he called bullshit and looked me in the eye. "There's no way you'd make it as a Marine," he said.

I'm pretty sure that that line was a recruitment strategy, rather than something the recruiter actually believed, but it felt like a slap in the face. What I realized later is that he likely said that to goad me into enlisting, and he probably said it to every recruit who came up to the table. If that was true, it worked, because my first thought was, *Watch me, motherfucker.*

I signed up on the spot. What I didn't know when I took the bait from that recruiter was that trust is central to the military, and especially in the Marines. Like a football team, like a cheerleading squad, like a functioning family, every part of the Marine apparatus depends on every other person doing their part, from the lowest grunt to the four-star general. Eventually, I would learn that under fire, and that lesson would be stamped onto my life with the stain of my brothers' blood. After I got to Parris Island, I would learn how to check my impulses, how to swallow my anger, how to earn trust. I'd fail that test one more time before I shipped out.

•————•

AFTER SCHOOL ENDED IN 2006, but before I left for boot camp, the track team had an upcoming statewide track meet, and I wanted to compete. Track was my springtime sport, and my events were discus, shot put, and relay. Coach Hodges wanted me there. He told the team straight up that we couldn't drive to the meet; we *had to* take the team bus. But he made an exception. For me.

I couldn't go with the team because my grandfather was in the hospital and I was with him when the bus was leaving. So Coach Hodges bent the rules and let me drive. But he also laid down the law for when I arrived at the meet: "You're going to give me your keys. You can't be driving people around, for safety reasons." Legitimate stuff.

This was a big deal. Coach Hodges wasn't just my track coach—he was the school athletic director and a math teacher. He is probably the most disciplined, military-looking guy that never served. A really consistent teacher and coach, steady as a rock. He was a huge influence on me because he was one of the few teachers who believed in me.

I should have made it easy for him to respect me in return, but I didn't. After leaving my pepaw in the hospital, I got in my white Trailblazer and drove to meet the team. When I got there, I parked my truck at the hotel where we were all staying and handed my keys to the coach, just as we talked about.

After we got there, coach called a team meeting so he could lay out some logistics stuff. The entire team packed into his room, fifteen of us or so standing or sitting on the bed. There was a big king-sized bed, and a TV on the left, and a dresser. And on top of the dresser were my car keys. They were just lying there, tempting me, the only thing that stood between a boring night watching TV in our shitty hotel room and a night of freedom on the town. I couldn't keep my eyes off them.

So when Coach Hodges wasn't looking, I reached out, carefully picked them up, and put them in my pocket.

I knew I shouldn't have done it. Obviously. My friends knew, too. They whispered, "You're crazy, you're crazy." I still recall the way my friend Karly said, "Oh, he's gonna be so mad," sounding shocked that I had done the impossible.

After the meeting, my friend John T., some other buddies, and

I jumped in the truck. We headed over to a gas station, probably to try to buy beer. The gas station couldn't have been far from the hotel, and it was the first and the last stop on our night of freedom. We had just pulled in, and what do you know, Coach Hodges showed up like a bat out of hell. I don't know where he came from—maybe he followed us, maybe he was coming out of the gas station, but all I knew was that he was standing next to the car, and he was fucking pissed. And then he spat out almost exactly the same words that the Marine recruiter told me in the high school lunchroom.

"The way you act, you'll never make it as a Marine!" he yelled at me.

This came from a man of few words, whom I looked up to probably as much as anyone other than my dad and my grandfather. When he said that to me, it cut right to the heart of my being. Every teenager has a few indelible moments that are cut into your memories, experiences that made you look at yourself and say, *I really have got to get my shit together*. For me, this was one of them, one of the biggest ones. He had put his trust in me in the simplest possible way, and I had failed him.

Right there and then, Coach kicked me off the team. He yelled at me to get back to the hotel, get my stuff, and go home. Those words impacted me more than he'd ever know. Look, I wasn't someone who shied away from being in trouble. And I wasn't bothered that he was upset at me. I was bothered that I let him down. Here was the other thing that really bothered me: he was right. I wouldn't make it as a Marine acting that way. Because if you can't be trusted with car keys, you certainly can't be trusted with the lives of your brothers, either.

PART TWO

DUTY

5

DRILLING DOWN

ROB

Be Afraid, but Don't Panic

My entire BUD/S class jumped two by two, fully clothed, from the diving platform into the water, until all 180 or so of us were in the pool. As the men swarmed into the water, our instructors bellowed at us without a break, screaming for us to find our boat crews, to tread water, to get undressed, to inflate our pants to float. It was pandemonium.

We had just finished one of the most grueling "evolutions," the term for different tasks on the BUD/S training schedule: the fifty-meter underwater swim. Afterward, we huddled, exhausted, on the concrete under a gray Southern California sky. That was when the instructors began yelling at us to pull on our boots, pants, blouses, and hats, line up, and get back into the pool.

None of us expected that. In BUD/S, there are SEAL candidates called "rollbacks" who dropped out of one class and joined the class coming up behind. The rollbacks from class 207 often told our un-initiated class 208 what to expect over the twenty-four weeks of the course. We rarely knew what was real and what was exaggerated. If some horrible evolution was coming up, like Hell Week, we usually heard details beforehand from them. We would just do what we were told to make it through this course. But no one had told me about this evolution, and I had no fucking idea what was happening.

I tried to get my bearings in the churning water, waves lapping my face as I looked around at the mass of swimmers to find the other six members of my crew. My waterlogged boots slowed my kicks and my clothes pulled me down as my classmates thrashed around me. Arms smacked the water, sometimes hitting one another on the head, on the shoulders. And then, at some point, I realized that the yelling instructors encircling the swimmers in the pool were pushing us together, herding us into a tighter knot in the water. Which was when I realized that pretty soon, none of us would have any room to swim.

The cluster of swimmers pressed tighter and tighter, until we were too close to one another to tread water. Slippery limbs slapped against the swimmers on each side, knees knocked under the water, shoulders wedged into backs and chests. We were nuts to butts. Every second, there was less and less space. With no room to swim, some of the men began to sink, forced under the surface by their struggling classmates. On the perimeter of the chaos, the instructors grabbed swimmers' heads and dunked them under the water. Their shouted instructions were contradictory and confusing, and didn't seem to have any point.

Around me, some of my classmates were starting to panic. There was no room to navigate or to find one another in the flailing tangle. As recruits sank, they grabbed whoever was next to him. That person grabbed on to the closest shoulder or arm next to him. Swimmers began disappearing into the writhing knot of swimmers. Some began screaming at the people near them, to get the fuck out of the way, deliberately elbowing and hitting them, which heightened the chaos and created still more panic.

I saw only one solution. I took a long breath to calm myself, and then exhaled. As the air left my lungs, I sank down between the bodies jammed around me. The pool was fifteen feet deep at that end, so I descended under the scrum of frantic limbs churning the pool water. From below, the hysterical activity on the surface looked more like a deepwater riot than a training exercise. I swam out from the center to the edge of the thrashing pack and then back up to the surface, where I could take a breath. *Good. Easy. Safe.* Until the instructors shoved me back into the middle of that watery shit-show. *Well this is stupid,* I thought.

———————————

I'VE NEVER BEEN AFRAID OF DROWNING. I suppose that's strange considering I grew up in a landlocked state and could barely do a breaststroke until nine months before SEAL training. Nevertheless, I've always been comfortable swimming and have never felt a fear of water.

Water is a strange thing. Aquaphobia, like other common fears, is widespread, powerful, and springs from the deep corners of our subconscious. But unlike, say, fear of public speaking or spiders or heights, there's a special kind of terror in being unable to breathe, suffocating as one's lungs fill up and fail and consciousness fades. Almost half of Americans are scared of the deep end of the pool, and that's water contained in a finite space, with ladders and lifeguards nearby. Imagine fear of the open water, of swimming in the ocean. Something like two-thirds of Americans are deathly afraid of the open water. Nobody knows what creatures are out there. I blame everything on *Jaws.*

I wasn't afraid. Just the opposite: I couldn't get to Coronado fast enough. I had pinned my hopes on it months earlier, and I was convinced I was ready. In my enlistment, I had been guaranteed three tryouts for BUD/S. During boot camp at Great Lakes, Illinois, I failed the first attempt, but succeeded on the second. After boot camp and a brief stint at aviation school in Tennessee, I flew back to Montana, then drove to San Diego with my friend Shawn, who was also headed for BUD/S.

We got there on a Thursday and drove straight out to Coronado. Coronado is a peninsula nestled into San Diego Bay, with luxury homes on the bay side and open beach facing the Pacific to the west. A bridge on the north end connects to San Diego, while a sandy road runs south along a narrow strip of beaches stretching past the Navy base and SEAL training facility at the Naval Special Warfare Center, and along an isthmus to the mainland.

When Shawn and I first arrived, we drove in my truck over the Coronado Bridge and then south to get a look at the Naval Amphibious Base, the Naval Special Warfare Center, and the infamous BUD/S obstacle course, known as the "O course." We were on a kind of reconnaissance mission, since we weren't expected until the following day. We scouted the Navy complex and the O course from the road, then turned around before we reached the mainland and returned the way we came, passing the Naval Center and the BUD/S "grinder" where the classes do PT, before continuing on and parking on the ocean side, near the luxurious Hotel del Coronado.

Being from Butte, I'd never been in the ocean or even gotten my feet wet in the surf. Maybe that's why the first thing I did was to walk down on the beach and look at the ocean. The sun had gone down, and Shawn and I went for a swim in the dark. Afterward, we sat on the beach, looking out at the ocean. As we faced the open water, we spotted lights bobbing on the waves. They were chem lights dangling from rubber boats paddling north. It was the BUD/S class 207, on the last night of their Hell Week. Soon enough, Shawn and I would be in those boats, too.

There's a mystique around SEALs for our toughness, for our knowledge, and for our combat experience. For our ability to push the limits of human endurance and strength, to operate with stealth in any environment, to survive under the most punishing circumstances. But there's another important skill—maybe the most important one—that's less obvious. That skill is staying calm and avoiding panic at all costs. Because when you're in the water up to your neck, or waves are crashing over your head, or you're tumbling through the air with tangled chute cords, opportunities for panic abound.

It would be years before I found out the purpose of the deep-end pool party that could have caused my classmates to drown. The instructors called it "the beehive." Somebody probably made up that name as a sick joke, but it's pretty apt. In a beehive, all the bees work together. In the BUD/S beehive, the way to avoid getting hurt is for everyone to stay calm. Which is hard to do when you're barraged with screamed orders intended to shatter nerves and sow panic. All it takes is one person to flip out and then everyone goes under. And when people freak out, things get dangerous.

At the time, I thought it was just a stupid exercise in keeping calm or learning to swim in your clothes or some shit. I found out much later that the beehive had adopted a more official name: "combat swimmer orientation." It turned out that the instructors were trying to simulate what would happen in a shipwreck combat situation, when a ship gets hit or sinks, and everyone gets dunked into the ocean, disoriented, constrained, separated from your crew, possibly fighting hostiles in the water beside you. It was supposed to emulate a worst-case, life-or-death, real-world maritime disaster. They wanted to see if we could maintain order and complete simple tasks amid complete chaos. Find one another. Stay afloat. Get out of the danger zone. And so they watched us carefully to see who handled their fear, and who didn't.

Fear is natural. Fear is healthy. Fear is fuel. It gives you adrenaline and heightens your senses. It can help you come out on the right side of fight-or-flight. It can work for you. In SEAL lingo, we call that a "heightened sense of awareness." I've had people ask me about combat, "What is it like to not be afraid?" My response is, "I don't know." I was afraid pretty much every time. And that's okay. My awareness in combat was heightened a lot.

But there's a fine line between fear and panic. Because panic is dangerous. And panic is contagious. And if one person panics, everyone starts to. It's the beehive mentality. You're either sliding into panic or you're finding calm, which is the flip side of panic. Calm can be contagious, too. You'll notice the way airline pilots talk in the middle of a turbulent flight. If there's stress or panic in their voice, it's almost guaranteed that it will spread to every passenger in the cabin. Imagine the difference between a pilot saying, "We are obviously experiencing some rough air," and, "WE ARE ALL ABOUT TO FUCKING DIE!" They stay calm so that you remain calm.

Now, there's danger in remaining too calm, in building up resistance to fear. The problem with not being afraid anymore is that you get complacent. You let your guard down. You get lazy. Mistakes creep in. And it doesn't matter what line of work you're in; mistakes can be lethal. Complacency kills.

Nobody understood this better than the BUD/S instructors, and it was their job to either teach us not to panic, or tell us to get the fuck out. They knew what was required to stay composed amid complete fucking chaos, and their job was to continually test our ability to maintain calm and equilibrium in the most insane circumstances. There was a notoriously hard-ass instructor at BUD/S named Instructor Woodie. His full name was Woodie Mister, and back in 1996, he was one of the few active SEALs with combat experience. He had my fair complexion, red curls, and deep crow's feet in the corners of his eyes that crinkled when he smiled. Not that we ever saw that, because he never smiled. He was legendary. Even before I started in class 208, there were rumors that you did not want Instructor Woodie to hate you, because he would drive you out of BUD/S. That he was a sadist who would stay on top of you like a barnacle on a rock, and he wouldn't let go until you were gone.

No shit, I watched him do that once. A classmate had mouthed off or said something disrespectful, and Woodie came down on him like Mount St. Helens. He ordered the kid to low-crawl from the O course up and over the sand berm on the beach, down to the water and into the surf, and then back, over and over. That might not sound difficult, but try low-crawling while covered in salt water and sand. For an entire day. I can still picture Woodie wearing his blue instructor shirt and holding a coffee cup, telling this kid that he would keep crawling until he quit, or until he was too physically broken to continue. Woodie kept it simple. The kid quit that day.

I tried to avoid Instructor Woodie. One of the few run-ins I had with him in BUD/S was outside a popular restaurant in Coronado about two blocks from the beach, when we had a night. At around 6 P.M., he was walking toward me down the palm-tree-lined sidewalk. I should have said nothing, or better yet, crossed the street. Instead, like a nervous jackass, I said, "Hooyah, Instructor Woodie." Which is how every instructor is addressed, always.

He stopped dead on the sidewalk. "What the fuck was that?" he shouted at me, glaring. I stammered something like, "I don't know, I was just trying to say hi." Sometimes the best thing you can do is shut your mouth. Never pass up an opportunity to shut the fuck up. He chewed me out and told me to fuck off. And fuck off I did.

Instructor Woodie wasn't a hard-ass for nothing. When he had chewed out the low-crawling loud-mouth, he explained to us that he was singling out this kid because, someday, we're going to work together for real and he didn't want dead weight on his SEAL team. If we were on a mission together, he didn't want someone beside him or behind him or in front of him who wasn't prepared, or couldn't keep from panicking.

BUD/S is filled with tests like that. One of the early evolutions is a truly demented evolution called "drown-proofing." It involves a series of exercises in the pool. Ten minutes of bobbing in the water. Five minutes floating. Then swimming the length of the pool. Then ten more minutes of bobbing. And then driving to the bottom of the pool to fetch a mask with your teeth. Doesn't sound so bad, except for one minor detail. Did I mention that all of this was done with our hands and feet tied?

One of the most difficult tests comes during the pool competency phase—or "pool comp"—when we learn to scuba dive. The course deliberately uses antiquated, leaking dive equipment that's much heavier than modern dive gear—again, just to fuck with you. The first time I used it, I began inhaling water, and had to figure out how to spit out water that infiltrated the respirator.

During the tests, we swam back and forth in the pool while instructors beat us up in the water. While we swam, they would come up behind us, unseen, and send us tumbling head over fin, pull off our masks, tear out our respirators, and—most insidious of all—reach behind our heads to yank off our respirator and tie knots in the hoses. Undoing this required taking off all your gear underwater, untying the knots, and putting the entire dive apparatus and weight belt back on, all while holding your breath.

I failed that test twice after an instructor tied an all-but-impossible knot in my hose called a "whammy knot." I had two more chances to pass the following Monday, and I did, to the annoyance of my instructor.

Of course, the real test of our ability to simultaneously handle chaos, extreme physical exertion, and exhaustion was Hell Week. Everyone who goes to BUD/S knows about Hell Week. It's probably the best-known part of SEAL training and certainly the most infamous. If the first weeks of BUD/S are intended to weed out the weak, Hell Week is a high-speed culling.

It begins at dusk on a Sunday. For us, it was our sixth week of BUD/S. We waited for it in tents on the beach. Although every member of every BUD/S class knows it's coming, no one is ever truly prepared. At about 6 P.M., the instructors swarmed among our tents in a screaming wave, detonating flash grenades and firing automatic weapons loaded with blanks, before tearing through the flaps and ordering the students in every direction. As with combat swimmer orientation, Hell Week is designed to be complete mayhem. It succeeds in every sense of the word.

Hell Week lasted for a hallucination-inducing five days, and it was not uncommon for the class to get only a few hours' sleep total that entire time, or even none at all, often while soaking wet and covered in sand from head to foot. We were forced to perform grueling tasks everywhere we went, like carrying our boats on our head or treading water for thirty minutes in the pounding surf or lying wet and almost naked on the metal pier in the biting wind.

The point of Hell Week is to prove to yourself that you can do anything, to keep from panicking, to keep from giving in to exhaustion or doubt or fear.

Your body can do anything if you will yourself to do it. You can do a lot more than you think. But if you let your mind quit, your body will follow. Once you mentally accept the fact that quitting is an option, you're probably going to quit. You're done.

The instructors knew this, and they psychologically probed our weaknesses, tempting us with hot drinks and rest if we would just . . . *quit. Do it. Do it. Fucking quit, I dare you.* At one point, an instructor offered me a hot cup of cocoa and told me how easy it would be to leave, to get a hot shower, and to fall into bed for the sleep I desperately craved. I looked into that dreamy, seductive mug of hot chocolate, and then handed it back.

Another time, we were shivering in the pool when the instructors said that if anyone needed to use the head in the locker room, now was the time. No instructors went with us when we doubled-stepped to line up at the stalls. A short distance away was the shower area, luring us with the forbidden temptation of a hot shower, which would have immediately led to expulsion. Shaking with cold, I looked at that hot steam, thought about getting in for a split second, and then decided against it. Because that would have been the end. A quick, gratuitous shower or a lifetime of results? Instead of a shower, I got the next-best thing: I had a guy piss on my hands one time to warm them up. Yes, you read that right.

As the end of Hell Week approached, my parents drove down from Montana, hoping to surprise me for making it through. After I made it to Friday, one of the instructors snuck them into the medical clinic where I was getting a checkup. I was so delirious with exhaustion that I looked right at them, decided that I was hallucinating, and walked out of the clinic.

BUD/S doesn't get easier after Hell Week. But it does become more relaxed, because there's an expectation that if you made it through that particular circle of Hades, you'll probably make it all the way through. I finally graduated from BUD/S in December 1996. After going back to Butte for Christmas, I headed to Army jump school at Fort Benning, where I earned my wings. Then I drove up to Virginia Beach with my friend Christian Lamb, who dropped me off at SEAL Team Two before he checked into SEAL Team Eight.

Nervous as hell, I walked into the front office, called the quarterdeck. I was directed to the training office, where the SEALs hung out when they weren't deployed. The veterans had a name for new recruits like me that show up every few months: "meat sticks." There were a couple of SEALs hanging around in there, and they were in full hazing mode.

One of them told me to go to the office, find a guy named Chris Kinney, and deliver a message to him. First, I had to figure out where the office was. "The office," it turned out, was JB's Gallery of Girls about a mile away, near Independence Boulevard and Pleasure House Road. Virginia banned nude or topless dancing anywhere, so JB's had a sign out front advertising "Stopless Go-Go" instead.

It was Friday, when the Team guys usually went there for beer and a few other reasons. Someone pointed Chris Kinney out, and I walked up to him and delivered the message that I had been instructed to say, word for word: "Petty Officer Kinney, my name is

Rob O'Neill from BUD/S class 208, and I just checked into SEAL Team Two, and I don't know who Rudy Boesch is."

In my memory, the music screeched to a stop, the dancers froze, and everyone in the joint looked at me. Rudy Boesch, I soon learned, was the most legendary frogman in U.S. history. He had been one of the very first Navy SEALs and had been command master chief at SEAL Team Two—my team—for about twenty-eight years. In a few years, he would become even more famous when he appeared on the reality show *Survivor*. A legendary bullfrog, whom I had never fucking heard of.

Kinney stared at me with the widest, most wicked grin I think I had ever seen, like a lion about to go to town on a gazelle, and said, "Oh, we're gonna have some fun tonight." They fucked with me all night long, and I ended up buying drinks for everyone in the bar that night. Several times.

That was my first hazing, and not the last. This didn't inspire any fear, though, just nervous jitters as I submitted to expected hazing, laughing most of the time. No, the real fear came soon after I arrived, when I drove into the SEAL Team Two parking lot and spotted a familiar tanned face topped with red curls.

As I got out of my truck, I came face-to-face with Instructor Woodie, the sadistic, no-shit frogman who rained down fire and brimstone and crushed souls in BUD/S. I had watched him beat down people and smash them into the sand, extolling the wisdom that he wouldn't dare be part of a team that had a weak link. Eventually, I would be in Bravo Platoon with him, but at that moment, all this meat stick could think about was what lay in store for me at Woodie's hands.

"Hooyah, Instructor Woodie," I shouted nervously. I was still banged up from the last time I had tried this.

It turned out there was no need to panic. "Hey, man, look, it's Woodie," he said with a wide, friendly smile. "It's just Woodie."

I had made it.

DAKOTA
Don't Even Try to Call Home

It was early morning when I got off the bus at the Military Entrance Processing Station in Louisville. All around me, nervous teenagers spilled to the curb with me—kids still in their sneakers and baggy jeans and T-shirts, wearing backward baseball caps and every kind of haircut. We had spent a relaxed night at a hotel, where we could watch TV and play video games and hang out with our feet plopped up on the lobby sofas. That was finished. In a few hours, we'd start new lives.

We spent the morning taking drug tests, medical exams, and aptitude tests before we raised our hands and pledged to defend the Constitution and follow orders, *so help me God.* Dad had come up from Columbia to watch me take the Marine oath of service. After the ceremony, he told me my mom had come, too, but she left before it was over.

When it was time to leave, I stood on the curb next to the bus talking with Dad. I don't really remember what we talked about, but I know he didn't get teary or anything. You can't shake my dad; he doesn't get emotional. After I said good-bye, the recruits piled back onto the bus, as giddy and naïve as before. I looked around all these guys and girls, who came in all sizes and shapes, and thought, *If they can make it, I can make it.*

That ride seemed to last forever, and it was raucous the whole time, all ten hours, with guys bullshitting each other and telling jokes, like we were on our way to summer camp. That is, until just before we got to Parris Island. It was hours after nightfall as the bus approached the entryway with its famed motto, "WE MAKE MARINES." None of us saw it, because the driver screamed at us to put our heads between our knees and shut the fuck up. As the bus drove through the entryway, that bus of teenage recruits went completely silent.

I sat there with my head between my knees, my heart pounding. I'll never forget the sound of boots pounding up the steps of the bus after the driver cut the engine. And then, total chaos. The bus erupted in screaming as everyone grabbed their bags as fast as we could, practically flying down the steps. Spittle flew in my eyes and mouth from the drill sergeants bellowing in my face as I ran as fast as I could off the bus into the darkness of Parris Island. It could not have been a more different exit than when we sauntered off the bus early that morning.

Under the bright glare of overhead lights, officers herded us like cattle into the intake building, where we were ordered to put all our belongings into a pouch. Insults aimed at fresh-faced recruits flew from every direction. Recruits who were slow, or short, or looked funny, they got it even harder. And then they herded us into another room to call our families.

Inside the room, fluorescent lights flooded the white concrete walls. A row of numbered phone boxes lined one wall. We stood heel to toe, my face about two inches away from the freshly shaved skull of the guy in front of me.

More instructions came at us: *You have three chances to make a call to your family—mother, father, sister, brother—and if you don't reach them, call the recruiter instead.* Except they don't tell us to call our family; they tell us to call our "next of kin," as if we're about to be killed in a firefight.

Then the sergeant ordered the first person in line to open up the phone box. These terrified kids started making their calls home, the drill instructors still screaming in their faces. There was no way the person on the other end of the phone couldn't have heard that screaming. When I reached the front of the line, I saw there was a piece of paper taped inside the door with instructions and a script that told me exactly what to say:

YOU WILL SAY THE FOLLOWING

1. This is recruit (last name).
2. I have arrived safely at Parris Island.

3. Please do not send food or bulky items to me in the mail.

4. I will contact you in 7 to 9 days by letter with my new address.

5. Thank you for your support. Good-bye for now.

I dialed the number for the farm. After a few rings, Dad picked up. It was probably 3 A.M. I doubt he could understand a word I said as I shouted the script into the phone, with the drill instructors berating me over my shoulder. And then as I ran off to the next processing station, the only thing I could think was, *What the fuck did I get myself into?*

———————•———————

I HAVE ALMOST NO CLEAR MEMORIES of what those months were like. The entire first week was getting processed in—physically training, but not drilling. No firearms. Just exercising and learning to march in formation. And getting yelled at—every minute that you're awake. More screaming than I ever would have thought possible. You're tested, torn down. And then eventually, the instructors scrape up the beat-down mess that's left over and build you back up into a warrior. Everything is a lesson, even if you don't know it at the time.

The recruits sorted the instructors into two types: first, there were the kill hats, who screamed at you for the sake of screaming at you. They're usually the newest drill instructors, and their job was basically to fuck with us 24/7 and keep us off balance all the time. That's the basis of their existence. Just like Rob's instructors at BUD/S, the job of the kill hats was to sow chaos and create stress, and force us to remain calm throughout.

Then there were the drill hats, who actually tried to teach us things, bless their hearts. Through the screaming, they were the ones trying to pound information into our thick heads. The ones who were supposed to turn us into Marines and leaders.

My drill hat was Sergeant Brady. I think he was an Amtracker, which meant he had been on one of the amphibious companies, and he'd taken part in the invasion of Iraq in 2003. Military guys wear their resumes on their uniforms, with the highest commendations on top. When Sergeant Brady wore his medals with his dress blue charlies, the medal on top of the stack was a Navy Achievement Medal with Valor. Which meant he'd been in some shit.

Sergeant Brady was a real good guy. I mean, it sucked having him as a drill instructor because he was hard on us, but all the guys knew that it's not about how hard somebody is on you. It's about the *reason*. Some people are hard on you to be a dick, and some people are hard on you to make you better. There's a big difference.

In boot camp, everything blurs together into weeks of suck. A few months in, the drill hats bring you out to an outdoor arena for your first taste of hand-to-hand combat. There isn't much that you look forward to in boot camp other than sleep and chow, but this is one of them. By then, the recruits are like starving animals let out of their cages—*it's on*.

The pugil sticks are poles that are about five feet long, with foam padding on the ends and in the middle. They're pretty harmless, but they're meant to simulate close-order combat with a rifle or a bayonet. One end is red, which represents a bayonet. If you get in a good hit with the red end, the fight's immediately over, just like it would be if you met the business end of a bayonet in actual combat.

Sergeant Brady brought us to one of the sparring spots, an outdoor arena surrounded by tall pine trees. Half-buried tires lined the pit, which was filled with mulch or sand. Chutes led into each side of the pit, and the platoons lined the edges. Everyone wore a mouthpiece, a helmet with a metal face guard, body padding, and a cup on your jock. Protect the jewels.

The instructors pitted the platoons against each other, and everyone wanted to win. Sergeant Brady yelled at us that if we were able to knock out the other guy's mouth guard, then we could call home. Other than that scripted call the first night, no one had called home. Don't try to tell me that there was a single recruit in there who wasn't dying inside of homesickness. We all were. So it was a pretty sweet incentive to come out swinging hard.

When it was my turn, I charged down the chute like a rodeo bull. As I came down, I saw the other guy come out of his chute at the same time. When the instructor blew the whistle, I hit the other guy with the end of the pugil stick as hard as I could. I just pounded and pounded and pounded the guy. I hit him so hard that his mouthpiece popped out. Bout over.

Sergeant Brady was all fired up. "See? Recruit Meyer gets to call home!" he bellowed at the others. And all day long, he kept coming up to me to ask, "Are you excited to call home?" I yelled back, "Yes, sir!" I yelled because I had to, but also because I was really fucking excited to hear a friendly voice.

That night, we were back in our squad bay doing our nightly cleaning when Sergeant Brady said, "Recruit Meyer, are you ready to call home?" My mind leapt. *This is the time, right?* "Yes, sir!" I shouted. I went up the squad bay to the drill instructors' hut outside the barracks and went inside.

Understand that recruits never went into the drill instructors' hut. Ever. But I went in, and there was the senior drill instructor sitting at his desk, and there was a phone next to him. Finally, a link to the outside world. He looked up at me, but instead of telling me to pick up the phone, he pointed to the window. "Open up that window there," he said.

"Yes sir," I said, and opened the window as he ordered.

"Stick your head out that window," he said. I stuck my head out the window. I was beginning to get a bad feeling. "Now yell 'home'!" he yelled at me.

I leaned out the window. "Home!" I shouted.

"Louder!" he said.

"Home!" I yelled, and now he was screaming at me, and I was screaming "Home! Home! Home!" over and over, my head hanging out the window, and I thought *This is some fucked-up shit* as I shouted out the window the name of the place I couldn't go or talk to, so loud that every recruit on the island probably heard me.

Finally, the drill instructor had enough fun. "Get the fuck out of my hut!" he shouted.

And that is what I did. I ran back to the squad bay, shattered but trying to keep it together. Unraveling inside.

Of course, no one was ever going to let me call home. That's the whole point, even if I didn't realize it. No one ever says, *Here's the lesson today, dumb-ass.* You're just left to figure it out for yourself.

To me, the takeaway was that your hopes can be crushed at any moment, that nothing's guaranteed, no matter who promises it to you. But it took a little longer for the other lesson to sink in.

———

WHEN GRADUATION CAME, my dad drove down from Columbia with my cousins for family day before the ceremony. When I wrote home, I mentioned Sergeant Brady a lot, and Dad wanted to meet him. So I got them together at family day, and my dad shook Sergeant Brady's hand and told him he wanted to take him out to dinner.

I hadn't graduated yet, so I was stuck at Parris Island while my dad and cousins went out drinking with Sergeant Brady that night in Beaufort, one of the nearby towns. And of course they got all in it and told stories and stayed out late having fun and it sucked because I wasn't there.

In the morning, on graduation day, I was up early with the rest of the graduates getting our dress uniforms ready. When I saw Sergeant Brady, he looked me straight in the eye and said, "Your dad's not coming. He drank too much and he went home."

This time I didn't believe him. He was fucking with me, just like he did with the phone call home, but now I knew better. When the graduation ceremony got under way, there was my dad and cousins out there with all the other families. As it turned out, I didn't need to call home, because home came to me.

That's when the second lesson from my pugil stick victory, the less obvious lesson, showed itself. As I looked out at my family, I realized that my reward for having made it through boot camp was the same reward as other Marines who were graduating that day, who also were looking out at their own families in the crowd. We all arrived at boot camp the same time, and we all received our prize at the same time. Why should I have been any different? Either everyone calls home, or no one calls home. And if you think otherwise, you're just the idiot with your head hanging out the window, yelling into the night at the top of your lungs, with no one there to listen.

6

OPEN YOUR EYES

ROB
Find Your Globe, Know Your World

Every soldier remembers his first mission. Mine was in 1998 when SEAL Team Two was ordered to Albania to guard U.S. diplomats and Navy admirals attending a ceremonial meeting with the Albanian president. The United States had received intelligence that the event might come under attack, so we were sent to guard the U.S. embassy and protect the diplomats and officers. The terrorist threat against the embassy hadn't come from some backwoods fanatic camping in the Albanian Alps. It had originated from a man whose name I'd heard but whom I knew little about: Osama bin Laden.

We sailed to the Mediterranean aboard the USS *Austin*, the amphibious transport that served as our base. Once off the coast of Spain, the *Austin* settled into a holding pattern called a "gator square." To get to Tirana, we packed into a monster CH-53E Navy helicopter called a Black Stallion. A row of seats ran down the middle of the cargo area, facing more seats against each wall. When the helos were full, there was almost no room to move. I was usually knee-to-knee with a SEAL or a Marine sitting directly across from me, and there was nowhere to look but down into your lap or straight into the face across from you. Making things really pleasant, lukewarm hydraulic fluid leaked constantly from above and soaked you from head to toe. We joked that if the Black Stallion wasn't leaking, you needed to worry.

When I took my seat, I found myself face-to-face with Woodie Mister, the BUD/S instructor. I was the M-60 gunner for the platoon, and I had five hundred rounds on me—one hundred in the gun, and two hundred on each side of my web gear. I packed a huge wad of Copenhagen inside my lip.

I was twenty-two, totally amped about my first mission, and completely inexperienced in the real world. I leaned over close to speak to Woodie to yell over the roar of the rotors how cool everything was, and accidentally spit my entire wad of Copenhagen in his face. I froze, expecting to get reamed out. He just kind of smiled and wiped it off. I wanted to lean over again to tell him, *Great. My first experience with combat and I'm gonna get killed by Woodie.* I kept my mouth shut instead.

We flew straight to the Tirana embassy housing compound, which had been short on security, and set up a perimeter. Later I set up a sniper observation position at the ceremony with the Albanian president, where I could identify potential threats. In the third phase of the mission, I returned to the embassy for security. We were in Tirana about five days total, along with a Marine reconnaissance platoon. While the Marines stayed in Tirana the whole time, we flew back and forth to the *Austin* to change up our gear and weapons for different duties.

It was a strange assignment. I had no experience with diplomatic protection—beyond being a glorified bodyguard—and I wasn't even equipped correctly: Some days I wore a drop holster that was mismatched for civilian clothes and carried an Uzi that was cool but was totally the wrong weapon. One day I wore a silly-looking plaid Oxford shirt and baggy acid-washed jeans, with my SIG Sauer—no shit—tucked into my belt. I looked like I was twelve. I didn't care. Even though I did not look the part, I felt like a badass and I was finally in the field and doing the work I had signed up for. I was the SEAL that I had set out to be.

And other than a lone gunshot near the embassy that we decided was probably a random drive-by shooting, the terror attack never transpired. But the mission was memorable for a different reason altogether.

Midway through the mission, I was in the embassy when a diplomat walked down a hallway toward me. And around him, forming a tight protective screen, was my future ▮▮▮, SEAL Team ▮▮, a group of operators who—unlike me—were *actually* cool.

But these men in front of me were no ghosts. They looked at ease and ready for anything. Sunglasses shielded their eyes, and they wore utility vests that cameramen or fishermen used, but there was no film or fishing lures in their pockets. They carried deadly weapons—inconspicuously, yes, but it was clear that they meant business. We nodded to them as they passed, but they didn't even acknowledge us.

After they continued by, I paused to watch them. *Holy shit,* I thought. *Holy shit.*

———   ■   ———

IT'S STRANGE WHEN I THINK about how my first mission was to guard against a threat from Osama bin Laden, and the mission I'm most famous for ended with killing him. Three years after Tirana, I was deployed to Naval Special Warfare Unit 2 in Stuttgart, Germany. I had just come back from a mission in Kosovo, part of the efforts to maintain the peace after the bloody war in the Balkans in the 1990s.

Being stationed at the Special Warfare Unit wasn't a bad posting. Though we were technically on sea duty because we were abroad, it was categorized as shore duty. We stayed in a decent barracks with a gym and TVs in common areas and a kitchen, and we received a per diem. And because it was Germany, there were lots of pubs where we could spend that per diem.

On the afternoon of September 11, 2001, I was writing an email in the second-floor operations office with a TV turned to CNN in the background. It was morning in New York. As I typed, the TV went to breaking news to report that a plane had plowed into the north tower of the World Trade Center.

What the hell's going on? I thought. A crowd of SEALs gathered in front of the TV. As we watched, we saw the second plane hit the south tower in the background, and a giant fireball erupt from the side of the building. It was a staggering, cataclysmic event unfolding live in front of our eyes, and brought the confusion into sudden, crystal-clear focus.

"Osama bin Laden," one of the SEALs said, and we all knew exactly what he meant.

We've been at war ever since. It is what we are trained for, and it's the reason the Teams exist. Every day since I arrived in Virginia Beach, I looked up at a sign during daily muster that read, "Are you ready for war today? You should be." It was ironic, because other than Vietnam the SEALs hadn't really fought before September 11, but we were constantly preparing for combat that never happened. Back then, when civilians asked a frogman what the SEALs did and got the cryptic, "I can't talk about it," the reality was that there was nothing to talk about. There were no secret missions, there was no midnight swims ashore with daggers clenched in the teeth shit. We joked that instead of following the credo "Train like you fight!" ours was "Train like you train!" And so I trained—for years—until I finally earned my trident around October 1997. But it wasn't until I deployed on the USS *Austin* the next year and flew to Albania that I realized how little I knew.

Tirana drove home for me that this was a real job, with real-world consequences. I realized that I could end up anywhere on the planet really quickly on missions that I couldn't even dream up, and that I needed to educate myself about the world and what we're doing in it. While I was on the USS *Austin,* I could have sat on the couch eating candy bars and playing video games for weeks on end. Instead, I spent hours alone at the metal tables in an unused berth below the chow hall, reading about everything I could get my hands on in the ship library. Books on diplomacy, on politics, about the Middle East, about the difference between Sunni and Shia Islam. Anything about the world that was spreading out ahead of me.

The first World Trade Center bombing had been five years earlier, so I was well aware of who bin Laden was. But I didn't consider bin Laden to be a tactical mastermind or a multinational terrorist. I thought of him more as a cartoon parody of a terrorist, like the vengeful Libyan gunman in *Back to the Future* who shoots Doc Brown. September 11 showed me how wrong that was.

After the 2001 attacks, we hoped to deploy immediately, but of course that didn't happen. There was so much chaos, and so much uncertainty, that it took weeks to even start to formulate the contours of the response. First, I had to return to Virginia Beach from Germany. And then the SEALs had to prepare for wartime missions, what the Navy called "training up," or "work up." Now we were no longer training to train; we were truly training for war. Basic patrol formations. Close-Quarters Battle (CQB). Land warfare. Mobile operations. Military Operations in Urban Terrain, or MOUT. Jump training. More dive training. Training for the desert. For the mountains. For jungles. For swamps. We didn't want to send operators to war unprepared, and we had to start from square one for the new

SEAL arrivals. Get the basics down. Crawl, then walk, then run. In the meantime, a bureaucratic reorganization changed SEAL Team Two to SEAL Team Four. Four became Two. Same guys, just different buildings.

I requested reassignment to another SEAL team. I wanted to join the cool-guy group that I had seen in the Tirana embassy in 1998. The screening board held only a few meetings each year, and mine was in spring 2003. After I completed the physical test—which was much more rigorous than the exam for the other teams—I was invited to sit for the screening board. After they grilled me, the board agreed that I was candidate material, and I was invited to try out with the class of 2004, almost a year away. If I made it through, I'd join the ranks for the most elite SEALs.

My first post-9/11 mission began in March 2003. Of course, our eventual destination had nothing to do with the War on Terror or Operation Iraqi Freedom. SEAL Team Four—my new outfit—had been deployed on the USS *La Salle* to Naval Special Warfare Unit 10 in Rota, Spain, when we were called up for a mission with Marines who were going to enter Iraq through Turkey. The *La Salle* was en route when the Turkish parliament voted against allowing U.S. forces from using Turkish air bases or deploying out of southeastern Turkey. So much for that mission.

Meanwhile, civil strife was reaching a peak in Liberia, on the coast of West Africa. For three years, armed factions had been battling to depose the president, Charles Taylor, who had been meddling in a vicious, bloody war in neighboring Sierra Leone. Liberia was destabilizing quickly and nervous U.S. diplomats and expats in Monrovia were looking for the exits. The *La Salle* turned around. Soon we were on a zigzag course for West Africa.

The mission was called Operation Shining Express. SEALs who had been expecting firefights with Iraq's Revolutionary Guard or hoping to chase Saddam Hussein found themselves instead in a midship briefing room hearing about potential threats in Liberia: sharks, saltwater crocodiles, hippos, and black mamba snakes. We thought that we had trained for every contingency in combat, but clearly there were some gaps in the SEAL program. I had no idea that hippos were the world's deadliest large land animals. And for the record: black mambas are no joke. They'll chase you. While I had trained for evading enemies, an eight-foot reptile pursuing me at 12 miles an hour was not one of them.

It was not exactly the daring post-9/11 assignment we expected. Rather, it was hydrographic reconnaissance, which was a fancy way of saying we went to map out the best locations for amphibious beach landings in case Marines needed to come ashore to rescue American diplomats, if ever it came to that. SEALs are trained to operate in secrecy, but this was the opposite of a clandestine operation. The Navy wanted to project an image of strength to deter any thought of attacks on the embassy or diplomats, so our ship, the USS *Kearsarge,* anchored about twelve miles off the Liberian coast, an intimidating offshore presence. To make sure that the American military presence wouldn't go unnoticed, we pulled in even closer, about five miles from the coast, as we prepared to go ashore.

We were definitely noticed. By the time our Zodiacs got to shore late one morning, thousands of Liberians waited to greet us. The locals knew that we were coming and came out in droves, along with photographers and reporters and television crews. Children did cartwheels on the beach, war-weary adults cheered for the arriving Americans, and curious rubberneckers crowded to get a look. One of the SEALs pumped his fist in the air as they arrived, to the delight of the crowd. A day or so later, we returned to shore—this time in helicopters—to scout out landing sites in case we needed to airlift embassy staff out. In downtown Monrovia, armed men walked around the streets with AK-47s. We eyed each other warily. They might have been militia members, but they might also have been civilians armed to protect their families during wartime. We could have drawn down on them, but that would only have escalated tensions. Very few people are combatants.

We were pissed at missing out on the start of the Iraq invasion. We wanted to be a part of history. In my disappointment, what wasn't obvious to me immediately was that we *were* a part of history. We were stepping into a volatile situation in a country with deep ties to the United States; the United States bought the land for Liberia to provide a place for freed slaves to return to Africa. The country exists because President James Monroe procured the money to buy the land. It was a valuable mission in a part of the world where I never expected to set foot, to play a role—a minor one, for sure—in a horrible war that terrorized a population of people who just wanted to live in peace.

After Liberia, we returned to Virginia Beach for more training. In 2004, I joined the next class to try out for SEAL Team ███. After months of more grueling training—Close-Quarters Battle (CQB); high-altitude, low-opening jumping and its cousin, high-altitude, high-opening jumping; and Survival, Evasion, Resistance, Escape (SERE) school; and a *lot* of hazing and pranks—35 SEAL Team ███ candidates remained out of the 60 I had started with. The next step was being assigned to a squadron. The assignments operated like the NFL draft; each squadron took turns picking from the candidates, informed by their members who were part of the training and watched us throughout. I knew what squadron I wanted and did some behind-the-scenes lobbying to get picked. I guess it paid off, because when the list was posted, ██████████ was next to my name.

My next mission was closer to what we expected in a post–September 11 world. In 2005, that squadron went to Jalalabad, Afghanistan, which was about ninety miles east of the capital, Kabul, and about twenty miles from the Pakistani border. It's a midsized city with a mix of cosmopolitan urbanites and extreme poverty, with low-lying buildings, crowded bazaars, and chaotic streets jammed with ornately decorated "jingle trucks," which looked like art galleries on wheels, and three-wheeled taxis called "tuck-tucks."

We had a safe house on a street nicknamed "Chocolate Alley," with walls topped with concertina wire on one side and gated compounds piled with sandbags on the other. It was near a roundabout with an enormous painted globe in the center, which we used as a local landmark for navigating the streets. We called it Chocolate Alley because the CIA and Green Berets also had safe houses there as well, and the local kids knew that they could expect handouts of candy and chocolates anywhere that there were Americans. The compound was a former motel. The senior guys had their own rooms; I shared one with a guy I went through selection with. But we had great showers. The plumbing was bad so we couldn't flush toilet paper. There was a red wastebasket next to the toilet. I'll let you figure it out. We had a very small pool, a little bigger than a jacuzzi, and a weight room. In what had been the lobby, we blacked out the windows, lined the walls with sofas and covered the floor with rugs, and endlessly watched episodes of *The Shield* and listened to bootleg CDs from the Jalalabad marketplace. When we went out, we covered up our T-shirts with local garb, a knee-length white shirt called a kurta, and wore black-and-white checked turbans on our heads. Sometimes we rode motorcycles, and we'd lounge in the bazaars eating shawarmas, unconcerned about al Qaeda ambushes or IEDs.

Our job was to collect intelligence on al Qaeda operatives, and if need be, bring them in for interrogation, operations that we called "snatch and grabs," for which we used a nondescript van. My favorite operation was when we picked up a suspicious Saudi man in the middle of the night from a house a few blocks from our own. He had a huge gut, and the T-shirt that stretched over it read, "It's not a beer belly, it's a fuel tank for a sex machine." Al Qaeda or not, he had great taste in tailgating attire.

One of our other missions was coordinated with U.S. Army Rangers, who had a sniper outpost at the Jalalabad airfield. The Army had taken over the airport, and the Rangers had a "recon and surveillance" operation, where they spotted suspicious activity at a nearby gas station. Their intelligence suggested that there was an al Qaeda operative laundering money out of the gas station, which they jokingly called "the Grab and Go," like it was a 7-Eleven in Dubuque, Iowa. Because the Rangers only had an observation outpost, they asked us if we wanted to bring the operative in. We were more than happy to oblige. Since picking up a hostile for interrogation was called a "snatch and grab," naturally the Rangers had a name for the operation: the "Snatch and Grab at the Grab and Go." Not a chance that we could pass that up.

We covered up with our kurtas and turbans on our heads. They weren't very convincing, especially with my red beard and blindingly white complexion, but the outfits only needed to be convincing for a couple of seconds, long enough to get through a doorway or into a room.

Four of us took the murder van from the safe house, drove across town, and rolled up at the gas station just as it was opening for the day. We popped open the van doors and ran inside. We scared the shit out of three guys working there who thought they were being robbed. We subdued them and kept moving through the gas station. Down a short hallway, there were two doors, one on the right and the left. I went in the door to the left, and too bad for me, because Mr. al Qaeda was behind the door to the right, sitting on rugs and counting stacks of money. Within seconds, he was cuffed and hooded and on his way out the door with us to the van. We drove him to the airfield, loaded him on a helicopter for Bagram, and then went back to the safe house to watch *The Shield*.

There was one more mission to perform before we left Jalalabad. This was a rescue mission to bring back Marcus Luttrell, the lone survivor of four snipers sent to do a reconnaissance mission in the Korengal Valley. Another attempt to rescue him by air had ended when the Taliban shot down a Chinook, killing all sixteen men aboard, including eight SEAL operators. We hiked over ten thousand feet in altitude in more than 100-degree heat to the village that was harboring Luttrell, only to have Rangers pick him up by helicopter in a parallel rescue effort just before we got there. We were in a hallucinatory state of exhaustion and dehydration by the time we got back, and slept for twenty-four hours straight.

My infant daughter had been born toward the end of my SEAL Team ▆ training, and I had been plucked from a ship where we were conducting live ordnance training and rushed to the hospital in Portsmouth, Virginia. I arrived at the delivery bed with five minutes to spare. When I got back from Jalalabad, she was a year old, and she was beautiful.

Being a father gave me a new perspective. No matter what mission I went on around the world, whether it was in Iraq or Liberia or Afghanistan, I found one thing again and again: most people don't want to fight. They just wanted to raise their families, to live without fear or violence. Anybody in their right mind would be scared to see me walking fully armed through their dark house at two thirty in the morning, uninvited. If someone had done that in my home, I'd blow them to bits. But these residents? They just had to live with it.

——————•——————

WHEN I WAS IN JALALABAD back in 2005, admirals and generals said to me, "There's never been a suicide bomb or a roadside bomb in Afghanistan, and there never will be." My response was, "Yes, there will." Within a year, the Taliban regrouped and began a resurgence with al Qaeda allies, and would gain back the territory that they had lost. In a few years, ISIS would be in Afghanistan as well. No matter what the intention is, the longer an army stays, the more likely that they will be seen as an occupying force. And that's exactly what happened to us. The United States is great at starting wars, but we're very bad at ending them.

When I saw SEAL Team ▆ in Tirana in 1998, those operators

had a kind of legendary quality in my starstruck eyes. They were larger than life. Mythic, you could say. In a way, all those descriptions would be right. Other than a few operations, such as a firefight that killed four SEALs and injured eight more during the 1989 U.S. invasion of Panama, the Teams had seen very little action in decades. They trained for wars that never came. The older bullfrogs from the 1980s and 1990s were so mad at us because they had seen almost no combat at all, and we saw it all after everything went to shit in the mid-2000s because of the Sunni Awakening in Iraq and the Taliban resurgence since Afghanistan. My operators and I saw more action and got more kills than in the entire modern history of the Teams.

But that didn't have to happen. I've thought a lot about the Jalalabad mission. Other than a few operations like the Snatch and Grab at the Grab and Go, and the attempt to rescue Marcus Luttrell, there wasn't that much for us to do in Jalalabad in 2005. The city was peaceful, even though we were right on the border with Pakistan's frontier. We had won. True, Osama bin Laden hadn't been caught, but he wasn't even in Afghanistan at that point; he had long ago fled into Pakistan. I believe that if we had left Afghanistan then, the country would not have become the quagmire that it did. If we hadn't invaded Iraq over fucked-up intelligence about al Qaeda, we wouldn't have lost more than 4,400 American lives there. Maybe we could have avoided all the bloodshed and tears that would plague us for years into the future. And then I could've become another bullfrog without any stories, telling anyone who will listen, *I can't talk about it. I refuse to talk about it. I just can't.*

DAKOTA
Know Your Blind Spots

After School of Infantry, I flew straight from Jacksonville, North Carolina, on a commercial flight to Honolulu, with about thirty or so other SOI graduates. We arrived in the middle of the night and boarded a bus that took us the twenty miles to the Marine Corps Base in Hawaii. I couldn't see much out of the windows as we drove over the mountains to the east side of Oahu. The base lies next to Kaneohe Bay on a peninsula about ten miles northeast of Honolulu, on the north side of a jungle-covered mountain range. It was paradise, and it was the last place I had wanted to be stationed as a Marine.

I had been to Hawaii once before, for a high school exhibition football game right before boot camp. *I hope to God I don't get stationed in Hawaii,* I had said to myself then, because it was so far away from Kentucky. Now here I was, 4,400 miles from home. When recruits graduate, the next step is called "joining the fleet," when active-duty Marines receive an assignment to either the Pacific or Atlantic Fleet. For me, that was the Pacific Fleet. I was sent to 3rd Battalion, 3rd Marine Regiment, an infantry battalion based at Kaneohe Bay with a long history going back to World War II. The battalion had deployed to Afghanistan in 2004 and spent eight months in eastern Afghanistan, including operations in the Korengal Valley, one of the most dangerous spots in the country. In 2006, the regiment went to al Anbar province in Iraq to secure the city of Haditha from insurgents who constantly attacked U.S. troops in that region. They would go back to Iraq in 2007, and I would go with them.

The Marines called the base K-Bay, and I arrived the day before Thanksgiving in 2006. The base is a couple of miles of lush lawns and palm trees, slung between high hills, one on the west and the jagged lip of an old volcano crater jutting up to the east. The entrance road passes ponds considered sacred to native Hawaiians on one side, and the Pacific War Memorial with an Iwo Jima statue encircled with flowering bushes on the other. Crescent-shaped beaches slide into turquoise water, and a golf course looks out over the Pacific, where you can see humpback whales swimming in the waves.

My quarters were not quite as idyllic as its surroundings. The bus pulled up in the parking lot of the barracks, Mackie Hall, in the middle of the night. When new Marines arrive, it's called a "boot drop," and I was one of those new boots. As I got off the bus with the other boots, I looked up at groups of Marines drinking on the balconies above. When I walked up the entrance, some of the Marines rained beer cans down on our heads before we went in to get our room assignments.

Mackie Hall was a horrible shithole. Four stories of concrete misery with balconies running the length of every floor. We called it "Crackie Hall," and it was infamous as one of the worst places to live anywhere in the armed services. I cannot emphasize what a rat den this was. The water ran brown out of the faucets, there was often no hot water, the clothes washers and dryers almost never worked, and the best hope for air-conditioning was to flap your arms to get the air moving. Mold infestations made Marines sick. During storms, the power would go out. Flooding, broken toilets, cockroaches as big as your fist, you name it.

Those were just the problems with the building; the inhabitants were another story. Fire alarms were routinely pulled as pranks, MPs had to break up drunk fights every weekend, Marines threw burning couches off the balconies, and sometimes they'd throw themselves off, strapped to a mattress to soften the landing. Every imaginable display of bad behavior could be seen there on any Saturday night. The entire barracks would turn out on the balconies, shouting "Mackie Hall!" at the top of their lungs, while Marines blew conch shells like a call to battle. A foul-smelling canal ran behind one side of the complex. We called it Shit Creek, and it was filled with broken or useless items—old TVs, chairs, washers and dryers, anything that wasn't bolted down— tossed in the water. Drunk Marines ended up in the water, usually on a dare but probably at the hands of bigger, more drunk Marines, too.

I wasn't twenty-one yet, so drinking wasn't as easy for me as it was for the other boots in the hall. I bunked with two other boots on my fire team, Cobb and Bevins. The fire team is the smallest unit in the platoon. Three fire teams make a squad, three squads make a platoon, three platoons to a company, three companies to a battalion, and so on. Cobb was from Massachusetts, a huge Patriots fan, a really funny dude. Bevins was quieter, more reserved. The fourth member of our fire team lived three doors down, my fire team leader, Lance Corporal Daniel Kreitzer.

There was something in Kreitzer's eyes that said *Do not fuck with me.* Coming from the School of Infantry at Camp Geiger, I thought I was all that, but I didn't know my ass from my elbow. Kreitzer owned me, as a result. When you're in the Marines, your life is not your own. Every part of your day is dictated by your team leader—when you sleep, when you eat, when you shit, and when you work. If your team leader ordered you to do something, anything, then that was what you did. So when everyone in Crackie Hall was getting drunk or doing some fucked-up prank, Kreitzer would order me to report to his unit along with Bevins and Cobb.

Instead of playing video games or dicking around, he'd drill us on medevac procedures. "Nine Lines," they're called. It's the universal format that's used to radio in a medical evacuation when someone's shot and bleeding and needs attention fast. Location. Radio frequency and call sign. Number of patients by urgency. Special equipment needed. All the way to number nine, which states whether there's hazardous contamination present at the evacuation site, such as a chemical warfare agent or radiation.

"Nine lines, nine lines!" he'd yell at us, and we'd go through the drill over and over again. That dude was so fucking hard. I hated him so much. And I owe him everything.

— • —

WHEN I ARRIVED AT K-BAY, the 3rd Regiment had only been back from Iraq for about a month. I could feel a cloud of death hanging over the Marines. The regiment had lost a lot of guys, and it took a toll on the unit. I went to memorials of men who died. I didn't know any of them, but I had to be there. Marines who had lost teammates and friends wore black KIA bracelets with their names, so I could look at someone and tell immediately if he had lost someone. With all the shit going on in Iraq, Marines who had seen their brothers die really couldn't confront their loss until they got back to the States.

I got to be pretty close to the other guys in the fire team, because these are the guys I would probably go into combat with someday. We had the only all-boot room in all of Mackie Hall, so that made us a special focus for attention. Senior Marines would come in and toss our room regularly, make us do push-ups, things like that. That made us tighter. I never really got to know Kreitzer—what he was like, where he was from, what teams he followed. There was something different about him. His demeanor didn't change much, and he didn't share much about himself. It took some time, but I found out what happened to Kreitzer. He might have told the fire team himself, or maybe I found out from someone else—I don't remember.

What I do know is that six months earlier, in May 2006, he'd been on a security patrol in Haqlaniyah, Iraq, when a roadside bomb went off as the patrol returned to their forward operating base. It was a big IED. Two members of the squad were badly wounded. One of them was Kreitzer's squad leader, Sergeant David R. Christoff. Kreitzer kept him alive long enough to be medevaced out. He died later at the hospital. Another Marine, Lance Corporal William J. Leusink, also died of his injuries.

I also knew this about Kreitzer: he hated IEDs. He hated how they maimed and shredded and killed anyone unlucky enough to be in their blast radius. He hated their vicious effectiveness in sowing fear and chaos. He hated the ruthlessness that they represented, planted among civilians whose deaths wouldn't mean shit to jihadis. I believe he was tormented by the deaths in his squad, and he didn't want it to happen to us or anybody else he knew. He forced our squad to knuckle down and train and study so that someday we'd get out of a firefight alive or survive getting blown up by an IED.

He forced us to do extra physical training, and then drilled us over and over on Nine Lines when everyone else in Mackie Hall was

fucking around. He made clear to us that while we hadn't been deployed yet, our time was coming. There was no doubt that we'd be
up next. Pretty soon we'd be walking on a roadside in Fallujah or
Ramadi, studying the dirt under our feet for IEDs and wondering
if the woman walking past us was a jihadi in a suicide vest. On one
level, the motivation to work so hard, to train as hard as you can, is
obvious—to stay alive, and to win the war. But here's what Kreitzer
showed us that wasn't so obvious: we weren't training as hard as we
did to save our own asses. We were doing it in case we needed to save
one of our other guys who gets hurt. We needed to be able to protect
one another. We needed to make sure that all of us got out alive.

I was worried that I would never see combat at all, though. I had
enlisted because I wanted to fight, and I wanted to go overseas. In
2006 and 2007, the wars in Iraq and Afghanistan looked to be winding down. If I remained in my assigned infantry battalion, odds were
that I would never see combat. But snipers, on the other hand, would
still be in demand for a long time.

I had found out that there was a sniper tryout—what the Marines call an "indoc," for indoctrination—coming up. An indoc is a
two-day introduction before you are accepted into a sniper platoon.
Kreitzer knew the indoc was coming up, and warned us against even
considering going because of all the time and energy he had spent
training us up. He felt like he had invested in us, and it would be a
personal insult to him if we left the fire team. He was furious when I
did it anyway and made it through. I was leaving the fire team, and
he felt like all of his efforts had been wasted on me.

It wasn't easy to stay out of Kreitzer's way for the week or so until
I was transferred to the sniper platoon, or after, because the sniper
platoon was right at the base as well. Kreitzer gave me the cold shoulder; he didn't need to say a word to let me know how disappointed
he was.

One of the perks of moving to sniper platoon was a housing up-
grade. After indoc, I packed up my stuff and moved out of Crackie

Hall to another barracks a couple of blocks away, upwind of Shit Creek, where I joined the other snipers. Sniper training was completely different from any other part of the Marines so far. Boot camp and infantry platoon trains your body, but sniper school trains your eye and your mind to pick out minute details and observe things that might otherwise be overlooked.

In one of the stalking drills, you lie flat in the grass and try to pick out things that are in front of you with your scope or your binoculars. It's a skill called "burning through," where you train your mind to ignore distractions in the foreground—blades of grass, weeds, leaves—that are crowding your line of sight, and focus like a laser on the target detail on the far side: the target, or the doorway he might emerge from, or a vehicle. I learned how to make a ghillie suit, the sniper's uniform that turns a man into a mound of grass or leaves or brush and lets me melt into the Hawaiian landscape. I practiced sneaking up on a target and taking a shot from two hundred yards while spotters scoured the area looking for me.

There was another exercise we would do at the barracks. I'd put five things in the refrigerator. Then I'd open the door, look at them for ten seconds, and then close it. Then I'd leave it and be gone all day. When I'd come back, I'd try to draw what I'd seen that morning from memory, every detail. One way I look at it is this: you learn the difference between looking and seeing. You can look at an object and identify what it is, or you can *see* that object and take in the details that help you understand it. Why is it there? How did it get there? Is it dangerous? Snipers don't look, they see.

My gamble on the snipers paid off. In July 2007, the battalion shipped out to Iraq. We ended up in Karma, which was about thirty miles west of Baghdad. I was there at the same time that Rob was, in the middle of the surge to try to beat back the Sunni awakening. We patrolled constantly to deter insurgents and build up intelligence that might help us find Sunni terrorist cells. Our compound came under mortar attack, and we couldn't figure out where the mortars were coming from. Eventually air support figured out that it was a bunch of guys with a van driving around, setting off mortars, and getting back in and driving away. After the aerial surveillance spotted them, it didn't take long to smoke them from the sky. We didn't have a problem with mortars after that.

I was only in Iraq for about forty-five days. What cut off my deployment and returned me stateside early didn't come from above but from the ground, and it wasn't an IED. One night when I was on patrol, I got an insect bite on my hand after sleeping on the ground. I didn't think much of it and figured that it was a sand flea; they bit us constantly. But after a day or so, it was obvious that it was something else, because my hand started swelling up. I didn't really want to go to the corpsman, the medical technician for the battalion, because he famously didn't give a fuck. He carried a bunch of bendy straws around with him, the kind that you use to sip from a juice box. When someone came to him with a medical problem, he'd hand them a straw and say, "Suck it up." I think I went to the first aid station when I returned to base. They immediately saw what the problem was: I'd been bitten by a brown recluse spider, which is venomous.

I went to Fallujah that night for surgery and had a second surgery after that. Afterward, I couldn't feel or move my fingers. But it got worse: the doctors recommended six months of physical therapy. I couldn't stay in Iraq, so I was evacuated to K-Bay to recuperate. It was a shitty way to go home, alone and without anyone in my unit. I had nothing to do but drink and do physical therapy. Because I was still underage, I would get older Marines to buy me booze. In one weekend, I would drink a bottle of Jack Daniel's, a bottle of Jim Beam, and a bottle of 99 Bananas, which is 99-proof banana-flavor schnapps.

In the fall, I made plans to go home to Kentucky for a week and connect with old friends. Before I left, I spoke to one of my best high school buddies, Justin Hardin, as I was on my way to one of my PT sessions. Justin and I had played football together, and he had gone to Hawaii with me for the game where I prayed that I'd never be stationed there. Over the phone, we made plans to hook up with other friends, go to a game, maybe see some girls. Just thinking about being home raised my spirits. After my physical therapy, my phone rang again. When I picked up, it wasn't Justin. It was his cousin. She told me that right after Justin and I talked, he was driving on a slick road, his car skidded off the pavement, and he hit a tree. The impact killed him. When she looked at his cell phone, she saw that he and I had just talked, and she wanted me to know that he was dead.

I took that leave in Kentucky, and then came home again for Christmas. While I was there, I was hanging out with some friends in the parking lot of the IGA in downtown Greensburg when I saw my friend Mary drive by. I was on the track team with her, and we took classes together. She was just a really great girl. A couple of minutes after she passed us, an ambulance went by with its lights. Pretty soon after that, we heard she had been in a wreck. I jumped in a truck to go to the hospital and got there just in time to see her loaded onto another ambulance to be driven to Louisville. She didn't make it. The doctors took her off the respirator the next day.

There was nothing I could have done to change the outcome of what happened to my two friends. But those two deaths were part of a long string of injury and accidents that one day would lead me to be a first responder. Fourteen years after Kreitzer first reamed me out for not being serious about nine lines and safety, I received EMT and firefighter certifications in 2020. Since serving, I had pulled over to assist with more road accidents than I could count. It wasn't like I heard Kreitzer yell "Nine lines!" in my ear when those things happened, but his sense of urgency that I needed to be prepared to help those in crisis around me has never left me.

●━━━━━━●

AFTER I RETURNED from Christmas in Kentucky and rejoined sniper platoon at K-Bay, I was still drinking. My platoon leader, Gunnery Sergeant Hector Soto-Rodriguez, had just come back from al

Anbar in Iraq, where he had been convoy commander for the commanding officer's security. He wasn't very tall, but he was lean with a long, serious face. He'd been a drill instructor, so he knew how to chew someone down to size. When I showed up drunk for a company hike one morning, he pulled me aside and told me to get my head out of my ass, so I did. I cut out the booze and redoubled my efforts on sniper platoon.

I impressed Gunny Soto so much that he put in my name for a meritorious promotion. When I was promoted to corporal, I made team leader. After fucking up with the drinking, I wanted to show Gunny Soto that I knew how to lead and that I could put together the best platoon of snipers that had ever existed. Soon after my promotion, we had our own sniper indoc. And one of the candidates who showed up was a guy named Castillo.

A short Latino dude with tattoos, Castillo had been a stripper in Las Vegas before he enlisted. I've seen it all in the Marine Corps, but this one was new to me. For whatever reason, he wanted to be a sniper. He obviously wanted to be there because he had signed up for the indoc, but at the same time, I didn't think he really took it seriously. Everyone liked him. Everyone but me.

Being a stripper wasn't his problem, in my mind. The problem was that he was soft, which meant he was fat. The problem was that he was a joker, which meant he didn't take things seriously. The problem was that he didn't put in effort, which meant that he was lazy. All of the excuses another platoon leader would've made I translated to him not being good enough. I didn't like his attitude, and I didn't want him in the platoon, let alone in my squad.

So after two days of hiking and grappling and runs on the beach, the indoc finished and we sat down to review the candidates. We evaluated their character, their physical strength, their mental condition, their ability to learn. And, still, I didn't want Castillo. Gosh, how I didn't want Castillo.

I voted against him being accepted. What do you know, out of everyone, Gunny Soto overrode me. But he didn't just do that: he put Castillo on my team of trainees. I was so pissed. As I saw it, my only recourse was making it my goal to break Castillo to the point where he had no choice but to quit the platoon.

The sniper platoons had higher conditioning standards than the regular Marine line units, and to me, Castillo didn't meet that higher bar. So I exploited that. My justification for beating on him was that he needed extra attention. He needed to do extra homework to catch up to the class. I could run forever, so I made him run forever. Every day, even on weekends, we'd do these punishing runs up and down the hills around the Marine base. I'd ruin his Friday nights by ordering him to meet me at 6 A.M. on Saturday for training. I didn't offer him any carrots to help him improve, only sticks to beat him down.

One day, I ordered him to do a long run with me up and down the hills. I could sense that he was at the end of his rope. After running every hill on the base, he was falling behind. He couldn't keep up.

So at a point where the road met the beach, I swerved left onto the beach. Now instead of pounding on pavement, our boots were shifting and sliding on sand. That was a whole other kind of shit, and I could tell it was almost over for him. Finally we came around a curve where the beach met the road, and instead of jumping back on the road, I kept going down the beach. And that was where he finally stopped.

"I'm done," he said, panting. "I'm done."

Mission accomplished. I had driven this crazy stripper from Las Vegas out of the sniper platoon. I couldn't have been happier.

"Well, go back and tell Gunny that you're done," I told him. I talked shit to him the whole time, telling him what a piece of crap he is, how glad I was that he hadn't made it. He didn't argue. He was completely defeated.

He went slowly to the company headquarters, went upstairs to Gunny's office, and told him that he was leaving. When he came back out, I saw him outside the building, and he told me that Gunny wanted to see me. I walked up to Gunny Soto's office like I had accomplished something. Like I had won.

"What's going on, Gunny? Good morning," I said.

He looked up at me, disgusted. "You know, I'm disappointed that I had you promoted to corporal."

"What do you mean? I'm out here trimming the fat off, right?" I said, surprised.

"I put you in a leadership position and trusted you with leadership. And I've watched you for three weeks prove to me nothing more than that you're going to take that leadership position and use it the wrong way," he said. Castillo didn't need to be torn down; he needed to be built up, he told me, because that's what leaders did. "All you showed me is that you're incapable of being a leader."

Even though I was a trained sniper, I couldn't see what was right in front of me. Soto had picked me up as I was turning into a drunk failure and had given me a second chance. Before him, Kreitzer had put me on a path that would make me a dependable Marine and, someday, an emergency responder. But I hadn't learned any of those lessons. Even though I was supposed to be training Castillo how to view the world around him, I hadn't been able to burn through and see what was right in front of me. I ran out of the company office after Castillo. I found him in the barracks as he was about to shower. And I asked him not to leave. And he didn't.

7

IN THE SHIT

ROB

Rule I: Don't Let Complacency Kill You

I went on kill missions almost every night during the summer of 2007, while the Sunni insurgency in Iraq was in full swing. Al Qaeda–aligned fighters had dug in across the country, and my job, along with other branches of special ops, was to find them and root them out. Over the summer, we hopscotched from base to base, landing wherever we were needed to tamp out insurgent activity. We started in western Iraq, at al-Asad Air Base in Anbar province, then carried out missions in Fallujah and Ramadi, and then went east to Baghdad, and finally northeast to Baqubah. We usually left after sundown to carry out the killings under cover of darkness.

We were part of the twenty-thousand-troop surge sent to Iraq in 2007 as sectarian violence was on the rise. U.S. Special Operations Command had realized that to defeat the insurgents who had aligned with al Qaeda and lit the country on fire, we needed to update our tactics in a war with rules that were constantly changing. We needed to try something different.

We joked that this was the Deployment That Never Was because we fell off the SEAL radar that summer. While we operated in Iraq under the umbrella of U.S. Special Operations Command and the Army, our commanders were occupied in Afghanistan, watching over SEAL Team ███ missions there. The group of us tasked to Iraq had become invisible to the Navy. Our command forgot all about us. Out of sight, out of mind.

Our base in Baghdad was at Baghdad International Airport, or BIAP. We had decent quarters. No TVs or amenities, like the Army Special Operations quarters, but we had comfortable beds and great air-conditioning and a world-class weight room. We'd sleep in the daytime to avoid the crippling heat and wake up for a dinnertime breakfast in the chow hall next to our barracks. Then we'd find out what the intelligence analysts had discovered that day, and whether we were going out.

When Army intelligence analysts identified a target, team leaders would gather in the Tactical Operations Center, which looked like every intelligence war room in the movies—analysts parked in front of rows of flat-screen monitors, with a platform in the middle of the room where the operations boss sat, managing everything. We'd brief in the main room, or in a side room, where we'd study aerial photographs, neighborhood maps, photos of the target and people around him: who they were, why they were important, what we had to do. We'd decide whether we were driving in or flying, or simply walking. We'd grid out the target buildings and the approaches to it. The insurgents often hid in urban areas, and sometimes squirreled into homes of noncombatants who had no choice but to let the fighters in. When we had a plan ready, we'd tuck away the maps and target photos into the plastic sleeves strapped to our arms, go tell our respective teams to suit up, and roll out.

One morning, the intel guys had picked up information about a bomb maker, who was in Baghdad and was almost sure to move if we didn't nab him quickly. I don't recall much about him, except that he was a top IED maker, which meant that he had American blood on his hands. To get him, we had to move fast, and that meant going out in broad daylight.

Baghdad in summer is a special type of hell. The sun blazed down from cloudless skies, and the temperature reached as high as 120 degrees. Water shortages and electricity outages gripped the city. The stench of shit from ruptured sewer lines was everywhere. We carried at least forty pounds of equipment, weapons, and water on top of our body armor and helmets. Within seconds of stepping into heat like that, I'd be in a full-on sweat. I'd freeze water bottles and carry them in a bandolier. Heat was only part of the problem. Sectarian violence was tearing Baghdad apart, and the entire city was hostile territory in 2007. There could be bombs underfoot or insurgents on rooftops anywhere we went. The delirium-inducing heat, the constant threat of violence, the hellscape of a city collapsing into anarchy, made missions into the city feel apocalyptic.

Since flying by helicopter into downtown Baghdad in daytime was impossible, we drove. We mounted up inside the high BIAP blast walls, assembling a long convoy of vehicles. My SEAL team usually rode in three Pandurs, which are six-wheeled, lightly armored vehicles that seat six plus a translator. Army Rangers went separately in four of their own vehicles, Strykers, which are bigger armored vehicles, with six Rangers in each. Dozens of us drove out of the airport toward the target. The convoy was like a freight train roaring at full speed through Baghdad's congested streets, stopping for nothing. Crowds scattered in front of us and vehicles full of frightened civilians pulled aside to let us pass. We were loud and visible and very conspicuous, and we know that at any moment, we could get blown up. Because of the threat of snipers, we kept the Pandur tops closed to protect us from shots from the rooftops above. Inside the sealed-up vehicles, we felt like meat in a smoker. We could roast inside while covered or keep the top down, get a bit of a breeze, but possibly get smoked a different way.

We reached the house, and cleared it, room by room. No sign of the bomb maker. I found the stairs and went up to the roof to set up security with a few of our snipers, looking out over the brick wall for any sign of hostiles or the bomb maker's movements. That was when we heard from the intelligence analysts: the bomb maker had been located at another house a few blocks away. We needed to move. This new location was so close that we went on foot, and the vehicles would follow us. We loaded our M249 squad automatic weapons while the Rangers carried everything from belt-fed M60s to rockets.

With weapons at the ready, we divided the patrol, and half of us went up each side of the street, scanning the rooftops and the windows overhead. In our eyes, every person was a potential suicide bomber; every vehicle could be a car bomb. We were woozy with the heat, and everyone was dehydrated and frustrated. Our missions were usually quick in-and-outs, but this was turning into a scavenger hunt that led us deeper into the city and farther from our base. When we left, it had been clear to me that we were the hunters. Now, as the chase dragged on with no sign of the target, I wasn't so sure who was hunting who anymore.

When we started the day chasing the bomb maker in Baghdad, we followed every rule. Our SEALs, Rangers, and Green Berets did everything by the book, exactly as we planned. But as the minutes ticked by, our patience wore thin, along with our resistance to cutting corners. As our target evaded us, we grew more frustrated, as the sun cooked us from above and civilians swarmed the streets.

There was still no sign of the bomb maker by the time we reached the second house. But minutes later, the intelligence analysts pinged us again: this time he was a few blocks away, in a third house. We mounted up the Pandurs and raced to the new location. We were on our way when the intel guys briefly lost track of the target. For a moment, he had disappeared. And then—you guessed it—we got another update: he had moved on to a *fourth* location.

The house was on the other side of a short bridge or overpass, and to get to it without helos, we had to cross the span. This was where we brushed up against our very own rules. *Never pursue a target over a bridge, especially an IED maker.* That was a huge red flag. Just a few months earlier, a suicide bomber—and maybe two of them—had blown up a truck in the middle of one of Baghdad's major bridges, sending cars into the river. At least ten people had died.

By now, my guys were pissed. They were hot and tired and were still carrying hundreds of pounds of weapons and equipment. The mission had turned into a cat-and-mouse game—the bomber had been messing with us all day.

That was when my team leader called it off and ordered us to turn back. "Breaking contact," it's called. Aborting the mission. What had started as a cut-and-dried snatch and grab was beginning to look more like a trap to lure four dozen or so of the most highly trained U.S. fighters in the world to this very bridge, so that he could blow all of us the fuck up.

If the team was angry before, they were on fire now. They flicked off their helmet chinstraps, shot us dirty looks, and grumbled, *Pussies.* They called us everything in the book. And not exactly under their breaths. *We could have got this guy, but we didn't because you're scared.* I got it—I understood why they were pissed. I was, too. But I didn't care. We had rules for a reason, and it wasn't so that we could do stupid shit and end up with dead squad members. My team never had a combat death, ever, and we weren't going to have any that day, either. Not on my watch.

My team stewed about in anger for a couple of days, and by the time their tempers cooled I caught up with a couple of my guys in the weight room. They were still bitching about it. *We could have gotten him, why did we stop, blah, blah, blah.*

That bomb maker we were going after until we stopped—what was his name again? I asked them.

They stared at me blankly. *I don't know, I don't care,* they said, annoyed.

What are your kids' names? I asked them.

They looked at me, surprised, and didn't say anything.

You don't even remember his name, I said. *You're going to forget all about this guy, but what if you never see your kids again because of some idiotic mistake or broken rule? Because what's more important— that we do something stupid and get killed trying to get a jihadi whose replacement is going to pop up tomorrow, or we follow our rules so we can eventually get home to see our families and maybe win the war, in that order?*

That shut them up.

I had learned this lesson early in the Deployment That Never Was. When we first began doing kill missions, we didn't have any experience. Everything was going to shit in Baghdad, sectarian killings were spiraling out of control, and the country was on the brink of civil war. Sunni insurgents had embedded among the civilian populations in Baghdad neighborhoods, and IEDs were killing U.S. troops left and right. It was a shit-show, and we were making things up on the fly.

At the start, we would land Chinooks and Black Hawks right next to the target building, announcing our presence by waking up everyone in a mile radius, and then we'd blow the door using explosives, waking up anyone who had slept through the helos landing. When we went in, we used white lights on our guns instead of night-vision goggles. The lights allowed us to move faster and see better, but it also meant we were easy targets for the enemy.

So we adapted. Instead of landing on top of the target, we would land out of earshot. Then we'd walk to the target. ████████████ ██████████████████████████████████████When we got to the house, we'd silently gain entry instead of blowing it open with explosives. There are quieter ways to break into the house than blowing the door.

But here was the problem. After we adopted those stealthier protocols, sometimes we would do that long walk in the dark only to show up at a target house and find it empty. Frustrated, we'd hike back out without fulfilling the mission. Night after night that happened. It felt like a waste of time. My team started to get pissed, and then they wanted to cut corners. *Fuck it, let's just fly to the target—no one will be there. And we'll go home and we'll have nice meals and we'll play Xbox.*

The next time, we reverted to our old ways; we took a Chinook and a couple of Black Hawks and flew directly to the target, just like before. Except this time, the helos were spotted before they could even land. I was in the doorway of the Black Hawk with my feet hanging down when the bullets start coming up at us from the ground. We hadn't even touched down and we were in a firefight.

We got our targets that night and then some, but we were lucky no one on our team got hit or took a stray bullet. All because we got frustrated and bored and wanted to get back to our Xboxes. Because we got lazy. Complacency kills, and you can't negotiate with a bullet that hits you in the head. The bullet doesn't care, nor does it compromise.

This isn't to say that rules can't change. It's okay to change the rules when you need to adapt to changing circumstances. Here's a great example. Since Vietnam, it's been a standard operating procedure in the military that when you breach a door, you go in fast and you go in hot. That way, if a firefight is ahead, you might as well get it started and get it over with.

Before I deployed to Iraq, I was training new guys in Close-Quarters Battle and telling them to do exactly that: go in fast. One of the guys raised his hand and asked, *Well, why are we going so fast through the door? Why don't you slow down and look around the room from the door before you've run in?* Wanting to put this guy in his place, my stupid ass answered: *Because this is the way we've always done it.*

"This is the way we've always done it" is one of the worst things you can say when you're running a team. When we got to Iraq, I realized the new guy had been right. Al Qaeda had been studying Army tactics, it appeared. They saw that soldiers entered quickly after they breached. So they had a tactical advantage: barricaded shooters knew to open fire immediately as soon as U.S. soldiers crashed through a door.

Army Special Operations lost a lot of guys that way. It wasn't because they were bad operators—they were incredible—but because we hadn't recognized that al Qaeda was observing our tactics and responding. So we adapted. We changed the rules.

Let's be real, though. Lives aren't on the line with every rule, and not every rule is a good one. Some rules are just plain stupid.

During a deployment in Afghanistan in early 2010, I had returned to Bagram from a firefight in Kandahar and was on my way to the chow hall when an MP stopped me. He informed me that I was not wearing the regulation reflective belt that was required at Bagram to increase your visibility so that, I guess, you don't get hit by a plane.

I had just come from combat where I was trying to hide from snipers, so the idea of wearing a reflective belt was funny. Well, at least it would've been if it weren't so stupid. There were other stupid rules, too. Like your firearms couldn't be loaded on the base. God forbid you'd have a bullet in the chamber in the middle of a war.

I asked the MP where I could get a reflective belt.

"You can get them at the PX for three dollars," he said. I thought that was funny, too, because I had a saying for my new guys, which was "Safety is free, so use as much as you like." *Except at Bagram, where it costs three dollars.*

"I'm going to have to cite you," he said. He wrote out a ticket and handed it to me. I looked at it and back at the MP. "Where do I pay this?"

"You don't pay it," he said. "You just get it."

It just kept getting better. "So I get a free ticket for not wearing a reflective belt?" I asked. He nodded. "Well, why don't you write me up another free ticket for littering?" I said. And I ripped up the ticket, tossed it in the air, and went to get chow. Rule or no rule, I'm pretty sure I got there just fine without a reflective belt.

DAKOTA
Rule II: Follow Orders Until You Can't

I had just zipped my brothers into body bags when I got the order to wash my hands. Four men on my team had been killed in the Ganj-gal Valley, and a fifth man would die a month later of his injuries. It was a grueling, seven-hour firefight that no one—not me, none of our guys—expected to be in. After we returned with the bodies of my team to FOB Joyce, our forward operating base, I had searched their pockets, taken out their personal items, and cleaned the dirt and blood from their faces as best I could before putting them in bags. Then I lay flags over the bodies so the PJs—the pararescuemen—could load them on an aircraft back to Bagram, and eventually, their families.

Every muscle in my body groaned with exhaustion, while my spinning thoughts turned over and over what I had just seen and what had gone wrong. I had shrapnel in my arm, and dirt and blood covered my clothes and were ground into every pore. My hands were sticky with blood, and my uniform was stiff and stained red. Some of the blood was from the men I had helped to safety, or whose bodies I had carried. Some was probably blood from a Taliban fighter I had killed. Some of it might have been my own.

As I left the landing zone, all I could think about was getting over to the Afghan side of the Joyce to help pack up their bodies. I had taken care of our dead, and now I wanted to help the Afghans with theirs. On the way across the base, I walked past the Tactical Operations Center, a plywood building where the senior officers oversaw regional operations and had made the fucked-up decisions in response to the ambush that our men had walked into. As I walked toward the Afghan side, I heard a voice yell at me.

"Hey, you need to wash your hands and clean up before you walk on this base," the senior officer said.

It wasn't as though that officer didn't know where I had just come from. Every asset on the base had been supporting me and the other soldiers and Marines trapped in the Ganjgal Valley over the seven hours of the firefight. My biggest problem there had been trying to save my teammates. And when I got back, the biggest problem for that motherfucker was that I needed to wash my hands?

Fuck you, I thought. I almost lost my shit. But I had just disobeyed a direct order not to go into the kill zone to save my teammates, and I might be facing discipline. I didn't say anything. I just found a lavatory with a sink and cleaned myself up.

———————•———————

HOURS BEFORE that officer told me to wash my hands, I had been pleading with my superiors for permission to help my team as they took heavy fire. I was a half mile away from the firefight, looking at the 40-millimeter grenade launcher on my truck that could have helped them escape from the net of Taliban closing around them. And then I defied the orders for me to remain in my place, and I went into the kill zone. I broke the rules.

One of the most basic tenets of the military is obedience. Even before I took a single step in formation in boot camp, I took the Marine oath of enlistment in Louisville and pledged to obey the orders of the president of the United States and the officers appointed over me. The military is not a democracy. Without obedience, there would be no military; it would be a bunch of mutinous men with guns at each other's throats. Following orders and adhering to the chain of command is what makes the military work.

During every step of my Marine career, I obeyed every order and edict I received, no matter how fucking ridiculous. Sometimes I argued, and sometimes I was a pain in the ass, but I never defied a commanding officer. I followed orders when I was sent to Kunar province to advise the Afghans. I had joined the Marines hoping to see combat, but not this kind: not an obvious ambush made worse because of incompetent commanding officers and idiotic rules.

I had arrived in Kunar over the summer, assigned to a Marine advisory team to the Afghan National Army. FOB Joyce, which was where my advisory team was headquartered, was about two miles southwest of Ganjgal. Joyce was the headquarters for a U.S. Army battalion whose purpose was to prevent incursions from Pakistan, whether it was Taliban or al Qaeda. My team operated out of Combat Outpost Monti, which was about ten miles to the north.

Team Monti, as we called it, wasn't there to fight, but to advise the Afghans on fighting the Taliban and establishing security in a dangerous area. The village of Ganjgal, in a valley of the same name, was an infiltration corridor between Afghanistan and the Pakistani border. It was a highway for black market smugglers and cross-border movement of Taliban. It was clear that in Ganjgal, allegiance to the American-supported Afghan government was weak at best.

A few weeks earlier, an informal truce with the Taliban had collapsed, and rockets had rained down on Forward Operating Base Joyce, setting off a fuel fire inside the base. To patch things up, Ganjgal's elders had asked Afghan National Army soldiers—Askars, in Pashto—to give money to the local mosque. Like a peace deal. It was called Operation Buri Booza II, and it was intended to show that the Afghan army was on the side of the villagers.

I had a bad feeling about it from the beginning. The only way to the village was up the gravel wash at the bottom of the horseshoe-shaped valley, ending in a box canyon with steep ridges on three sides. My team—along with about sixty Afghan soldiers and thirty border police—was going to walk to the village to deliver the goods, while the vehicles would stay behind. The reasoning for leaving the vehicles behind was that the mission was supposed to be clandestine, but it couldn't have been a more perfect setup for an ambush. Despite the obvious risks, the plan went ahead. At the last minute, I was taken off the team and tasked with providing security, which pissed off me and my team members. I tried to convince the senior officers to send me up in the vehicles with the patrol, but I was denied.

While I waited at the mouth of the valley, Team Monti left before daylight on the operation with the ninety Askars. Every U.S. movement coordinated with the Afghans was certain to be leaked to the Taliban, and this operation was no exception. As the delegation approached Ganjgal, all the lights in the village went out. A few minutes later, the gunfire began. The peace mission had walked straight into a trap.

During the course of the night, some sixty Taliban had entered the villages and taken up positions in an elaborate trench system, and they were ready when the team walked up the valley floor into the village before daybreak. Within minutes, the gorge had become a valley of death, with Taliban machine gunners firing down at the Afghans and the Marines from behind rocky crags and out of the trenches, mortars, and rocket-propelled grenades raining down in every direction.

When the firing broke out, I was down the valley with support vehicles. When I called up to the officers in the village, asking for permission to enter the valley with the truck-mounted grenade launcher, most didn't respond, and when one did, he denied my request. I just sat there, tearing my hair out as I listened to the voices of my team screaming over one another over the radio. At the same time, officers at Joyce dithered about whether to send artillery shells over. Requests for air support were also denied, because of new rules of engagement around civilians.

This story has been told again and again, by me and others, but what's worth repeating is that when the time came, I defied direct orders not to advance into the valley to retrieve the Marines and Askars who were getting cut to pieces. The thing is, I knew I would go in there even before I asked for permission. I didn't have the confidence in the officers who ordered me to stay put and not to enter the kill zone. I knew what needed to be done, and I had made up my mind to enter the valley and help rescue our pinned-down men.

It took more than five hours, but one of the helos finally spotted their bodies in a trench close to the house where they had been pinned down from the start, stripped of all their equipment and weapons. I ran to the trench with Army captain William Swenson, who belatedly received the Medal of Honor for that day as well. I carried two of my team members' bodies out; the Afghan army soldiers carried the others. We left the valley in an Afghan truck with the bodies of Team Monti in the back, and when we got back to Joyce, I went to get the body bags myself.

I don't disrespect authority; just the opposite. But I question those who wield their authority the wrong way, or for the wrong reasons. I want to know the reasoning behind a rule or an order before I follow it. And if the person who's giving an order can't give the reasoning behind it, then I'm damn sure that that person isn't cut out to give it.

On September 8, 2009, in Ganjgal, the reasons behind our orders were completely fucked. And the commanders back at the Joyce Tactical Operations Center who could have sent air support, who could have sent artillery, who could have sent ground support, tied themselves up in fucking knots trying to follow rules. Because of that, my four teammates and eleven other men were cut to pieces, and seventeen more were wounded.

Those men died because generals have put policies into place that try to generalize about every situation. Instead of individual thinkers making decisions on the battlefield, you've got rules of engagement, rules of engagement, rules of engagement. It's part of the reason we haven't been able to prevail in Iraq and Afghanistan. The military has tried to plan for every contingency, to make rules that apply in every circumstance. The problem is that you can't generalize everything and make a rule for it. Once that happens, thinking stops.

I loved the Marines, still do. It made me who I am today. But it's a bureaucracy. Just like any giant, bloated organization with thousands of people spread across the world, if you stick your head in any office, I guarantee there's going to be a Kathy in there that just likes to bust a flex to make people do dumb shit. Make rules and make demands for no reason other than the fact that she can. Everywhere I went in the Marines, at every base and FOB, there were rules that didn't pass the common-sense test. Which was why that officer yelled at me to wash my hands after carrying bodies out of a firefight.

Deference to authority might even be the downfall of our country someday. People don't think for themselves anymore. They swallow what's in the media and generalize about what they see around them, attach labels and slogans. If we're going to stay the freest country in the world, individuals need to unburden themselves from others' opinions. They need to think for themselves. I don't think that's something that we're born with—it's something that's nurtured. It's something that we have to learn. I think that in some ways, everything in my life up to that point, all the micro-decisions that I had made, led up to that decision in that moment of crisis to do what was right, rather than what was expected.

I paid a price for what happened in Ganjgal. After that day, I stopped sleeping. I was lost in a fog of exhaustion and anger during the day, while out-of-control thoughts spun through my head at night. Finally, the Marines sent me stateside for treatment. In late 2009, I was about to leave for home. I had left FOB Joyce and was at Bagram for a couple of days before shipping out to Kentucky. It was right after Thanksgiving, and it was cold. To keep my hands warm, I stuck them in my pockets on my way to the chow hall.

"Hey Marine!" Across the street, a first sergeant yelled in my direction. I looked around, but I was the only Marine in sight.

"Yes, First Sergeant," I responded.

"You know it's against regulations to have your hands in your pockets!" he shouted at me.

"It's cold outside, First Sergeant," I said. "Why can't I have my hands in my pockets?"

"You can't have your hands in your pockets in case you need to salute," he snapped back. Being a smart-ass, I said, "Marines don't salute in combat."

"We salute here," he told me. By now, he was up in my face screaming these regulations over and over at me. Unless I wanted to risk a court-martial, there was nothing that I could do but take it. I would be on my way home in a matter of days, to try to get my head straight after surviving one of the worst enemy attacks in years in Afghanistan. As I sat there, with this desk jockey screaming in my face, all I could think was, *Man, you don't even leave this fucking wire. I've been out fighting. I've been out in combat and you're sitting here worried about my fucking hands in my pockets.*

Rob got a ticket for not having a reflective belt. I just got reamed out. I didn't argue any more. In Ganjgal, I had broken the rules when I needed to, when the stakes were real. Sometimes, the stakes are too high not to break a rule. Sometimes, like on a cold day in Afghanistan right before I was about to return home, the stakes are too low. After the first sergeant was done tearing me a new one, I walked off. It was still cold, so when he was out of sight, I put my hands back in my pockets.

8

CHOOSE TO CONNECT

ROB

Don't Shoot the Sleeping Man

I didn't see Osama bin Laden right away. My night-vision goggles cast the stairwell of the compound in Abbottabad, Pakistan, in amber light as I crept up to the third floor behind my point man. Just before we entered the building through the open carport, the lights had winked out in the building and throughout Abbottabad, snuffed out by God or the CIA. Whoever got there first. In the darkness, about half of the assault team had entered the building and eight SEAL Team █ operators from the squadron started up the stairs, surveilling the interior through the eerie luminescence of their goggles. I was near the back of the procession as it moved up the stairs to the second floor. The first floor had been cleared quickly before I got there, so I had a front-row seat to watch cool guys do cool stuff. Two by two, the operators had peeled off to secure rooms once we got to the final set of stairs to the third floor. Now there were just two of us: my point man and me.

Just before I got there, there was a flicker of movement behind a curtain, and the point man fired up at it. We paused on the stairs, momentarily uncertain of whether the two of us should advance alone. I squeezed the point man's shoulder, and we moved quickly up the last steps. The point man swept the fabric aside. Two women on the other side screamed. My point man lunged toward them and pushed them out of the way, acting as a human shield in case they were wearing suicide vests. I swiveled to the right through an open doorway.

As I pivoted into the doorway, I could see Osama bin Laden standing in the dark bedroom at the foot of a bed, a glowing presence in the ghostly hue of my goggles. He wore a robe and was taller and leaner than I expected. He was also older and grayer than in the pictures from a decade earlier, but he had the same mournful face and long nose. He was standing behind one of his wives, Amal, nearly looming over her. I don't know if he was using her for a shield or something else, but it didn't matter. I shot him twice over her shoulder. One of the shots split open his head. After he fell to the floor, I shot him one more time and heard him take his last breath, saw his tongue loll out of his mouth. I could smell the inside of his skull, like the funky odor of an animal's entrails.

Amal had been shot in the leg somehow, and as I helped her to the bed alongside the wall, I noticed a boy standing in the dark, looking up at me. It was bin Laden's son, Hussein. He was two years old, I found out later.

I picked him up as gently as I could and put him on the bed next to Amal. Behind me, the other members of the squadron spilled in the door of the bedroom. I stood there for a moment in shock. One of my boys put his hand on my shoulder. "Are you okay?"

"I think so," I said. "What do we do now?"

He laughed at me and said, "We do this every night. We've done this hundreds and hundreds of times."

"You're right, I'm back. Holy shit," I said.

"Yeah, you just killed Osama bin Laden. Your life just changed. Now let's get to work." Then I snapped out of it, and we got back to work.

———•———

SINCE I'VE LEFT THE NAVY, people come up to me all the time and ask me to sign pictures of bin Laden with his face crossed out. Or they ask me to sign their paper targets from a shooting range, with bullet holes peppering his picture. There are even fake Rob O'Neill signatures that people sell online to cash in on the craze: a big lie for a small payday.

If anyone deserved what he got, it was bin Laden. He deserved it because he was a mass murderer who was never going to stop murdering. But he also had children; he had family. He had people around him who loved and admired him, even if he was despised throughout the world. It's not hard to take aim at a picture printed on a paper target at a gun range. But imagine looking down the barrel of a gun at a family portrait, of bin Laden and his wives, and of his children and parents. Who would want to take that shot? Who wouldn't hesitate knowing that a child would be involved?

When I'm asked to sign those pictures, I always tell people that there are real lives and emotions connected to what happened in Abbottabad. *I killed this guy in front of his kid, man. This is not a fucking game,* I think. And then I hope that the boy was too young to understand or to remember what happened, and that he might forget seeing his dad's head blown open right in front of him. But if we're being honest, I don't think you forget that kind of thing.

The War on Terror created a warrior mentality that was ubiquitous in the United States, regardless of whether or not you are a soldier. Of course there was Rambo and Arnold Schwarzenegger and Steven Seagal before September 11, but that soldier-of-fortune attitude is everywhere now. "Warriors" on Instagram pose with their muscles and guns and beards, but the fact is that most of the people who say "I like to kick in doors and shoot fuckers in the face" have never actually done it.

I have done it, more times than I can count. More times than I can remember. I killed a lot of people in Iraq and Afghanistan, a lot more than the one I'm most famous for. And I will tell you this: being responsible for so much death is a burden that I wish upon no one.

Make no mistake: I have respect for anyone who raised their right hand and served. Lots of veterans have seen bad combat and I respect the shit out them. But we all also know the deal. Not everyone is a door kicker. In any chow hall in any branch of the service, it's easy to spot the difference between the combat vets who have seen some shit and the noncombat vets who have clean uniforms and laugh while chewing their sandwiches. When the guys come in covered in dirt with a thousand-yard stare, sit down without talking, and then leave, those are the guys who have seen some really bad shit. It just doesn't go away. You have to just deal with it. The dying changes everything.

Dakota and I both remember the first person that each of us killed. It's something that's seared into your memory, a recollection that never fades, but often crystallizes, as the years go on. For me, it was winter of 2006, in Ramadi. We were on a joint operation with guys from Army Special Operations and commandos from the British Special Boat Service (SBS), which was the Brits' version of Special Forces. It was bitterly cold as my guys from my squadron hiked from the drop-off site to the target. Along the way, we passed a grape orchard. The grapes looked good enough to eat, but I lost my appetite when I saw huge rats scurrying on the vines.

As we arrived on the outskirts of Ramadi, dogs started barking—not one or two of them, but dozens of them, whipped into a yelping frenzy all around us that continued throughout the operation. As we crept up on the target, the D-boys and SBS arrived in helicopters, like we were used to, and landed next to the building. The noise probably woke up everyone in the neighborhood.

Once inside, one of my guys and an operator from the SBS shot and killed a gunman peering at us down a darkened hallway. The SEAL asked the Brit, "How's that guy?" The Brit briefly shined a light into what was left of the gunman's face and said, "He's fucked, mate." It was the first time I had ever seen someone killed in combat, but it wasn't the last time I'd hear, "He's fucked."

A few minutes later, we could hear our snipers shooting from nearby rooftops. One of my guys exited the building with me. We were covering each other in the yard, panning the area around the building, when two gunmen popped out of nowhere. Each of us shot one, killing our first guys at exactly the same moment. Years later, he was a groomsman at my wedding.

All of us in the SEAL Teams—anyone who's in a position to kill someone—wonder how they're going to react the first time they take a human life. When I killed him, my first thought was, *Holy shit, I'm in the club.* It was a similar feeling to when I shot my first deer. I wasn't sure if I felt bad about killing my first buck, but it was a rite of passage: I was a hunter. When I killed that man, I wasn't sure if I felt bad about that, either. I mentally recorded the milestone and said to myself, *This is what I do now.*

That was my very first kill, but I remember the last one, too. After we got bin Laden, I already knew that my career in the Teams was over, but I extended my stay after 17 SEAL operators and a total of 31 Americans, including the dog, died in the shoot-down of a helicopter, Extortion 17, in Afghanistan. I couldn't leave the Teams when so many of my friends had just died. So I stayed on, and moved to another squadron.

On that mission, we were stationed at a forward operating base in eastern Afghanistan. The base was at six thousand feet altitude in the bitter cold of winter. It was the opposite of my deployment in Jalalabad six years earlier. Our base came under mortar attack daily; there were few missions, and little to do at the base. As Christmas came and went, I thought about my family constantly. One of my girls packed a suitcase and set it by the door of our town house in Virginia Beach, because I had promised to take them on vacation when I got back after Christmas. The suitcase sat by the door for three months.

My last mission, and my very last kill, came during surveillance of a house in our area. Our intel guys reported to us that each night five men would pile into a pickup truck, drive around the southern tip of a mountain, turn east, then wait by a road that was regularly used by Americans. They were probably Taliban fighters, and they were most likely hoping to ambush American troops on the road.

I suggested that we observe them on Friday, which is the Muslim day of prayer. If the men did something that day, it was *definitely* an ambush. That meant they would be there on Saturday, only that time we would be there as well. Surprise, surprise, they went out on Friday, and we got ready to meet them the next day.

We inserted a kilometer away and hiked to the road before dawn. We set a few snipers above and found a hiding place behind some rocks, where we broke out some Cuban cigars. It began to snow as we waited, puffing on our stogies. I heard one of the pilots who was observing from high above say that they were on the way and the sound of the Nissan's engine up the road confirmed it. We watched the vehicle arrive with the five Taliban. I put down the cigar and stepped into the road. When the driver saw me, he stopped. I yelled to him to get out of the car. Instead, he tried to reverse, but the wheels spun in the snow. Then everything went hot. The front passenger door popped open, and one of the five men jumped out with a machine gun. One of my guys in the road opened fire on him at the same time that the sniper above shot the driver in the head. The men in the back of the car scrambled to get out, and everyone, including me, opened fire. When everyone had stopped moving, I went back to our hiding spot, picked up my cigar, and kept smoking.

I'm not telling this story because it was memorable, or because I feel bad about it; I'm telling it because it wasn't, and I don't. I don't know which of the five men I actually killed on the road that day. Maybe I killed more than one. Maybe I didn't actually kill any of them. I don't know. The only reason I remember it is that it was the last one. Because when it was done, I felt nothing. There was no adrenaline. There was no fear. Killing had become routine. That was the moment, on that steep Afghan roadside with a cigar smoldering in my mouth, that it became clear to me that it was time to retire.

Among all those people that I killed, there's only one face that I think about every single day. It's the face that I see when I lie in bed awake at night, unable to sleep. And no, it's not bin Laden's.

It was a man in Baqubah, about thirty miles northeast of Baghdad. This was during the Deployment That Never Was in 2007, when we were going out every night, cleaning out nests of al Qaeda–linked Sunni militants and sleeping during the day. I was the acting team leader for the mission, so all the decisions rested with me. And all their consequences, too.

We set down and then walked from the drop-off site. We crept past darkened houses and down alleys in an urban neighborhood until we reached the target, a big, two-story building. Nobody saw or heard us come in. Remember: *rules*.

I was the first one in the door and when I came in, I surprised a guy with a gun in the middle of the living room. I shot him.

When the gunfire began, everything started moving. Not faster, just more efficiently, briskly. The team came in behind me. There were doors to the left and right, and a third one straight ahead. I went through that door alone. That's called a "one man entry"; you're not supposed to do that.

Inside the room, I hugged the wall as I entered. There was a bed with a man and a woman sleeping, and an AK-47 lay next to the sleeping man. I quietly circled them until I reached the foot of the bed. The man was on my left and the woman on the right. Then the man woke up.

He was angry, or startled, or both. He jumped up and threw himself at me, trying to kick me. I called out "One more" for backup. Otherwise, I didn't do anything for a moment. Behind me, I heard my buddy observing the kicking man say, "Is this guy fucking serious?" I laughed. *I think so.*

And then I saw the man reach for the AK-47 next to him. I warned him, "Don't do it. Don't do it." But he kept reaching for the gun. And then I shot him in the face. After he fell back into the bed, I turned on my light, which is attached to the barrel of the gun, so I could see more clearly. And while I had my light shining on his ruined face, that was when his wife woke up and saw her husband next to her on the floor, his face blown off, and she screamed.

That's the guy I think about every day. Sometimes I think about him in the middle of the night, when a sound in the house wakes me up next to my sleeping wife. He's the guy who I wonder about. Al Qaeda didn't usually sleep with their guns—they would bury them outside at sundown, so that they could feign innocence if the house was raided while they were sleeping. We found IED materials in the house, but not everyone in houses like that was automatically guilty—al Qaeda would embed themselves in Sunni houses whether the owner liked it or not. So I wonder whether I had to kill that man, or whether I could have disarmed him without hurting him, without killing him with his wife beside him.

The interpreters told the women in the house not to leave until dawn, and we left the bodies there, so the families could bury them in the morning. It's strange to think that in a different time, and in a different place, I would have been happy to sit down with that man over coffee or a beer, and talk about ourselves, and our families, and the directions that our lives had taken. Maybe we would have shaken hands, and parted as friends, and the memory of that man that would stay with me wouldn't be the image of his shattered faced and his brains splashed onto his pillow, but of his smile. In that different time, in that different place, he'd still be alive today, walking back to his home and to his kids and to his life.

DAKOTA
Look into Their Eyes, Then Pick up the Rock

Everything had come apart at the seams in Ganjgal when I learned that our team was still stuck somewhere in the valley. For more than three hours, I dodged machine gun bullets and RPG fire, hoping to still find Team Monti alive. As I drove with my translator and motor transport chief, Staff Sergeant Juan Rodriguez-Chavez, in our Humvee, buzzing Kiowa helicopters dove and spun overhead, machine gun fire ricocheted around us, and RPGs streaked down from Taliban positions. When we ran low on ammunition, we had returned to our casualty collection point to get more ammo and guns.

At the collection point, dazed Askars who had walked out of the gorge milled in groups among the vehicles. I searched the faces of those who had escaped; I was looking for my team. My friend Dodd Ali wasn't among them, either. He was an Afghan army NCO who spoke better English than the typical Askar, so I often went with him because he doubled as a translator. He and I had been on more patrols together than I could count. My translator questioned the Afghans, and they told him that Team Monti was still somewhere up the valley. They hadn't made it out.

We went back up into the valley in our Humvee with more ammo for our .50-caliber gun. An Afghan policeman followed us up the wash in a Ford Ranger. After another return to the casualty collection point, a second Ford Ranger joined us, this one with Captain William Swenson, the border police advisor, and Second Lieutenant Ademola Fabayo, the operations manager for Team Monti. As enemy fire rained down on us, we careened along the terraces stacked along the valley walls, trying to find Team Monti and our Afghan allies. I was also watching for Dodd Ali, hoping that he might have holed up somewhere safe.

About halfway up the valley, our convoy paused to take stock of the situation, and I switched vehicles, hopping into the beat-up Ford Ranger with Swenson. Bullet holes peppered the vehicles, and driving over the wash had destroyed the shocks. As he drove, he shouted into his radio trying to direct the helicopters overhead.

As the Ranger bounced and slammed among the terraces, I spotted a motionless figure. I yelled at Swenson to stop. Swenson had a torn ligament and had taken shrapnel in the legs, so he stayed in the truck as I jumped out and ran toward the body. It was lying at the foot of one of the terraces rising up from the narrow gorge. I climbed up the terrace wall, following its curve. As soon as I reached the body and saw the hands, I knew it was Dodd Ali. We had given him green fingerless gloves that I saw on the motionless hands of the corpse. I turned him over and saw that he'd been shot in the face. He's a small guy—too small for his body armor—and I got ready to hoist him up and carry him away.

As I did, I felt something hit me in the back of the head. It was a tap, something to get my attention. When I turned and looked up, I saw a Taliban fighter standing over me. He wore a flak jacket over his long shirt, and he had a huge beard. He was a big dude, and he was pointing an AK-47 at me. He was telling me to stand up, to drop my rifle, and go with him.

Fuck that, I thought. *Not a chance.*

———————

I TELL THIS STORY about the Taliban fighter as often as I can. Not because it's a glorious story about combat, but because of how it changed me. Rob and I talk a lot about how we've had moments in combat where we've turned a corner and saw something in ourselves that we hadn't seen before, or maybe didn't want to see. Rob remembers killing the guy in his bed next to his wife. I remember fighting this Taliban soldier to the death in the Ganjgal Valley. I can't get his face out of my head.

Up until September 8, 2009, I was always the guy who wanted to get in fights, who was itching to get into combat. Even if something went sideways and I got myself in trouble, I could call in my friends to rain down hellfire from the sky. You can say anything you want about the U.S. military, but one thing no one can disagree with is that American forces have superior firepower on their side. When a fight went bad, artillery and high explosives and rockets and white phosphorus and every kind of aerial bomb you can imagine can make things right.

Rob remembers the first man that he killed, and I do, too. It was at Combat Outpost Monti, where my team was based, in August 2009, the month before Ganjgal. I had just shaved and showered when I heard RPG explosions outside the walls of the post. The rockets were falling short, but the fact that we were under fire meant that there was a direct line of sight to the camp. Whoever was firing the grenades could see us, and he was close.

I went up on the corner sentry post and set up my M240 machine gun and lookout. I spotted this guy firing the RPG from the side of a mountain, and as soon as I got him in my crosshairs, I stitched him with the M240. I fucking nailed him. Afterward, I laughed about it with the staff sergeant next to me. The man I had killed wasn't real to me; he was just a far-off object, a figure running across a hillside, until he wasn't running anymore.

Let's face it: empathy is not something that's taught in the armed services. The Marines only teach how to take lives, but there ain't no classes to help new boots understand what it means to take a human life on a philosophical level. I think that's why so many people come back from war fucked up, because no one's prepared them for the emotional consequences of their actions. They don't understand why they feel so torn up, and no one helps explain it. You're taught rules for taking a life, but not what it does to you. Under military rules of engagement, I'm required to ask a commanding officer for permission to fire on another person unless there's an imminent risk. In my view, if I have time to call a CO to ask for permission to shoot someone, I probably have time to resolve a situation *without* killing that person.

It doesn't help that a lot of killing in these wars happens at a distance. It's not a person in your sights a thousand yards away, or a half mile overhead, or someone on a rooftop down the street—it's a target. Maybe it's an infrared blur that a drone pilot sees on a screen twelve thousand miles away in Nevada. I've never asked those guys how they interpret their kills, and part of me doesn't want to know.

Almost no one looks into the eyes of a person that they're about to kill anymore. Shooting someone from far away is akin to hunting an animal. That's what happened to me that day at COP Monti. I was excited to have my first kill, to have my training come to something, but I didn't have to go and pick up his body parts afterward, or shovel him into a grave. He just fell where I shot him, and that was it. A video game; his body might as well have disappeared.

It's different when you're looking into another human being's eyes and killing him with your hands. In that personal struggle, all the other differences fall away. American versus Taliban. Islam versus Christianity. Invader versus invaded. None of that matters when all you're trying to do is to draw your next breath. The person whose eyes you're looking into wants the exact same thing as you: to live.

The person who helped me understand this better than anyone was the man whose body I tried to reclaim at the foot of the terrace, Dodd Ali.

We spent so much time together that we became almost like brothers. He spoke pretty good English, and I spoke a little Pashto, so we had ourselves a little team that didn't require a translator. He had a nickname for me—Meyeda—and he was always cracking jokes. He told me that his parents had opposed his joining the Afghan army because it was so risky, and that he had snuck away to enlist against their wishes. Right before Ganjgal, he had reconciled with them. After the mission, he was supposed to go home to see them for the first time since he enlisted.

He was a devout Muslim, and like all the Askars, he prayed five times a day. He would stop whatever he was doing—even if it was in the middle of taking fire—to get down on the ground, face Mecca, and pray. Commanding officers discouraged us from talking about religion with the Afghans. They worried that it would lead to misunderstandings or conflict, instead of dialogue. But I talked about it with Dodd Ali, because that's what friends do.

We were talking over dinner one night, probably about a month before Ganjgal. I often ate dinner with the Askars on their side of the base. We would gather our meals and climb up on the roof of their chow hall. The view from there was spectacular. I could see the snowy peaks of the Hindu Kush, and after dark, the stars stretched in a shimmering curtain of light across a sky that seemed to go forever.

As we ate, Dodd Ali explained to me that in Islam, Jesus was considered a prophet. Not the son of God, but still a revered holy figure. That difference was all that lay between Islam and Christianity, he said. And all the bloodshed between the two religions, all the hatred, all the killing, was over a slightly different interpretation of one man's place in two related religions. He thought it was bullshit that Muslims and non-Muslims were killing each other over that, and that the Taliban were using religion as a justification for fighting. And he also told me that he would never let me die for his country before he did.

Before that conversation, I never thought about what I might have in common with our enemy in Afghanistan. On the most basic level, it seemed like I shared nothing with the people we were fighting, or the ones we were defending, for that matter. Dodd Ali showed me otherwise. I mean, I don't feel sorry for any of the guys I killed. Not in the least. But not feeling bad doesn't mean I can't humanize them. If I had hit the point where I didn't feel anything when I killed somebody, I would have become nil. I would have ceased being a person.

And that's what might have happened if it hadn't been for the Taliban fighter standing over me and Dodd Ali's body with an AK-47, yelling at me to go with him. I was in a crouch, with my rifle on my left thigh, looking up at him. When I raised my arm as if to surrender, I pulled the trigger on the grenade launcher and a 40-millimeter grenade thumped into his chest from about two feet away, knocking him backward. He staggered and fell. The grenade didn't explode—they don't arm unless they travel thirty-two meters—but I swore he was dead.

I was wrong. I leaned over Dodd Ali again planning to hoist him up on my shoulder and bring him to the Ranger. That was when I felt the Taliban fighter's hands around my neck. At the same time, I knew that between him and me, there was a live grenade that could go off. He was strong and had a powerful grip on my throat. I could feel myself starting to pass out as he throttled my windpipe. I began to fade, and as I relaxed, he let up his grip.

When he did, I ripped his arms away from my neck, wrestled him over onto his back, and pinned his arms with my knees. I began reaching all around me, fumbling for anything on the ground that I could hit him with. That was when my hand closed around a rock about the size of a baseball.

All I could think about was hitting that motherfucker. I raised the rock and smashed him on the left side of his head. Then I just started hitting him across the face as hard as I could, over and over, fueled by rage coursing through my veins.

I had hit him about six times when we made eye contact. As I sat there with the rock in my hand, looking at the face of this soldier I was about to kill, the world around me went silent. In that second, I didn't see hate or anger or fear in his eyes. I saw that he had given up. He knew what was about to happen. He knew that he was never going to see his family again, or his wife and kids, if he had any. I thought, *I don't even know this guy. I don't hate him.*

Then the world flashed back on and I raised the rock again and I went back to killing him. I smashed the left side of his face to pieces, caving in his eye socket and smashing in his teeth like a pile of old bones. If I hit him once, I hit him fifty times. I don't know how long I hit him. It couldn't have been very long, but it was long enough. I could hear the sound of him choking on his own blood, until finally he stopped breathing. It seemed like forever.

Once he was dead, I finally began trying to get Dodd Ali's body to the truck. I couldn't get a good enough grip on him, so I began slowly dragging his body back around the terrace, to where Swenson was waiting for me. As I made my way around the curve, bullets began snapping past me again as I came back into the line of fire from above. I'd pull a few meters, stop and rest, pull a few more meters. When I finally reached the Ranger, Swenson helped me get his body into the back of the truck.

When the day was over, and I was back at Joyce, it wasn't just the bodies of Team Monti that I helped clean up. Afterward, I went over to the Afghan end of the camp and did the same thing with their KIAs, too. One of them was Dodd Ali. Like with my own team, I washed his face as best I could, tried to remove as much of the grit and blood of war as I could. His mother was going to see her boy for the last time, and instead of the joyous homecoming and reconciliation, they were going to prepare his body for burial.

I respect people who have fought in gun battles. What I don't respect are people who brag about being a gunfighter and have never looked an adversary in his eyes before taking his life. Because that's something else completely. Like Rob says, there are a lot of people out there telling war stories these days, going on about all the things that they did, all the people they killed. I tell the story about the Taliban and the rock whenever I can because there are so many stories that are being told out there that make it like it's a cool thing to go kill another human being. And you should know by now that it's not.

After I was nominated for the Medal of Honor, parts of my story have been questioned, and Monday morning quarterbacks have raised doubts about whether I killed that Taliban with a rock. None of that bothers me, because I know what I saw that day in the valley, and I know what I did. Here's what I have to say to that bullshit: unless you were there, you don't know. And let me tell you why I can say that: because when I close my eyes at night, it's the eyes of that Taliban soldier that I see, looking into mine, knowing what was coming, and that he was about to leave this world and enter another. Night after night, I look into the eyes of a dying man, and every time that image replays in my mind, I don't see an enemy: I see myself.

9

———•———

PRAISE

ROB
Don't Sit in the Front Row

As our Chinook thundered through the Pakistani night sky toward Jalalabad, I sat against the fuselage in the dark interior of the helo, my wristwatch counting down the minutes until we reached the Pakistani border and crossed into safe Afghan airspace. Osama bin Laden had taken his last breath minutes earlier, and his corpse was zipped into a body bag on the stealth helicopter fleeing for the border somewhere nearby. I was wedged between two SEALs, still wearing my night-vision goggles. A few seconds after we took off, the SEAL on my right asked me the question I would hear over and over: "Who got him?"

"I did," I told him.

He stiffened in his seat, as if he wanted to salute me, and thanked me instead. Then, from the other side of me, a can of Copenhagen floated into my field of vision. The SEAL holding it had taken the shot that saved Captain Richard Phillips from Somali pirates who seized his ship in the Indian Ocean in 2009, a mission that I had been on, too.

"Now you know what it's like to be a hero," he said.

Word had leaked out even before we arrived in Jalalabad. After we landed, I walked through the helicopter hangar so I could throw out the bottle of piss that I had used to relieve myself during the flight. A couple of mechanics who saw me whispered and pointed at me as I went by. From Jalalabad, we flew the body to Bagram, where the enormity of what had happened began to truly sink in. In a hangar at the airfield, we sorted the items that we had collected from bin Laden's compound, then wolfed down sandwiches as we watched President Obama announce bin Laden's death live at a press conference at the White House. As Obama talked about the mission, bin Laden's body lay a few feet away from me, body bag unzipped. Surreal doesn't even begin to describe it.

After a debrief with the shooters on the mission, we went to the other side of the base, showered, had some pizza and bourbon, checked our email, and then returned to the hangar to get ready to return stateside. Bin Laden's body was gone, loaded on an Army transport to be disposed of in the Persian Gulf. Our C-17 back to Virginia Beach was ready for boarding when the ground force commander who had led the mission pulled me and my point man aside.

He looked every bit the SEAL, and I believe that after September 11, he spent every minute of his waking life planning to kill bin Laden. I think he always knew that he would get the call to lead that mission, and that when he did, his team would get the job done. He brought us into a room off the side of the hangar. He had a bottle of whiskey, probably Jack Daniel's, and poured shots for both of us and one for him. "Great job, guys," he said very simply, and we knocked it back. Then we got on the plane for home.

———

FROM THAT POINT ON, my time with the SEALs would be different. More monumental. All of us who had chosen to go to Abbottabad had gotten out alive, and we would now be the best twenty-eight friends who had ever lived. We could do no wrong. We would be a brotherhood within a brotherhood. And none of us would ever talk trash about the others.

What a load of shit that turned out to be.

The Teams are a small community, and word got around quickly that *O'Neill got him.* Resentment and jealousy began to fester almost immediately, both within my squadron and with the other squadrons that hadn't been sent on the mission. I found out that on the night after bin Laden was killed, a bunch of SEAL wives were out at CP Shucker's, a bar in Virginia Beach that's a favorite for SEALs. When the ▮▮ Squadron wives saw on the TVs that bin Laden was killed, they started giving a toast to their guys: *Cheers, those are our husbands,* they gloated, before someone corrected them. *No, no, no, that was* ▮▮ *Squadron, not* ▮▮ *Squadron.* Apparently, the wives didn't like that too much.

The backbiting started almost as soon as we got back. When we landed at Naval Air Station Oceana in Virginia Beach, SEAL Team ▮▮ operators who hadn't deployed met us at the base's secret entrance. One of them—the future commanding officer of the team—ran down the center of our airplane and high-fived each of us like an NFL player greeting fans out of the tunnel. When we got to the team room, someone from another squadron broke out a bottle of Johnnie Walker Blue Label. "I was saving this for a special occasion," he said. "I think this is it." Everyone traded stories about what happened, about who did what. Afterward, a bunch of us went to the Ready Room and continued the celebration.

The next morning, I called my ▮▮▮▮▮▮▮▮▮▮ master chief, and told him I would be in a few hours late because I wanted to spend some time with my kids. And that's where everything started to sour. He was pissed at me because I wanted to come into the office late. I didn't understand it. We had killed the man responsible for the worst terror attack in U.S. history, and I didn't really think it was that urgent that I come to the office that morning to fill out forms so

I could claim my fucking travel per diems. Just in those few hours of my absence, word was going around that O'Neill would never come into the office again, that my head was too big and that I felt superior to other SEALs. This was less than a day after our return. Soon the lies would be flying fast and furious. That I had been bragging about what had happened. That I hadn't actually killed bin Laden. That I was planning to write a book. That I talked too much. That I had broken the SEAL code of silence.

The resentment only got worse as the spotlight fell squarely on us. Within a few days after our return, defense secretary Robert Gates flew to Virginia Beach to thank the twenty-eight of us. We gathered in the big conference room ███████████████. Things got weird. Only those of us sent to Abbottabad were allowed in; members of my squadron who hadn't been on the mission weren't permitted to attend, let alone members from other squadrons. And this was *after* the mission. I'm talking master chiefs, high-level E-9s that wanted to listen in and were turned away at the door. More pissed-off people. More jealousy and anger.

In a way, Naval Special Warfare Command stoked that tension with its emphasis on SEAL anonymity, on the notion of the quiet professional who does his job without seeking praise or reward. There was an expectation that no one should seek recognition or fame for what we did collectively. There's nothing wrong with that, but the problem was that our anonymity was gone even before we got back to Virginia. I was constantly getting hammered for talking about what had happened in Abbottabad, even though everyone was talking about it. It was the worst-kept secret in the Navy.

And the anonymity only grew harder to preserve. After they flew us down to Tampa, a constant parade of visitors came to Virginia Beach to shake our hands and hear about the mission. They would get a tour of the facilities and see the memorial for all the fallen team members and the piece of the twin towers of the World Trade Center that we have on display in front of our headquarters. There's a room with a bulletproof window where they can watch a live-fire exercise. We called it a dog-and-pony show, and I'm sure the naysayers used the same phrase. Me, I was fine with it. I was happy that the story was getting out there, and I thought the exposure was good for us. The more secretive guys got very uncomfortable with this, though, because we were all over the news.

I think that our official recognition from the Pentagon may have been influenced by that pressure to maintain a low profile. President Obama had said we could get any military award that the U.S. government bestows for having killed the man who ordered 9/11 and caused the death of so many Americans. Instead of the Medal of Honor, or even the Navy Cross, my ground force commander suggested silver stars for all of us. That was nice, I suppose, though I already had one. I can't help wondering if he might have put in for silver stars simply because the prestige of Medals of Honor for everyone would have attracted too much attention. There's nothing wrong with silver stars, but personally I think I would have gone a little higher. Call me crazy.

When we eventually went to Central Command to receive our Silver Stars, everyone at the damn organization wanted to sit in the room to watch. They tried to keep us nameless and faceless. Instead of calling us by name when we went to claim the stars, they called us "operator one," "operator two," "operator three." I loved that because I was "operator six," ████████████████ which had a nice ring to it. I was also happy with it because for a moment more, it maintained our anonymity in front of the appreciative crowd.

Within a week of the raid, they flew us to Fort Campbell in Kentucky, because President Obama wanted to personally thank us. He also wanted to give us the Presidential Unit Citation, which is awarded to entire military units whose members have collectively shown heroism in combat. I had two of those already. It's not the Medal of Honor, but it's a prestigious award that requires the same level of heroism as the Navy Cross, Distinguished Service Cross, and the Air Force Cross. I was particularly happy with this because it was a unit award, an award for what we did as a team. That was all I ever wanted.

When we flew into Fort Campbell, it was a blazing hot Friday afternoon. We quietly disembarked at the rear of a building near the airfield. On the other side, a huge crowd was waiting for President Obama, who was scheduled to speak to the 101st Airborne in a hangar after meeting with us. Since our identities were still secret, we entered the building out of sight of the crowd.

We were shown into a nondescript classroom with a small stage in the middle. Our chairs were on the right side of the room, but it wasn't just my squadron there. On the left side were members of the Night Stalkers, which is the badass name for the 160th Special Operations Aviation Regiment, the Fort Campbell–based helo crews who flew us into Abbottabad the night of the raid.

Most of the twenty-eight of us waited in our chairs while the president received a briefing in another room with a scale model of the compound so he could visualize the raid. I was in the front row, for no good reason. While sitting there, an Army officer walked up right in front of me, stopped, and saluted. There was no question that he had singled me out. My heart sank. *I do not need that right now,* I thought. His salute shone a spotlight on me at the same time that I was under scrutiny from those within my own squadron; it really pissed me off that he violated my anonymity while I was accused of bragging and bringing attention to myself. My identity as the shooter was not public, so it was a mystery to me how this guy found out.

After the officer saluted, the room got awkwardly quiet, and a pit filled my stomach and stayed there until the moment the president walked into the room with Vice President Joe Biden. "Hey everybody," President Obama said in his booming baritone. Members of his cabinet came in as well and stood behind him, lined up against the wall. I'm not sure if the secretary of agriculture was there, but I know for sure that Hillary Clinton wasn't.

It's not a typical day when the president casually strolls out to say hello. This was fucking cool. When people today ask me if I'm a Democrat or Republican, I tell them I'm an American. That was exactly how I felt that day. Obama had made the hard decision to send us in, and he deserves credit for that. However I felt about Obama's politics, the man was cool, calm, and honorable. And any president, no matter who he is, should be honored as such. And for the record: whatever criticisms people have about Biden, about his gaffes and his generosity with hugs—it's untrue. Biden's just a good guy. He's fun. He's like the smiling grandfather whom you're always happy to see at holiday time.

The president praised us for the successful mission and thanked us, and then he presented us with the Presidential Unit Citation. It was a certificate, and he gave it to us collectively, as a group. We gave the president a gift, too. One of our guys had carried an American flag into bin Laden's house on the raid, planning to give it to Obama if the mission was successful. We had it framed, and just before the ceremony, we all signed it with our call signs. After the president's comments to us, we presented it to him.

Now, Donald Trump was not the first president who likes to talk a lot. Most presidents like to give long speeches, and they like to hear themselves talk. I'd put Obama in that category as well. But I think Obama lost all ability to speak when we presented him with the flag. For once, he was momentarily speechless. Then he looked at Joe Biden.

"So, Mr. Vice President, you think I can find a nice place to hang this?" he asked Biden.

"Mr. President, I think it'll look great in your Presidential Library one day," Biden said.

I'll never forget what Obama said next. "Fuck that, this is going over my bed." Now, I can't say with completely certainty that that's precisely what he said, but I'm 95 percent sure those were his exact words. Okay, maybe 80 percent sure.

One of the operators had brought a second flag on the mission to give to George W. Bush, and we had signed that one, too. When the operator asked Obama to pose with that flag, the president said, "Oh, is that one for me, too?" Not knowing how to diplomatically say no, the operator gave the president that flag as well. So Obama ended up with two flags, and W got none. Very awkward.

Afterward, I lined up to get my picture taken with the president and the vice president. While they had been briefed, I don't think they knew who had shot bin Laden; if they did, they didn't let on when I talked with them. We chatted a little bit. I wish I could remember what we talked about, but I do remember briefly discussing fishing. Biden must have asked me where I was from, and when I said, "Montana," he told me he wanted to go fishing up there.

"Well, my dad will take you," I told him. Because the first thing my dad offers people is to go fishing. And I can guarantee you this: if Joe Biden went up to Butte and knocked on my dad's door, he'd invite him in, give him a beer, then a rod and reel, and they'd head out to the river to fly-fish. My dad would never vote for Biden, but he'd sure as hell take him to catch some beautiful brown trout.

At the very end, we gathered around the president and the vice president for a group photo, with the flag in the middle. And the formal ceremony ended, and we dispersed. For about fifteen minutes, operators and Night Stalkers clustered around Obama and Biden, chatting them up and asking questions, and the stiff formality turned into a casual, cocktail-party type of atmosphere, with lively conversation from around the room, laughing, a lot of milling around.

Afterward, Obama left the room and went out to the massive hangar, where 2,200 members of the 101st Airborne were waiting for him. After a long, rambling introduction from Biden and a very short one from the 101st commander, he greeted the units by name, cracked some jokes, and then got down to business.

"This has been an historic week in the life of our nation. Thanks to the incredible skill and courage of countless individuals—

intelligence, military—over many years, the terrorist leader who struck our nation on 9/11 will never threaten America again," he said. He talked about his visit to Ground Zero in New York the day before, and then talked about meeting all of us. "And today, here at Fort Campbell, I had the privilege of meeting the extraordinary Special Ops folks who honored that promise. It was a chance for me to say—on behalf of all Americans and people around the world—'Job well done.'" And the audience broke out into cheers and applause.

And then he went on to repeat the mantra that would follow me for the next three years and beyond, that had the power to turn SEAL against SEAL in the brotherhood: "They're America's 'quiet professionals'—because success demands secrecy," he said. It's an interesting thing to say, when you think about it. *Success demands secrecy*. Certainly that's true in the lead-up to a mission, but what about afterward? What about after all the bullets have been spent and the bodies have been carried away—does it still need to remain a secret? It was a question I'd wrestle with for the next three years.

When I think back on that hot Kentucky afternoon, it was one of the last times I felt as though all of us on the team were still together as a team. That day, we were still the brotherhood that we had hoped to join when we were fainting with exhaustion during BUD/S. We basked in the praise of the president, and outside that drab classroom, with thousands of people cheering, even though they didn't know any of our names, or what role any of us had on the mission, or who had taken the shot that had killed the nation's most wanted man for a decade. There was a sense of unity like I had felt on September 12, 2001, a feeling that no matter what happened, we were united behind a common purpose. A year later, so much of that would change, and the jealousy and anger would rear its ugly head. But then, right then, it was perfect.

I was standing with another operator from the mission, and one of Obama's top staff members—maybe his chief of staff—sidled up to me. "Hey, who got him?" he whispered in my ear. It was the same question that I had gotten from the other squadron operator in the seat next to me after we took off from Abbottabad. I had a different answer this time.

"We all did," I said.

DAKOTA
Leave the Sword in the Library

In August 2011, I was working at an optics company in Austin when a colonel from Marine Corps headquarters called. At that point in my life, the last thing I expected when I picked up my phone was to hear someone from the Marines on the other end, so I figured I was probably in trouble for something. The colonel said he needed to talk to me and asked for my home address so that he could meet with me. *No way*, I said. I flat out wouldn't give it to him. If I was in deep shit, the last thing I wanted was to make it easy for them to find me.

I didn't want the Marines coming to my home, but I agreed to meet the colonel at the Hilton hotel near the airport. I got there early so that I could see who was coming to meet me when they came in the door. Inside the hotel, I walked into a massive atrium with full-sized trees sprouting from the planters and a circular bar in the middle. I chose a café table that had good sight lines and a couple of escape routes in case I needed to get the fuck out of there in a hurry, and I waited.

A few minutes after I got there, a tall, bald Marine officer came in, looked around, and spotted me. He came over to my table and introduced himself as Colonel Otto Rutt. He sat down and opened up a big white binder.

"You know," he said, "we need to start planning because you're going to be getting the Medal of Honor." The secretary of defense had signed off on the award, and it was on its way to President Obama's desk for his approval.

If the colonel had told me he was an alien who had beamed in from the future, I would have been less surprised. Up until that moment, I really didn't have a clue what he wanted to talk to me about. There had been rumors about my name being put up for the Medal of Honor, but I thought it was a bunch of BS. I figured I had a better chance of buying a scratch ticket and winning a million-dollar lottery jackpot. As far as I was concerned, this was a case of mistaken identity. "I think you got the wrong guy," I said.

No, he told me, he didn't. Then he described the medal, about how they were going to have a ceremony where the president was going to hang it around my neck, and this and that. "Your life will never be the same again," he told me, as if that was a good thing.

I'm pretty sure that he didn't like what I said next.

"Yeah, I don't want it," I told him.

"Well, you don't really have an option," he said.

"Then just tell him to mail it to me," I said. "I don't want this medal. I don't deserve it."

"Well, the president of the United States believes you deserve it," he said.

Things started going downhill from there. "If I deserve it so much, if I'm a hero, then why don't you go tell my teammates I'm a hero?"

Let's just say that the conversation ended kind of badly. The second you mention dead soldiers, it ruins the mood. The colonel left the hotel with his white binder and I went back to work and tried to forget all about it.

I wasn't being modest when I said I didn't deserve the medal, and I wasn't lying when I said I didn't want it. Gosh, I *didn't* want that medal. My guilt over what had happened in Ganjgal—that four of my guys had been killed when I had been tasked with providing their security—hung over me like a poison cloud. It crept into every corner in my brain and invaded my sleep. Ganjgal followed me everywhere; it stalked me, and when it found me, it produced crippling anxiety attacks. I won't lie—I drank myself numb to get away from that anxiety. From the first moment that I learned I was receiving the medal, everyone kept saying, *Your life will never be the same again.* Well, no shit. My life had already irrevocably changed; I sure as fuck didn't want it turned on its head all over again. I just wanted what happened to me to go away. I just wanted the Marines to go away.

But the Marines didn't go away. They simply backed off a little and gave me a bit of breathing room following that conversation in the hotel. Finally, after some back-and-forth with the colonel, I agreed to attend the ceremony and accept the award. But on one condition: only if the dead members of Team Monti, the ones killed in Ganjgal, also had graveside ceremonies at the same time. They agreed to that.

Soon after, things started moving ahead. I had switched jobs and I was traveling in Atlanta when I got another call on a Friday. This time the call was from the White House. "You're going to be receiving a call from the president on Monday around eleven fifty A.M. Can you be on a landline an hour prior? We're going to call every fifteen minutes to make sure the line's clear."

"Well, no," I told them. "I gotta work. But he can call me on my cell phone."

They did not like that at all. Landlines were very important to the White House. "We can't do that. We can't do that," they kept telling me. "You have to be on a landline."

"Listen, you don't pay my bills anymore," I said. I finally convinced them that the only way the president could reach me was on my cell phone, and they agreed to do that instead. They told me the president would call at 11:50 A.M. on the coming Monday, right around my lunch break.

By that time, I was in Indiana on a job site pouring concrete. Before the call, I took my lunch break early along with my cousin Troy, and a buddy named Adam. We went off to eat at this gas station in the middle of nowhere, eating crappy food and waiting for my phone to ring. Adam looked at me and said, "Do you think the president knows that he's going to be calling you and you're going to be sitting in some shithole gas station?"

Except that he didn't. 11:50 A.M. rolled around. I had my cell phone out, ready to pick up the moment it rang. Then it was 11:51, and the minutes kept rolling by. No call. Nothing. We finished our lunches, our break was over, and the president still hadn't called. We didn't know what to do. "Do you want to wait?" Troy asked.

"No, let's go back to work," I said. It didn't really matter to me. What mattered to me was getting back to work so I could pay my damn bills, instead of waiting around for a phone call about an award I didn't want. As we were driving back to the job site, my cell phone rang. It was the president's aide calling to tell me that the president had gotten tied up. She asked if he could call back in a little while.

"Look, I'm going back to work," I said. "I don't know if I'll hear the phone because I'm busy, too." Thinking back on it, it's pretty ballsy that I compared my work schedule to the leader of the free world. I arrived at the job site and got back to work. I was greasing a Bobcat, probably lubricating the loader or something, when my phone rang. Now, trying to answer your cell phone in the middle of any kind of physical work is hard. Imagine trying to do so when you're up to your elbows in engine grease. When I finally got my greasy hands on the phone and answered, I heard that deep voice on the other end.

"Dakota Meyer?" President Obama said.

"Yes," I said.

"This is Barack Obama," the president said.

"Hey, what's going on?" I said.

We talked for a little while. It wasn't a long conversation. He told me how proud he was and that he was looking forward to meeting me and my family. And then I went back to work. I didn't think anything was going to change in my life.

Right.

Later that day, my phone started going nuts with calls from reporters trying to reach me. I just ignored them and erased the voice
messages. I was practically in hiding. I didn't tell anyone where I was
because I didn't want reporters around. The Marine Corps kept calling, too, asking if I wanted a PR team there to help with the media.
And I told them point blank, I'm not talking to any media. Just leave
me alone.

Of course, the media eventually caught up with me. I had returned to Kentucky for a job installing a new lawn at a house, and I
was running the Harley rake to get the rocks out of the soil. A Harley
rake is a big machine that looks like a cross between a tractor and a
riding lawn mower. It chews up the topsoil and pushes all the rocks
to the side so that you have nice, even soil for a new lawn. They're
loud and they're dirty and they kick up a lot of soil, and you have
to stay pretty focused on what you're doing. At some point I looked
up from the Harley rake I was running. When I did, I realized there
were news people everywhere swarming the job site, and I hadn't
heard a thing because of all the racket from the machine. I don't
know how they found me. One reporter came at me and told me that
my mom wanted to do an interview, so either my mother could do
the interview, or I could. *Oh, shit*, I thought.

Sweaty and covered with dirt, I did the very first interview of my
life on the front porch of a complete stranger who had no fucking
idea who I was or what was going on. After that interview aired, the
Marine Corps stopped asking me if I wanted PR help. They just sent
a team to straighten up the public relations mess I was making.

I had about five PR people around me all the time. I gave them
hell when they first showed up. They were constantly on me, wanting
to coach me about interviews. I was horrible to them. I would make
them talk to me while I was working. They had to chase me around
job sites to try to get me to listen. It was terrible what I put them
through. I still feel bad for them.

I was about a month out from the ceremony, and it was a complete shit-show. I hit the bottle hard because it was the only way to get through. I had never given a speech or an interview in my entire life, and all of a sudden, that was all I was doing, all day long. It got to the point where I started drinking around 5 A.M., before my days started at 6 A.M. with interviews and speeches that lasted all day until 9 P.M., and then I'd drink until 2 A.M., and get up and do it all over again. I was giving these speeches, and I had no clue what I was doing, and then add on the fact that I was drunk. I am not lying when I say I was drunk the entire time. The PR team was with me 24/7 making sure I didn't do anything stupid. They would even sleep in my hotel room because they were petrified that I was going to sneak out in the middle of the night, and they'd have to hunt me down and bring me back like a crazed inmate from an insane asylum.

About a week before the ceremony, I was in D.C. when the president's speechwriter called me to say he was touching up some details for the day of the ceremony; he asked me if there was anything else I wanted to add before he delivered the memo to the president. Being the smart-ass I was, I told him to tell the president that I was going to be in town all week. "If he wants to grab a beer, he can hit me up," I said.

I'll give the speechwriter this: he had a sense of humor. "You really want me to say that to him?"

"Yeah, why not? What's he gonna say? No?" I joked.

"I promise you, I will ask him," the speechwriter said. I didn't really think about it again.

The day before I was supposed to get the Medal of Honor at the White House, I was giving a speech to Marines at the parade grounds of the 8th and I Marine Barracks in D.C. when my phone rang. As usual, I was drunk because it was the only way I could get through any of this craziness.

Since I was onstage, one of my PR handlers answered my phone for me. She listened for a moment, and probably turned white as a sheet, because she walked up to the podium, interrupted me in the middle of my speech, and pulled me off the stage. "Hey, you need to take this call," she told me, and handed me the phone. It was the White House, and the aide on the other end said, "Hey, the president wants to have a beer with you tonight at five P.M. What type of beer do you like?"

"Well, I'm classy," I said. "I like Bud Light."

He sniffed at that. "We're not drinking Bud Light," he said, "but I'll find you something else."

When I got off the phone, the PR handler started freaking out. "Who was that?" I told her and then she really freaked out.

"How are we going to get you in there? You're wasted." And it was only about two hours before I had to be there.

Fuck it, I thought. *I'm gonna get blasted with the president tonight. We're going to be doing keg stands.*

I'd been sweating like a pig in the heat, so she sprayed me with cologne to freshen me up. She poured water down my throat and tried to make me eat something. "I just hope to God that they don't do a Breathalyzer before you get in there," she said.

When we got to the White House, the staff had me wait right outside the Oval Office. While I stood there, all these people were staring at me. One woman came up to me and said, "Are you nervous?"

"I don't know. Does he have a gun?" I asked. "I've been in worse situations." I thought that was funny as hell, but she didn't seem to think so.

Finally, the president came out, and shook my hand. He had taken his coat off, and he unbuttoned his cuff links and rolled up his sleeves. Then we walked out of the Oval Office and onto the stone terrace alongside the Rose Garden.

He led me over to a plain, black metal patio table with a couple of chairs, set into a corner of the terrace, with a tall hedge between me and the Rose Garden, and some red flowers in a planter behind me. A waiter came and poured us pints of beer. Apparently there's no Bud

Light in Washington, because they served White House Honey Ale, which turned out to have come from the president's own home-brew kit. Coming from Kentucky, I'd say he definitely got props for making his own hooch. We kicked back, drinking the president's home-brew beer like a couple of buddies. I felt like I was talking to a good friend. We talked about the future, what I should do, my education, things like that. And there it was again: he told me how my life was about to change in both good and bad ways.

After a while, he apologized and said that he had to get ready for his next appointment. He had only drunk about half his brew in his mug. "Is it going to offend you if I don't finish my beer?" he asked me.

"No," I said, not really registering that the president of the United States was asking my permission to leave his beer unfinished. "That's a man's decision."

"Let me tell you why," he said. "I can't finish it because I've got a speech after this."

"Man, I usually try to drink six or seven before my speeches, so I don't know if that's a legitimate excuse." He almost died laughing.

We got up from the table and walked back into the Oval Office, and after he said how much he was looking forward to seeing me again the next day, I exited out into the office of the president's secretary. That same group of people was there, waiting for us and looking anxious. "How did it go?" one of the women asked.

"He's a lightweight," I said. "He's fucking wasted. He's drunk. Good luck with him." She looked completely fucking mortified.

The next day, my whole family was in town for the ceremony, along with about 120 of my closest friends. As we got ready to walk into the Oval Office, my grandma was on my grandpa not to say anything stupid to the president. My grandpa was a conservative Bush supporter, and he had no filter. None at all—whatever he thought came right out of his mouth, like a cartoon. We walked in, and of course—*of course*!—my grandpa grabbed the president by the hand, pulled him in close like the older generation does, and looked the president right in the eye. Remember: my grandpa was the loudest person I've ever met in my entire life.

"Listen, if you knew half as much about this country as people like my grandson do, you wouldn't be making the decisions you're making right now," he said to the president.

My heart almost stopped. He had done exactly what Memaw told him not to do. Obama could have been offended, but he wasn't that kind of guy. He just rolled with it and laughed, and said something like, "You're probably right."

The president signed the citation, we posed for photos, and then we walked to the East Room of the White House, where we held the ceremony I'd been dreading. I stood with my hands behind my back, while the president delivered his speech at the podium. When the president finally put the medal around my neck, sweat was dripping down my forehead. I won't lie—I was drunk then, too. We drank the White House out of beer. I think I had five or six before the ceremony.

Just like the day before, the president was gracious and funny. I couldn't help but crack a smile at his jokes a couple of times, but most of the time I stood there wishing I was anywhere but there. The truth is that it was hard for me to be up there getting that medal. I didn't want it. I didn't think I deserved it. When the president read the citation itself, I felt as though I was living that day all over again. It was a relief when it was all over.

Afterward, there was a big reception. Obviously, it was a big deal being in the White House, and everyone was pocketing everything they could find that had the presidential seal on it—napkins, forks, anything they could get their hands on and that would fit in their pockets. After the ceremony, I walked into a bathroom. And while I was in there, I overheard a couple of Marines bullshitting at the urinals.

They were talking about a sword hanging on the wall in the White House library called the "Washington Presentation Sword." It was a beautiful saber that some French volunteers in the American Revolution had commissioned, and the French donated it to Franklin Roosevelt in 1933. As I listened to the Marines, they were saying, "Hey man, do you think we can get that sword out of here without anyone noticing?" All I could think about was how I had to get the fuck out of that bathroom before somebody thought that I had stolen it.

I'm still amazed when I think about how often I was told that my life was going to change because of that medal. Obama was right. Nothing was the same again afterward. Not by a long shot. And not in the way that the president and other people praising me intended. After the ceremony, reporters began questioning the whole story of what happened at Ganjgal, claiming that parts were embellished or made up. That I had never killed the guy with the rock, and maybe hadn't killed any Taliban at all. That I couldn't have saved as many people as I claimed. Questioning why I received the medal and others who had acted bravely in the battle hadn't. Even before I received the award, I knew I didn't want it. Receiving it made that notion feel even more true.

Now the medal belongs to one of my daughters, Sailor Grace. It was just lying around one day and she grabbed it. "Here, you can have this," I told her. So she wears it around as a necklace. If she can get some enjoyment out of that medal, then she can have it. That's why I gave it to her. About once a week, I take Sailor Grace and her sister, Atlee Bay, to the Chili's near our house in Austin. It's a family ritual. It's Sailor's favorite place to eat. She usually has these little pizzas or chicken strips. She likes the peaches for dessert.

Before we go, she grabs the medal by its blue ribbon from where she keeps it—her diaper bag or her toy chest—and puts it on. It dangles around her neck when we drive over and sit down to eat. If anyone asks her why she's wearing an award, she tells them she won it.

It's her medal now. No disrespect to Obama, but I hate the medal. I hate every aspect of it. I don't want to be known as anything other than a dad. I hope I never have to talk to Sailor or Atlee about why I got the medal. I've already made that decision. I'll never bring it up. Obviously, they're going to find out what it means someday. When they do, maybe I'll tell them that it's for something that their daddy did a long, long time ago. But it won't be a long conversation. And when it's over, I hope she puts it back in her toy box, which is where it belongs.

10

HOMECOMING

ROB
Everyone Has a First Day

Rivulets of sweat dripped down my collar as I paced behind a curtain in a Hollywood, Florida, convention hall in October 2012. On the other side of the curtain, seven hundred airline pilots in the enormous room faced the stage, waiting to hear me deliver the first speech of my life. With a few minutes to go before my talk, I walked back and forth out of sight of the audience, clutching my note cards in one hand, running through my comments, and struggling to stay calm.

As the minutes ticked down, I pulled out my cell phone to call a friend who, unlike me, had done a lot of public speaking. I asked her what the key to a good speech was. "I'm not going to bullshit you," she said. "The key to speaking is three glasses of red wine. *Not* two and *not* fucking four—*three*." I checked the time. I still had a few minutes to go. I slipped out the back, took the elevator up to my suite, and cracked a bottle of red wine in the bar. And then I downed exactly three glasses as she instructed and hurried back downstairs. When I got back to the hall, I texted my friend. *Done.*

A few minutes later, I heard my name and introduction, and I walked out to the podium to thunderous applause from the audience.

Behind me, a huge screen displayed my name with the title of the speech, "Never Quit." My cheeks emitted a warm glow from the wine, which took the edge off my nerves, but once the applause died down I became conscious of the crowd, of the bright stage lights beating down on me and the microphone clipped to my shirt, and I briefly wondered, as the room tilted, *Am I going to faint?*

Everything in my life had changed. I'd been out of the Navy for two months without a pension or a real plan. After the high of the bin Laden raid, jealousy and anger within the team had forced me to leave behind the only adult job I ever had. My wife and I had separated, I was living outside Washington, far away from our two daughters, and I had no idea how I was going to support them, pay their rents, or buy them clothes.

Now I was stepping out onto the stage to talk about being a Navy SEAL, something that would have been unthinkable a few years earlier, and which some of my former teammates saw as an unforgivable betrayal of the SEAL ethos of being the "quiet professional."

As I began to talk, the hall fell silent. I squinted through the bright lights and peered into the sea of faces. Then I heard it among the whistles and cheers, from somewhere deep within the middle of the crowd. "Hey squid!"—the Marine term for Navy sailors. I was being heckled by a friendly audience. In that moment, I knew everything was going to be fine.

———

WHETHER YOU'RE CEO of a Fortune 500 company, or you're a terrified fourteen-year-old stepping into a high school homeroom for the first time, or you're the SEAL ███████ operator who shoots bin Laden, we've all faced the anxieties of being new. There's no one in the world who hasn't closed one chapter of their life to begin another.

The day I stepped out onto that stage in Hollywood was a first day in my new life as a public persona. I didn't choose how it was going to happen; it chose me. Almost as soon as we returned from

Abbottabad, resentment over the raid began to build, starting the day after we got back to Virginia Beach. As word spread about who had killed bin Laden, the brotherhood that I expected to last a lifetime began to fray immediately, corroded by jealousy and resentment. It wasn't just within my squadron, either, but between my squadron and others that felt they'd been cheated out of the assignment. The environment had become toxic.

I wanted to leave at the end of my obligated term of service in January 2012, but I couldn't because disaster struck. About three months after the bin Laden raid, a Taliban RPG shot down a Chinook with the call sign Extortion 17 in Afghanistan. Thirty-eight people died, including fifteen members of another squadron. It was the single largest loss of American life in the entire decade of the Afghan war. The deaths included a close friend of mine, Rob Reeves. The last time I had seen him, I had visited his house and turned down a glass of red wine he had offered me. It was one of my biggest regrets that I never shared that glass with him.

Morale collapsed as we went from planning missions to planning funerals.

Because of the huge loss of combat experience when Extortion 17 went down, I extended my service for one more deployment, to augment the overseas forces. I couldn't leave in the middle of such a massive loss, though my squadron was no longer hospitable to me as a result of the jealousy and backbiting over the bin Laden raid. The master chiefs knew that my squadron had become toxic for me, so another squadron's master chief asked me to become one of his team leaders for an upcoming deployment to Afghanistan. I remember the meeting in the ███████████ team room when they asked me if I wanted to jump to ████. "One hundred percent," I told them. It was a complete breath of fresh air. A clean slate.

But even with the team switch for me, I found it just wasn't the same anymore. While I was overseas in Afghanistan with another squadron, our missions no longer had the urgency they once had. We were supposed to be going after high-value targets, like rooting out a Taliban-allied shadow governor of an Afghan province, or al Qaeda–linked militants. We usually found out that was bullshit. While I don't doubt that our intelligence showed some links to militants, in reality we were sometimes killing low-level Taliban sympathizers and wannabe mujahideen who basically were just local street thugs. If we had gone to their houses in the middle of the day to sit down and have a conversation, no bullets would have been fired. But by smashing in through people's doors in the middle of the night, we guaranteed that there would be a firefight, and the body count would rise, and the generals could claim more militants were dead. Each time the intel analysts suggested a target, we would vote on whether to pursue it. I sometimes voted against those operations. I was usually outvoted.

This made me not care anymore. I was starting to get complacent and bored, and boredom plus complacence can be deadly. Remember that.

I later found out that during that last deployment to Afghanistan, my former teammates ████████████ were holding meetings to talk trash about me, claiming that I was going to cash out. I also found out that wives of SEALs in Virginia Beach were gossiping about how I had a book deal supposedly worth $17 million. I don't think they knew how book deals work. Even for a former president, that would be pretty lucrative. In a way, they were right—a SEAL was secretly working on a lucrative book. But when the book about the mission eventually dropped, surprise! It wasn't mine.

There were also rumors, conflicting stories about who had killed bin Laden, and suggestions that I was claiming credit when someone else had fired the bullet that killed him. I decided a long time ago that I'm not going to talk shit about my fellow SEALs. I have no doubt who killed bin Laden: I'm the one who killed him. ████████
███
██████████

After I got back from that last deployment, I had accrued so much leave time while overseas that I was able to use it at the end of my service, for what's called "terminal leave." It gave me time to spend with my family, to go out with my wife even though we were separated, and to sort out my impending departure from the Navy. It also allowed me to stay out of the way of my former teammates.

Maybe more importantly, it gave me time to figure out what to do when August 2012 finally rolled around and my career as a SEAL would come to an end. The cold reality was that the Navy wasn't going to look after me. I already knew that I wouldn't get a pension because I hadn't stayed for twenty years, but I discovered that even my kids' health insurance was going to disappear the day my service ended. I was more than a little bitter at how little the Navy offered on my way out of the door. *Here's a plaque. Thanks for your service. Now get the fuck out.*

My whole world was changing, but not in the way that I had imagined. Right before I left the Navy for good, I began actively avoiding my teammates. I would run into them at the Kroger in Virginia Beach or at the Ready Room, a bar that's popular with SEALs (and popularized in the 1990 Charlie Sheen movie *Navy SEALs*), and I'd get nasty looks and comments.

One night at the Ready Room, there was another SEAL there who I had been drinking with cordially just a week before. Since last seeing me, he had watched a clip of me on YouTube. Now he was so angry he looked ready to fight me.

"What are you so mad about?" I asked him.

"You didn't kill him!" he yelled at me.

"You weren't there!" I told him.

He snapped out of it. "Oh, that's a good point," he said.

Fucker. Those were the kinds of guys that started this shit. That was the negativity that I tried to stay away from.

As we prepared to leave Virginia Beach, the place that I had called home for more than a decade, I sent my daughters to another city with their mother, the first of several relocations for them. Because of our separation, they were better off with her, but it was also a security issue. I knew that eventually the whole bin Laden story was going to come out big-time, and when it did, everyone around me would be at risk. But it hadn't yet. It would be another two years. In the meantime, they would be safer without me around.

And then I left Virginia Beach myself. I packed everything that fit into my car and drove north to Washington. I'd done that drive many times, but this time was different. As I crossed over from Virginia to D.C., I remember thinking, *Well, this chapter of my life is over.*

I was experiencing what a lot of vets go through—leaving the armed services without knowing the next step. Without the structure or safety net of the military. Without anyone telling me what to do anymore. I didn't have a lot of experience with the private sector. What would I do? Sell sunglasses for a living? Insurance? I had no idea what normal people did in life.

I thought that it would be easy to figure out the next steps, that something would magically present itself. I was lucky to stumble on a gig with a lobbying firm called Potomac Partners, which gave me a lifeline by putting me on a retainer to build connections with members of Congress, both Democrats and Republicans.

In another stroke of dumb luck, I got an introduction to the CEO of Leading Authorities, a D.C. speakers' bureau. When I went to their offices to talk with them, I told them stories about my missions. Eventually the conversation turned to the bin Laden raid. As I walked them through the details, they began paying closer attention, until one of the company officials interrupted me.

"Wait a minute, I think we're catching something here that no one's really saying out loud. But if you are who I think you are, I don't know how to price you for a speech," he said.

"What do you mean?" I said.

"It'd be like if we hired the guy that killed Hitler," he said.

"But Hitler killed himself," I said.

"Exactly," he responded. And then his eyes lit up as if to say, *But imagine.*

At that time, there was no way for me to talk about the raid or my role, because it was still classified. I told them I wasn't comfortable talking about the bin Laden raid. But I still gave speeches. That first speech in Hollywood, Florida, came in October 2012, about two months after I had left the Navy. I survived the speech and the good-natured heckling from the audience, just like I survived the beehive, and drownproofing, and Hell Week, and the bin Laden raid. Like most people, I've had a shitload of first days. First day in BUD/S. First day with SEAL Team Two. ██████████████████████ Like everyone else, I was scared until that first day was over. Then there was another speech, and another speech, and another. Then the fear went away. I had survived the transition to becoming a civilian.

When I gave those speeches, it was always as one member of the SEALs. I talked about missions that were known to the public, like the rescue of Captain Phillips from Somali pirates in the Indian Ocean or the rescue of Marcus Luttrell. I described the lessons that I drew from missions. Preparation. Following rules. Saying good-bye to my kids. I didn't talk about my fellow SEALs. I didn't talk about anything classified. I certainly didn't talk about Abbottabad or Osama bin Laden. But just talking at all as a former SEAL put a target on my back with respect to my former teammates.

For the two years after that speech in October 2012, I maintained my anonymity as the shooter. I did give one interview about it, to *Esquire,* which published a story in which I was identified simply as "the shooter." I liked the article, but I hated the headline, "The Man Who Killed Osama bin Laden . . . Is Screwed." It made me sound like I was whining, but I wasn't.

All of that changed in fall of 2014. November 3 was another important first day for me—the day that I went from being the anony-mous shooter to being unmasked as the one who pulled the trigger.

The details of my role in the raid still weren't public then. Other than the *Esquire* story, I hadn't discussed it publicly at all. But word had spread ever since we returned from the raid. It was the worst-kept secret in the military.

I had begun to waver about staying anonymous after a New York congresswoman convinced me to donate my SEAL ▇▇▇▇▇▇ uniform to the September 11 museum in New York. She brought me to meet privately with a group of constituents who had lost family members on 9/11. After the meeting, some of them wept. It was the closest thing that they had to closure for their loved one's deaths, and because of the SEAL ethos of the quiet professional, the story of what happened in Abbottabad had never truly been told. The event brought me into the orbit of Fox News reporter Peter Ducey, who brought a camera to film the meeting. Afterward, I started to ask myself, *Why can't I tell this story? Why shouldn't the American public know more about what happened to the man who declared war on the country?*

I went back and forth, never sure what the right thing to do was. I even talked to a half dozen or so former SEAL teammates for their opinions. Some urged me not to; others encouraged me to. On balance, I decided I did want to go public—but carefully and strategically.

The result was the Fox special *The Man Who Killed Bin Laden*. The network scheduled part one to air on Veterans Day, with part two to follow the day after. In the weeks before the show, we made preparations to get my family to safety, far out of the public eye. Just like in my speeches about preparation, I got ready for the moment when my identity would become public. Those preparations ranged from PR coaching about how to conduct a hostile interview to making arrangements for my daughters' safety, so they would be far from the spotlight when it finally fell on me, and completely insulated from any fallout or threats. It was an anxious time. Not only was I preparing to become the most famous operator in a clandestine world that claimed to prize secrecy, but I also had to get ready for the target that would be on my back from anyone who wanted to avenge the death of bin Laden.

And then everything fucking blew up. The week before the show was scheduled to air, my phone began exploding with messages and texts while I was in an airport hotel in Raleigh, North Carolina, where I had come to spend time with my seven- and ten-year-old daughters before the world turned upside down. It was morning, around 9 A.M. Bleary with sleep, I glanced down at the screen and my heart sank. A website focused on Special Forces had just outed me as Osama bin Laden's killer. It wasn't just my name; the site also published a link to my photograph. The article was essentially a preemptive broadside against me for going public. Using the very best journalistic practices, the author—who ironically used an anonymous pseudonym, "Frumentarius," which was a name for spies in the Roman Empire—didn't bother to try to contact me. Better to just dangle my name out there and see which terrorist tried to smoke me first.

That was the start of the worst week of my life. It wasn't me I was worried about; it was my two daughters sleeping in the other bed, who were getting on a plane that morning to meet their mother in one part of the country. I was getting on a flight back to Virginia Beach, which was sure to be a barrel of monkeys after this shit. If my face wasn't already all over the Internet, it would be soon. And that meant my daughters might be sucked into a vortex of unwelcome publicity along with me.

After we got to the airport, I pulled my Redskins cap low over my sunglasses. As we hustled through the terminal, I glanced around carefully, looking for my face on the TVs blaring news in the waiting areas and watching for anyone who might be taking a picture of me along with my girls. My daughters wore sunglasses, too, along with bandannas around their necks that they could quickly pull up over their faces if someone rushed up to us with a cell phone or a camera to take a picture.

The girls knew the drill. We had trained for this. If they were with me when something happened, if I was attacked or drew some kind of unwanted attention, they would quickly pull the bandannas up over their faces and just drift away, as if they didn't know me. They knew that I had done dangerous things for a living, and that I could become a target. Keeping my face down, I reminded them in low voices of the drills we had practiced, how we had trained for this moment. They were never scared.

When I got them onto the plane, I was able to breathe a sigh of relief as I headed to my own gate. They were gone, and soon they'd be relocated for good with their mother, with new last names and no connection to me. After I left them at their flight, I boarded my own plane for Virginia Beach. Originally, I had planned to just slip in to deliver my planned speech and then slide out again. Now it was impossible. After the news broke, a couple of SEAL ▓▓▓▓▓ guys attended the event, and I talked to one of them without realizing that he was there to keep on eye on me.

Then it was on to Tennessee, to deliver a speech for the Chamber of Commerce in Maryville. By now my name was everywhere, and national press was there to see if I had anything to say. I didn't. "I've had my phone and computer off. Anything interesting on the Internet?" I asked the audience. They thought I was joking, but I wasn't.

The day after that, I flew to D.C. That's when the shit really hit the fan. All the negative news began pouring out, and every ugly, shitty allegation about me came out. How I had lied about shooting bin Laden. About how I had been thrown off the team, about how I was destroying the credo of being the quiet professional. But until the special aired, I had to keep radio silence and say nothing. No responses, no comments, no tweets. Over the weekend, I holed up in a Northern Virginia hotel room with bottles of whiskey and read every word, fuming but powerless to do anything. I had a lifeline: over the weekend, I called to bitch to the same friend who had given me advice on getting through my first speech. She had suggested three glasses of red wine before: I think I had a little bit more Jack Daniel's than that over the weekend.

After the Fox interview finally aired on November 11 and 12, things immediately got better. Colleagues who had been talking about me behind my back watched the show and softened, contacting me to tell me that they were impressed. When I was able to speak publicly, a lot of the negativity receded.

Not all of it, though. My detractors are still out there, along with others who haven't come to terms with how the secrecy of the SEALs has fallen away. And make no mistake: that secrecy *has* fallen away. After Captain Phillips and Marcus Luttrell and the bin Laden raid, lots of SEALs have stepped up and gone public with books and movies and podcasts. Here's what Navy Special Warfare Command doesn't want to admit: the SEALs have needed more publicity for a long time, to gain more recruits and bolster their ranks, but the so-called "quiet professional" credo didn't permit SEALs to capitalize on their expertise and experience after they left the Teams. So the SEALs wanted publicity, but not the type that benefited the SEALs themselves. Because I was one of the most high profile, I took a lot of shit for it. I still do. But that doesn't bother me, because I know who my brothers are, and I know that everyone sometimes needs a helping hand when their world turns upside down.

In 2018, I flew to Miami for a speech. The country singer Tim Montana, who's a friend of mine and a fellow Butte native, had a show at a honky-tonk bar. He invited me to come down for the show. It's a big warehouse-sized bar and music venue. After I got there, Tim hauled me up onstage and introduced me to the audience as the man who killed bin Laden.

The audience roared their approval. And then I heard a voice in the crowd screaming, "You! You! You!" I looked out over the audience and picked out a familiar face, a guy named Phil. He had been my BUD/S instructor in 1996, he had been on SEAL Team Two with

me, ████████████████ and he'd been my squad chief ████████
████████. I'd known him for my entire career. He was a SEAL that
we called a "one percenter"—a minority of super-achievers within the
SEALs who seemed to be able to do anything. He was about to leave
the Navy, just like I was in 2012, and he was shitfaced.

He was so drunk that he was screaming that he didn't like me
anymore, that he hated me. I pushed my way through the audience
to him and asked him what was wrong. He was so wound up that
he barely made any sense. All he could say was, "I love you, but I hate
you. But I love you, but I hate you. I hate you."

I tried to calm him down by asking some questions. "Are you
still in?"

"I retire after thirty years next week," he said.

"What are you going to do?" I asked him. He told me he had
no idea. Just like me, six years earlier. "You need a job, give me a
call," I went on, "because the Navy's like everything else in life: it's
so important when you're there, but once it's over, it's fucking over."
After that night, I never found out how things ended up with Phil,
or what he's doing now. I hope he landed on his feet, and that he
had his own first day after he left the Teams behind. But I'll tell you
this—if he hasn't found his sea legs yet, and he needs a helping hand,
he's welcome to give me a call, no matter where he is. Whether or not
he hates my guts.

DAKOTA

If Someone Holds Out a Hand, Take It

When I returned from Ganjgal with the bodies of my teammates,
all I wanted was to get back to what I was good at. After the battle,
there was no real reckoning for me. COP Monti received constant
intel that Taliban were about to attack the post, and so I went back
to running patrols and getting in gunfights every other day. I didn't
think much about why I never slept anymore. The way I saw it, I felt

awful about having survived. Other soldiers and Marines got PTSD. Not me. I got an adrenaline shot of guilt.

The problem was that other Marines and officers around me didn't see the grounded, high-functioning warrior that I was supposed to be. They saw a Marine who was obviously in trouble—a Marine who was making bad decisions and taking risks that could end up getting me or my fellow Marines killed. They saw a Marine so tied in knots over what he had seen, a person so emotionally self-inflicting he might've had a death wish.

The person who saw that first wasn't a Marine, or even a man, for that matter. She was an Army psychologist named Captain Katie Kopp. I'm pretty sure I first saw her when I was on my way into the aid station at FOB Joyce, right after I came back from Ganjgal. The freezers were there behind the building and I went in to check on the availability of space for the bodies of my teammates.

Captain Kopp was a combat stress specialist who had flown to FOB Joyce after she heard word that something terrible had happened up in Ganjgal. Her base was at Forward Operating Base Fenty in Jalalabad, and she was the brigade psychologist for about a dozen camps and posts, including Joyce and Monti. She was tight with the brigade physicians, who would tip her off that some shit had gone down somewhere and that she might be needed.

She arrived at FOB Joyce right away after she heard about what happened in the valley. She always went to the memorials of the soldiers and Marines killed in her region. She was friends with the battalion surgeon at Joyce, so the aid station was her first stop to find out about combat survivors who might need help. It wasn't really her approach to talk to warfighters immediately after combat; she preferred to hang back and wait a day or so.

I remember seeing her at the aid station as I was on my way in to check on the freezers. She's hard to forget. She was a freckled redhead with glasses and a big, wide smile, and was the only woman who ever visited COP Monti, and one of only a few at FOB Joyce.

She asked me if I wanted to talk to her, and I told her no and kept going. Gosh, how I didn't want to talk to her. Because I knew that if I did, the trajectory of my whole life might be changed.

———•———

THERE WAS A PART OF ME that stayed behind in the Ganjgal Valley. That fight changed me. The death that I had seen, most people will never see in a lifetime. I had picked up my lifeless brothers from the ground, and driven out of that valley with their bodies, the only one on my team left alive. I was supposed to be there with them, and as far as I was concerned, I should have died fighting next to them. The weight of guilt for having survived crushed me. I lay awake, night after night, as the events of that day endlessly rolled through my skull. I was struggling hard, harder than I ever had before.

In the aftermath of the battle, the shit-show really began, with multiple investigations into what went wrong in Ganjgal. I never talked to the investigators; I was never asked. But one person I did talk with was Katie Kopp. Technically, I wasn't required to talk to her; it was voluntary. But there's a phrase in the military when something is expected and optional at the same time: you're "voluntold" to do it. Well, I was voluntold to see Captain Kopp. I didn't make it easy for her, though. During the mission debrief in the chow hall in COP Monti, Captain Kopp put all our chairs in a big circle to talk about what happened. She wanted me to talk, to spill my guts about my feelings, but I didn't. I barely said a word.

Of course, I didn't just think that I was all right—I *knew* I was all right. I just wanted to get back to what I was good at. Captain Kopp didn't see it that way, though. She saw all the red flags waving, all pointing toward me and a need to be reconciled. When she kept coming around Monti, it was hard to dodge her. I would spot her in the chow hall, and she would ask around about my behavior. She was no bullshit: if she wanted something, she got it. And if she didn't know how to get it, she found out.

What I wanted more than anything else was to stay right where I was. What I didn't realize was that she wanted that, too. She was doing everything she could to try to find a way to keep me in Afghanistan as I wanted, and also help me cope with what had happened in Ganjgal. The problem was that doing both of those things together was impossible—there was no way that I would be able to make it to the end of my deployment in those circumstances. I just wouldn't admit it.

I was doing my best to make it through, but it was obvious to everyone around me that I was falling apart. The company commander at Monti would tell Captain Kopp, *Check on Meyer, he's not doing well.* I was seeing her about once a week for therapy, as well as a psychiatrist, but we weren't getting anywhere. I'd argue with her about how much I was to blame for my teammates' death. She'd ask me how much of the responsibility for their deaths was mine, and I'd say "one hundred percent."

"But you didn't shoot them yourself," she said.

As far as I was concerned, I had.

Around December, she and my superior officers made the decision to send me home for treatment. I was dangerous—I was doing reckless and careless things out on missions, and it was obvious that I was trying to punish myself, maybe even get myself killed. Suicide by Taliban. So she arranged for me to get treatment at an inpatient VA program in Kentucky immediately after I got back to the States. An arrangement like that is unheard-of—no one goes out of theater straight into residential treatment. She was pulling strings for me left and right.

The only problem was me—I didn't want to go, and she didn't want to force me. Dragging someone kicking and screaming out of theater is no way to convince a Marine to get better. One day we were in the rec room at Monti, which has a Ping-Pong table, a TV, a bookshelf, and some chairs. I made a deal with her: we'd decide with a Ping-Pong match. If I won, I stayed. If she won, I went home for treatment.

A couple of other guys watched as we started playing. I thought I was pretty fucking smart to give myself an escape route. I also thought I was pretty good at Ping-Pong. It turned out I was really shitty, and she was *really* fucking good. She beat my ass hands down. I was going home, and boy was I pissed about it. The lesson? You're never as good as you think you are.

An escort brought me back to Germany, and from there I flew back to the States, where I arrived in the snowstorm that brought Atlanta to a standstill. Within a few days of returning to Columbia, I drove north to Fort Thomas, which sits right across the Ohio River from Cincinnati, to check into the Department of Veterans Affairs' inpatient PTSD clinic for an eight-week program. The clinic was in the hospital, in a big brick three-story building. I was allowed to leave on the weekends, but once I went in, I had basically committed myself. I bunked with a Vietnam-era vet named Bob, a stand-up guy who called me "sarge." He said I could always call him if I needed help.

Bob and I shared a plain room with white walls, two beds, and lockers to keep our wallets safe. The programming went all day and consisted of a lot of bullshit about mindfulness and well-being. We'd sit in a big circle, and the doctor would go around and ask how each of us was doing.

How are you doing today, Dakota?

Good.

Good's not a feeling, Dakota.

Real good.

There was an art therapist who asked us to draw pictures of our feelings. She asked me to do that one time, and I drew a huge black circle on one side, and a box with a checkmark in it on the other side. *What did you draw, Dakota?*

I pointed at the black circle. *This place is a black hole,* I said. I turned the piece of paper over. *I'm here because I'm checking a box.*

I didn't want to be there. I felt like I didn't *need* to be there. And it didn't do anything to help my sense of guilt, because guys were still getting killed in Afghanistan. The only way to get back to them was through the clinic. If I made it through, I could get back into theater. So I gritted my teeth, sat in circles, and exhaled into a Breathalyzer every other day.

I made it through, and I graduated. But my grand plan to go back to Afghanistan never happened. The closest I got was to fly to Okinawa to reconnect with what was left of my Marine detachment that had gone to Afghanistan as an embedded training team. While there, I looked through the belongings of my four dead teammates, which had been stored in lockers in Okinawa, to send items home to their families. Word had gotten around about what had happened in Ganjgal, and guys would come up to me to tell how sorry they were.

After I got back, I never did re-up for a new contract. I'm sure the Marines wouldn't have let me. I was drinking constantly. And I was fighting. I was an endless keg of fury that never drained. One night, my cousin Troy and I went down to Sixth Street in Louisville to go to bars. I got wasted, and I swear I got in three different fights in five minutes. I don't know what set me off. Maybe I thought someone looked at me funny. I was just so angry that it didn't fucking matter what anyone did. Nobody could have stopped me, least of all myself.

One guy was just walking down the street and we exchanged words. I chased him, and his cap flew off onto the ground. I picked it up and said, "Here, try to get it back." I put it on and kept yelling at him, "Come and get it." He told me to keep it. That night at the Hilton hotel, I smashed every exit sign I could find with my fist. When I woke up, I was lying in a puddle of blood.

Another time, I tried to fight with my cousin Steven. What happened between us showed how fucked up I was, because I loved Steven. We had been close growing up, but after I returned home, we grew apart. I tried to call him a lot, and he'd never call me back. In my mind, he had turned his back on me when I needed him, but the reality was that he had gotten married and had a new baby and was overwhelmed with being a new parent. I couldn't see that at the time, and instead I just let my resentment toward him fester and grow.

Eventually I did connect with Steven, and we made a plan to go to the track to see some horse races. Of course, I drank. And when it came up that we hadn't been in contact for some time, I called him out, and then I blew up at him. Thinking back on it, I think I was planning for that to happen. I was so full of rage and grief that I aimed that sentiment at whoever was around me and unloaded on them. That day, it was Steven.

I'll never forget the look in Steven's eyes. He was looking at me in fear, saying, *I don't want to fight you.* It probably took five guys as big as me to hold me back, and as a result I had bruises all up and down my neck and shoulders and arms from where they were holding on to me. That was the first time I realized how scary I was.

Eventually I tried to kill myself. In Afghanistan, Captain Kopp believed that I was suicidal, but back then, I turned that self-destructive force outward and tried to put myself in situations where I might get killed. This wasn't an option at home in Kentucky, and my story almost ended the same way it did for twenty-one veterans a day back then: with a gun to the head. Early one morning, I pulled my truck into the parking lot of my friend's shop, so that he would find my body when he came to open up first thing in the morning. I sat there for about five or ten minutes before I sent a text message saying good-bye. Then I took my Glock out, put the barrel to my head, and pulled the trigger. And nothing happened, because someone in my life had the sense to see this coming and had unloaded my gun. What do you do after that happens? I drove home. Once I put the car in gear, there was no going in reverse. That doesn't mean that everything got better.

If anything, getting the Medal of Honor made it worse. I was so racked with guilt that at first I told the Department of Defense officials that I didn't want the medal or a ceremony. They could just mail it to me. The whole story's funny in a lot of ways: that I was greasing a Bobcat when the president called. That I had a beer with him at the White House. But the fact is I also drank the whole week before the ceremony. I was drunk for my speech to Marines the day before, and I was drunk when I went to the White House for a beer with President Obama, and I was drunk during the medal ceremony.

Everyone told me that my life would never be the same after the Medal of Honor. President Obama told me that. They were all right. But not in the way that they might have expected, or for the reasons that they expected.

The day that truly changed everything was the day that my daughter Sailor Grace was born in Alaska, which just happened to fall on the anniversary of the death of my friend Mary Kate. As I look back on it, I realize that when I say that nothing good came out of Ganjgal, that's not completely true. My daughter was a direct result of what happened to me that day, and here's why.

After I received the medal, Rob and I began giving speeches through the same speakers' bureau, Leading Authorities, which represents a lot of high-profile veterans. In late 2014, I went up to Alaska to do a show with Sarah Palin, and that's where I met her daughter Bristol. I saw her again in 2015 at Shot Show, a big gun show in Las Vegas. Shot Show is just a big drinking fest, and we connected and started dating after that.

Now this is a chapter of my life that a lot of people want details about. How Bristol and I got engaged, then broke up, then got married. All our fights, all our tweets, all our fucking drama that was all over TMZ and *People* magazine and *Us Weekly*. Our season on *Teen Mom OG*, which was a special kind of shit-show. But to me, none of that matters. She's the mother of Sailor and our second daughter, Atlee Bay, and they'll never hear me say a bad thing about her. No matter how terrible things got with Bristol, no matter how much fighting we did, I am forever indebted to her for bringing both of our children into this world. Women are made to be so much tougher than men. They're just the most resilient creatures that God ever created. I will always be grateful to her.

I wasn't at the bedside when Sailor was born. I was thousands of miles away, and I found out about the birth on Twitter. Because of all the turmoil that had happened before the birth, Bristol required me to establish paternity, so I did. When it was clear that I was Sailor's father, I could finally see her. By then, it was around March 2016. Under the agreement I had with Bristol, I had to have someone with me when I was with the baby. So I flew up to Alaska with my aunt Cindy, and we stayed at the Embassy Suites, because it had rooms big enough for the two adults plus a baby. The night before I saw Sailor, Cindy and I went out and bought everything we would possibly need for a newborn—diapers, formula, bottles, toys—everything.

I was petrified, like every new father is. Before I got up there, Sailor was an abstraction. I knew I was a father, but I didn't feel like one yet—she was thousands of miles away. As I got closer to her, I got scared thinking about whether I could be a decent father. I hadn't seen Bristol since she had left me, right before the wedding. When we drove up to the house, I walked in, and I sat down on the couch and Bristol put the baby in my arms, and I just remember thinking, *Holy shit*. I couldn't keep my eyes off this tiny, defenseless baby who was now my responsibility, whose entire existence now depended on me making wise choices, on owning up to the duty to look after a human life.

I was up there for four days. Under the agreement we had, I wasn't allowed to have her overnight, so I would drive an hour from Anchorage to Wasilla, pick up Sailor, drive back to Anchorage to spend the day with Sailor in the hotel, then bring her back at night. Back and forth, back and forth. When the four days were up, I got back on a plane for Kentucky.

Here's the important part. When I finally flew home, I couldn't sleep on the plane. I was so tired, emotionally and physically spent. But it wasn't because of images of Ganjgal in my head. It was because of images of my baby girl. All I could think about was how I needed to get home and shut down all my businesses because they were distractions from my ultimate goal: being with Sailor. If I had to take a job at McDonald's, I would do so. If I had to sell everything I owned and live out of a cardboard box, I would do that, too. That was where I wanted to be. That was where I needed to be.

Sometimes you can draw a line that connects all the milestones in your life, straight as a bullet, that shows how point A leads to point B and C and so on. It's linear, and it's direct. But sometimes that path isn't straight. Sometimes it goes in circles, doubles back, gets caught in knots, before that line ends up where it's supposed to. I'll never forget that the reason Sailor ended up in my arms was that someone showed me that tangled path forward, even if I didn't know it at the time.

In January 2018, I pulled into the parking lot of an H-E-B Grocery in Austin, turned off the engine of my truck, and pulled out my phone. Almost exactly nine years after I left Afghanistan, I was in another dark place in my life. Not the first, and not the last one. I was going through my divorce with Bristol, and everything seemed to be falling apart all over again. I could feel the pressure building inside me, like an overinflated tire.

Even though everything in my life was in turmoil, I chose that moment to call Katie Kopp. I needed to do something to release the burdens on me, or at least one of them, to make something right. She was someone who had done right for me, and all I had given her in return was anger. I had left Afghanistan full of grief and guilt, instead of gratitude to her for seeing something in me that I hadn't. While there were plenty of problems and mistakes I couldn't fix in my life right at that moment, there was one that I could.

Sitting in my Toyota Sequoia, I pulled up her contact information and sent her a text, asking if I could call her. She was stateside now, at Fort Carson, and she texted me back and told me to go ahead and call.

She picked up immediately. She was in her office in Colorado Springs. She sounded surprised to hear from me. We hadn't been in contact since December 2009, but over those ten years she'd followed me in the news, as the details of my private life were dragged through the headlines. She'd read my first book and found out that I had tried to kill myself. I was surprised that she even remembered who I was.

"I just had to thank you," I said. I told her that I think she saved my life by sending me home, even if I didn't agree with her at the time. "I have two beautiful daughters now, and I have no doubt that I wouldn't be here today living and having them if it wasn't for you."

And then she said something that shattered me. "I thought you hated me," she said. It was like a punch in the gut over the phone. Like I said: Captain Kopp was *no bullshit*.

"No, it just took me a long time to mature enough to come to grips with it," I said.

I don't remember what all else we talked about. We probably chewed the fat a little bit about where our lives had gone, and what we were doing. She had become a parent as well since we had last seen each other. Before we hung up, she thanked me, and told me that she was proud of me.

After we ended the call, I went in and did my grocery shopping. Later, I thought about what she said, and how she thought I hated her. I felt terrible that she believed that. Of course I didn't hate her. I hated the idea of failure. I hated that my team was dead and I wasn't. I hated the idea of going home to face that. But I didn't hate her then, and certainly not now. I was still conflicted about being sent home, wondering if I would have been okay if I had stayed in Afghanistan. But even if I wasn't sure about what she did, I could never hate a person who made a hard decision on my behalf, who gave me so much later on in life that I never could have foreseen. Every time I look at my two girls, I think about how lucky I am that Captain Kopp took an interest in me, held out her hand, and then beat my ass at Ping-Pong.

11

RECUPERATION

ROB
Don't Ask the VA for Help

In 2015, I went out to celebrate my friend Joseph's birthday in Dallas, right before I moved there myself. We met at an upscale bowling alley that resembled a nightclub, with music and soft blue lights and an impressive bar with top-shelf whiskey. There were about ten of us bowling, enough for two lanes side by side. I bowled with Joseph, a very funny and very gay friend who's a riot to be around.

I had probably bowled about five or six balls, enough for a couple of frames, when I went back to the rack and reached for a ball. As I hefted one, I heard a pop and felt something give in my arm. It was like the sound of a cucumber snapping in two, and loud enough to have been heard over the racket of falling pins and gutter balls. Joseph heard it. Everybody heard it.

I tried to shake it off and bowl the damn thing anyway, but the ball just slowly rolled into the gutter and down into the pit. A metaphor as good as any. As I went back to the group, Joseph stared at me in shock, his mouth agape. I think he was stifling a laugh.

"You've got to be kidding me," he said.

"I probably need to go to the hospital," I groaned.

He understood. But he also understood why this was so funny: after four hundred missions with the SEALs and no injuries, I had hurt myself in a family bowling alley, hefting a ball that a five-year-old could have picked up. No wounds in Fallujah, in Baghdad, in Baqubah, or Jalalabad. I expected to die in Osama bin Laden's compound in Abbottabad, and instead walked away without a scratch. Go figure.

I left the bowling alley as soon as I could, but I didn't get my arm looked at immediately. I knew enough about VA bureaucracy to know to go to the one where I was registered, and that was in D.C. It took a couple of weeks to get back to the capital because I had a busy travel itinerary for speeches and doing commentary for Fox News. When I finally did get to my doctor in D.C., he ordered an MRI. And that was when things got interesting.

———————•———————

EVERY VET HAS A VA STORY. Vets pay a high price in a lot of ways through their service. They pay a price again when their service ends, they come home, and try to make sense of the bureaucracy of the VA. For anyone who says, "Health Care for All," I would suggest they try getting a checkup at the VA, and then see what they think about a national health care system.

The VA was in the news a lot around this time. The year before, it had gotten in deep shit with Congress when it turned out that the VA wasn't reporting long delays for veterans who needed to see a primary physician. The scandal centered on the VA in Phoenix, where some vets died while they were on waiting lists to see their physicians for checkups.

Before the Great Bowling Fiasco of 2015, I had some experience of my own with the VA. By that, I mean I had experience getting screwed. As soon as I left military service, my care switched from the Navy to the VA system. Here's one of the quainter aspects to the VA: all the notifications about appointments come by snail mail. No calls, no email. When you're moving a lot, that means you don't get your notifications. That means you miss appointments. That means your care is constantly interrupted, if it ever starts at all.

Because the VA used the U.S. Postal Service—another stellar government service—I missed appointments for evaluation for PTSD. Appointments that I never knew I had. As a result, no one's ever determined whether I have PTSD from all my combat deployments. I was lucky never to have gotten a physical injury during combat. But I can't say for certain whether I've paid a mental toll for killing other people night after night, for years on end. I simply don't know, because I've never been to get an evaluation. A lot of guys look for that answer at the bottom of a bottle.

One time I sat on hold in a hotel room, trying to get through to a live person at the VA. After an hour waiting, I suddenly heard the click of someone taking me off hold—and then the line promptly went dead. I shit you not. Since I've got 100 percent combat disability, I could get care if I needed it, but without a diagnosis, care would never occur. It's a chicken-and-egg situation of health care that so many soldiers, and nonsoldiers alike, are privy to. Eventually I just gave up, just like a lot of vets do, but I still would like to know if my government service has driven me fucking crazy. Maybe I would if someone would pick up the phone.

My bowling injury in Dallas demanded immediate attention, though, and I needed that MRI of my arm. Within a couple of days, a big bruise appeared on my arm right above the elbow. Obviously, it was a bad injury. After I returned from Dallas, my dad joined me for a while in D.C., where he'd been helping me manage my post-SEAL life. When I finally saw my doctor, he poked the bruise a couple of times and ordered the MRI. It was probably the result of accumulated years of stress on the ligament. It could have happened at any time. It was just a coincidence that it happened while I was doing my best Big Lebowski imitation.

On the day of the MRI, Dad drove me to the Washington, D.C.,

VA Medical Center, which is off North Capital Street in the middle of the district. In the distance, you can see the basilica of the National Shrine of the Immaculate Conception, which is kind of comforting for an Irish Catholic boy like me. The hospital is also close to a large veterans' cemetery, which is less comforting.

The VA Medical Center in D.C. is not an uplifting place. It's about as cheerful as the inside of a morgue. Sad to say, it felt more like a homeless shelter to me than a hospital, full of hangers-on who congregated in the lobby until they were booted out and let back in the next morning. When I was in line for coffee, a dude came up to me and panhandled me for two dollars.

"I'll buy you something," I offered. "I'll get your coffee or doughnut."

He wanted cash. "No, I want McDonald's," he said. Apparently, beggars *can be* choosers.

When I went up to radiology with my dad, I handed him my cell phone to hold during the MRI, but I kept my wallet with me in my pants pocket. There were two techs in there, and I followed their instructions: clothes off, robe on, no metal, get on the gurney, slide into the MRI tube. Straightforward. I folded up my clothes and put them on a chair, got into the robe, and climbed onto the gurney. As I lay inside the machine, the techs told me over the intercom that they were having some technical problems. I waited awhile. Finally, they told me everything was working.

After they completed the scan and the gurney slowly rolled me back out, I got out of the johnny and got dressed. Back with my dad in the radiology lobby, I felt in my pocket for my wallet, and it wasn't there. I looked around, to no avail, and then asked my dad if he had it. He said he didn't, so I walked back and asked the techs if they had seen my wallet. One said he didn't know what I was talking about. I noticed that the other one wouldn't even look at me.

My dad and I searched that tiny waiting room for an hour, maybe an hour and a half. We searched around the seat where I had been sitting probably a hundred times. No wallet. So I walked back to talk to the techs again. This time I was a little more direct. "Hey guys, I work at Fox News and it'd be a shame for me to talk about you guys and what you did. So hopefully it shows up, huh?" And we left.

"I guarantee you that my phone rings in about ten minutes," I told my dad. And it did. The techs had "found" it right where I had left it, in a spot I had searched over and over again. I'm just glad I had my dad hold my Rolex.

That wasn't the end of it. After the MRI revealed a torn bicep, I needed surgery to repair the tear. I got that in the VA as well. While I was in the recovery room, I passed the time by texting updates and tweeting. I was still groggy from the anesthesia. The doctor came in to check on me and see how I was doing. He pointed to my phone, which was resting on my chest.

"You might go back to sleep because you still got some medicine in you. Don't leave that phone on your chest. Someone will take it," he said. I didn't doubt it.

It turned out that the D.C. Medical Center had other problems beyond employees with light fingers. Two years after I was at the center for my MRI, the VA fired the director of the medical center. Not once, but *twice*. He was fired the first time after the inspector general found less-than-sterile conditions and shortages of medical equipment. Then the federal protection board that hears appeals from fired employees ordered him reinstated. After President Trump signed new accountability rules, the VA fired the director a second time. Six months later, the IG released another damning report that found all kinds of other problems, not the least of which was that instrument and supply shortages put patients' lives at risk.

My experiences just reinforced my belief that if you want good health care, don't look to the government for it. I'd like to say most people in the government really do care about how veterans are treated. And I think the VA doctors and nurses, by and large, are excellent. The problem lies with the administrators and the clock watchers who don't give a shit about veterans, who care more about lunchtime and quitting time. I've told congressmen that if they want to see what the VA is really like, skip the choreographed, prearranged visits and instead go unannounced on a Wednesday at about 10 A.M. Take a walk around then. They can buy the guys in the lobby as many quarter-pounders as they want.

I don't know what the solution is, and I'm glad that I'm not in charge of trying to find one. The VA is dealing with a lot more than they ever have before, because we have so many troops coming back with problems. Many of them have real problems, but let's face it, there are guys trying to game the system and prove they're combat disabled, because everybody wants to get paid for disability. I mean, it's a fucked-up system. The reality is that for a lot of vets, it's the only option. Some vets swear by it and will defend it to their dying breath. I respect that. But it doesn't mean that we can't improve what we've got, or keep looking for something better. Our vets deserve that.

If there's one consistency that I've found, it's that vets don't want to be pitied, and they don't want to be seen as victims, no matter how serious their injuries. I really admire another Navy SEAL who epitomized that attitude. He was a guy named Jason Redmond, and he'd been shot in the face and arms in 2007. When he was at Bethesda Naval Medical Center for recovery, he posted a note on his door for anyone who came to visit, whether it was a friend or a politician looking for a photo op. Here's how the note read: "ATTENTION to all who enter here. If you are coming into this room with sorrow or to feel sorry for my wounds, GO ELSEWHERE."

Something that helps vets get through their recoveries, whether it's at the VA or somewhere else, is a sense of humor. Navy SEALs are some of the funniest guys I've met in my entire life, probably because they have to take so many risks in their work. Sometimes it's kind of gallows humor, because in theater, you never know when you're going to get blown up or take a sniper's bullet. Humor gets us through firefights alive, and it gets us through amputations and surgeries. Humor also allows us to survive the federal bureaucracy. (If you haven't noticed, this screed about the VA is not for you to take pity on me or any of us veterans; it's for you to laugh at the hypocrisy and ridiculousness that is the federal government. Laughing yet? Good.)

After I started on the speaking circuit, I worked with a consulting firm called Potomac Partners that organized events with the Miss USA pageant contestants. One of the events they pulled together was a visit to Walter Reed Army Medical Center in D.C., before it merged with Navy National Medical Center and moved to Bethesda. While there, I met a young Marine who had just returned stateside with serious wounds. He had both his legs blown off, he was in pain, and he had a lot of drugs in his system. I went in to talk to him. While I was looking around the room, I noticed a Marine Corps flag hanging on the wall. Everyone in his unit had signed it, wishing him a speedy recovery. As I looked at the flag, I noticed one inscription. It read, "Wagner loves the cock." That seemed like a pretty strange thing to write as a get-well note, so I asked him if his name was Wagner.

"No, no, that's someone else," he said. "Marines just write that."

He told me the story behind it. "Wagner Loves the Cock" is an inside joke in the Marines. It's our generation's version of "Kilroy Was Here" dating back to World War II. Back then, U.S. soldiers drew a little doodle of a cartoon man peeping over a fence, with a long nose drooping down, along with a phrase that became the calling card of military personnel everywhere: "Kilroy Was Here." You could find it in lavatories, bunks, foxholes—anywhere that there were bored GIs with pens.

"Wagner Loves the Cock" is kind of an X-rated version of Kilroy. Apparently somewhere back in the day, there was a guy named Wagner who hated his chain of command—the COC. So someone scrawled in a bathroom stall, "Wagner Loves the COC." Some smart-ass Marine, of course, edited that to say, "Wagner Loves the COCK." Marines, being mature and upright citizens, began writing this wherever they hit the head—latrines, stalls, and porta-potties across the globe.

Wherever there's a Marine and a shitter, someone's written "Wagner Loves the Cock" inside.

"Yeah, it's kind of funny. General Mattis was in here yesterday and saying hi to me," the soldier went on, referring to General James Mattis. "He asked me the same question. 'Are you Wagner?' I told him, 'No, we write this in the head, sir.'

"So General Mattis told me, 'Well, I've never seen it in my head, son,'" the kid went on. And no shit, the private first class said to the four-star general, "I have a feeling you and I use different shitters, sir."

I don't remember what the kid said after that story, but I'd like to think that he cracked up laughing as hard I do every time I think about what he said. Humor won't bring back legs, but it might make loss a little more bearable.

NOW HERE'S THE PART of this story that's not so funny for me, and that's hard for me to talk about. Humor also masks a lot of pain. SEALs, along with warfighters in every other branch of the military, are irreverent and crack jokes about everything, because we haul around a lot of ugly shit that we've seen and done. Some of us have seen things in our service that only another soldier or SEAL or Marine can understand. Things that give us nightmares. Things that make us hit the bottle. Things that whip us in a rage for no reason.

Thanks to the fucked-up bureaucracy of the VA, I was never evaluated or treated for PTSD, despite four hundred missions where I watched men's heads explode like watermelons, or bodies stitched in two with machine gun fire, or children who saw their parents killed in front of them. By the time I left the Teams, I was numb to killing; it didn't mean anything to me anymore. In 2019, Dakota and I started to notice that something had changed for both of us. That we were acting differently, that the pain that we had been carrying with us for years was taking a toll on our lives.

Those of us who have served aren't unique in that respect. Lots of people, men and women, hide their grief and their pain for all kinds of reasons. Dakota and I—we saw that something was happening in each of us, and it wasn't pretty. When he went to one of my speeches, he saw me break down in the middle, and tried to figure out how to cut the speech short and get me off the stage. I'm the guy who was supposed to be laughing and joking all the time, and suddenly something was pushing up in me that the people around me didn't recognize. Something I didn't even recognize at the time. People told me that I needed to cut down on my drinking, but that wasn't really the problem.

In August 2020, I began to fall to pieces. That was when I got on a Delta Air Lines flight amid the coronavirus pandemic, took a selfie of myself without a mask, and tweeted it. I post a lot of things on Twitter that get people riled up, and this was one of them. The reaction was immediate, and the backlash was fierce. Delta banned me, people across the country condemned me, and for a moment, I became the poster child for COVID deniers.

I'm not writing this because I want sympathy, or because I'm apologizing. I was trying to be funny, and in retrospect there was no good reason for it, and I paid a price. But the reason I'm mentioning this is that the backlash sank me deeper into the dark pit that Dakota had noticed years earlier. I drank more, I fought with my wife more, I got even more angry and belligerent than usual. And after a drunken afternoon on Cape Cod, I raged about swimming with sharks and said stupid shit and ended up sleeping on the couch. And then I flew off to Montana to be by myself.

My wife saw what was happening. While I was in Butte, stewing in rage and frustration, she called to tell me that she had found a doctor who was doing experimental therapy for people with PTSD. The doctor wasn't sure that he wanted to take me on. I was high profile and well known. Maybe a little too well known. But he agreed to see me.

After I got back to the east coast, I did about five or six sessions with him and talked about all the anger in my life and the drinking and the trolling I did on the Internet. And then one afternoon, I lay down on a couch—I can't say where—put on Bose noise-canceling headphones, and took two small pills. They were MDMA, or methylenedioxymethamphetamine. It's also called ecstasy. Clinical trials into using MDMA as a treatment for PTSD have been going on in the United States, Canada, and Israel, but this wasn't one of those sanctioned trials.

For five hours, I listened to classic guitar with my eyes closed. My wife, Jessica, sat by my side holding my hand; I could feel her weight shifting on the sofa next to me. A therapist was there with me the whole time, overseeing the process. I only got up once to use the bathroom, and otherwise spent the entire time replaying in my head all the terrible things I had seen and done in Iraq and Afghanistan. When the drug wore off and I opened my eyes, all I could feel was a sense of deep peace, something I hadn't felt in years.

Like I said at the beginning, everyone's got a VA story. At the end of the day, my VA story isn't about some idiots who took my wallet and rifled through it, or that a guy panhandled me in the lobby of a hospital. My VA story is that I never received what I needed the most, which was attention to my invisible wounds, the ones that were there before my bicep popped in the bowling alley and the ones that were still there after that bicep healed. That I had to go completely outside this crazy system to get some help, and that when I did, it was on a couch listening to Eddie Van Halen through some Bose headphones, using a treatment that's illegal in the United States. As far as I'm concerned, it should be available to anyone who needs it . . . legally.

I know what you're wondering—whether it worked. I have an answer for that. The answer is that it did. After the treatment, I went golfing with my wife. On the second hole, I made a terrible shot, and the ball sliced hard to the right and disappeared into the woods. A month earlier, I would have yelled and cursed and tried to break my club over my knee like a cartoon golfer. That day, I just watched the shot, then looked at my wife, and said, "Well, that was unfortunate." Then I proceeded on, up the fairway, and on to the next hole.

DAKOTA

Don't Fear the Toad

In 2016, I dropped most everything in my life to try to be a father. After the drama of my breakup with Bristol the year before, the birth of Sailor Grace brought us back together. We married in June and I left behind my family in Kentucky to move four thousand miles to be with Sailor in Alaska. I moved in with Bristol just up the street in Wasilla from her mother, Sarah. Though I slimmed down my businesses, I was still running my construction company in Kentucky from Alaska, and I was traveling all the time to speak and make appearances. I was putting up with her crazy family, trying to make a living, and never getting any sleep. My life was a shit-show. Sometimes my days felt like I was back inside the war, trapped behind enemy lines.

One day in October 2016, I was at home alone. Sailor was at day care while Bristol was at work. My desk was in the corner of the playroom on the second floor. I was on my computer, probably answering email, when a panic attack consumed me out of nowhere.

Panic attacks can hit with no warning, like a truck that comes out of your blind spot and T-bones your car when you're not looking. It's hard to describe, but it felt like a crushing weight on my chest, a compression that squeezed out my breath and constricted my throat. My heart raced, my hands trembled, and waves of dizziness and nausea washed over me. Nothing made it better. I tried standing, then sat down again. Up and down, up and down. Finally, I lay down on the floor and shook and couldn't keep from crying.

No matter what I did, I couldn't get it to stop or calm myself down, and there was no one there at the house to help. I tried to focus and breathe, and when it didn't get better, I tried to get downstairs to the telephone. With each step, the attack worsened. By the time

I reached the bottom of the stairs, I was scared to death. I thought maybe I was having a heart attack.

I finally reached for the phone and called the VA in Anchorage. I got a woman on the phone and told her who I was. "I need some help. I'm not asking for anything," I told her. "I just need, maybe, a blood pressure medicine or something to get my anxiety under control."

That's when the conversation went downhill. "Do you have a case manager here in Alaska?" she asked me.

"No, I don't," I told her.

"Well, okay, so here's how it's going to happen," she told me. "You'll get an appointment with a case manager in two or three weeks. And then after that he'll schedule you with a physician. So then a couple weeks after that, you'll get a physician and then you can go to that physician and he can help you with a referral to a psychologist."

I couldn't believe what I was hearing. "If I live like this for five weeks, I'll be fucking dead," I told her.

"Well, the only other option you have is to go check yourself into a psych ward," she said. That was when I hung up.

———————

WHEN I SAID the panic attack had come out of the blue, the opposite was actually true. I had lived with these feelings so long that I thought they were normal. But what was different this time was the intensity. It crippled me there in the house.

This is the experience of a veteran with the highest disability status possible at the VA. I'm considered 100 percent disabled, and I have a Purple Heart and a Medal of Honor. You'd think nobody would get better treatment than me. But no shit, there I was—I was looking at weeks, maybe months, with no help, for a debilitating condition that had, at one point, almost made me take my own life. If that is how they treated me, I could only imagine what it'd be like for soldiers and Marines and sailors who aren't in the headlines and hadn't had a medal hung around their neck by the president.

After I hung up on the lady at the VA in Anchorage, I never did call back. I was done with the VA. While I was still active duty in 2009, I had been in PTSD treatment at the VA in Kentucky thanks to Katie Kopp, the combat trauma psychologist, but honestly, it didn't do much for me. I learned some useful tools to help me cope with PTSD, but it didn't relieve any of my anxiety or trauma.

After the panic attack in Wasilla, the anxiety attack relieved itself the way it usually did—coping with it, waiting it out, probably some drinking, and eventually some anti-anxiety medication. It didn't really register with me at the time, but I had gotten caught up in the same issue that had gotten the VA in trouble in 2014—long wait times. Gosh, I might have been one of those statistics if things hadn't turned out differently for me. After my experience, I wouldn't take my dying dog there. The VA was completely dead to me.

After I realized the VA wouldn't help me get better, I contacted friends and asked them for help. A friend connected me with a nurse in Boston who sent me a device called Alpha-Stim that reduces stress and anxiety by stimulating the brain with mild electrical shocks. It's called cranial electrical stimulation, and so many vets began using it that the VA released a study about it about two years after my panic attack. It was pathetic that I had to ask friends for help when a big governmental behemoth, one that I paid for with my service, was supposed to be there for vets like me.

I wasn't shy about saying so. In November 2017, I got invited to a meeting of VA officials at the Eisenhower Executive Office Building, which is next to the White House.

The meeting consisted of a roomful of VA officials talking about problems within the department. Except they didn't talk about the problems. As the officials went around the table, they started patting themselves on the back for how successful their programs were.

As I listened, I got fired up and interrupted all the self-congratulations to throw some water on the meeting. I told them that none of the VA program, none of its efforts have been successful if twenty veterans are killing themselves every day. If that's the yard-stick for success, then that's just the start of the problem. I chewed them out bad. They all just looked dumbfounded, like no one had ever told them they were doing a shitty job. I didn't expect an invitation back, and, guess what, I never got one.

The electrical stimulation helped, but for me it was only a short-term solution, like putting a Band-Aid on a snakebite. You have to strap the electrodes onto your head almost every day for as long as an hour, so it's not exactly convenient. Two years after the Wasilla panic attack, I knew I needed something more. By then, Bristol and I had moved to Austin. Neither of us wanted to admit it, but the marriage was collapsing. I was sleeping a lot of nights in my truck, parked outside a Best Buy in a shopping center outside Austin. I didn't want to go back to the booze, which had turned me into a monster that scared everyone around me. I had to do something to help me cope with my anxiety and panic attacks.

I knew I had reached rock bottom one day when I drove out of the shopping center and pulled up at a stoplight. It was around rush hour, and there was a line of cars in front of me at the red light. And then behind me, there was a guy in a little car. And he laid on his horn. He got on that horn and wouldn't fucking stop.

Don't do it, Dakota, don't do it, I said to myself over and over. Behind me, I could hear those honks, and it felt like my head was going to explode. *Don't do it, don't do it.*

And then I looked in the rearview and I saw his car door open. He put one leg out and popped his head up above the roof to figure out why the traffic wasn't moving. That was when I slammed my truck into park.

It was as if I blacked out because one minute I was jumping out of my truck and walking back to the car, where I grabbed that mother-fucker and slammed him on the side of his vehicle. And then the next thing I remember, I was miles away from the Galleria, at another stoplight. Except that now, I was behind the little car, instead of in front of it. And I had been following him. I don't know why; I don't know what I planned to do. Those minutes had dissolved into a place that was both so empty and full of rage that it had forced my logic into a vortex. I said to myself, *This is not okay*. I turned around and drove home.

I needed to do something. Like after the Wasilla attack, I asked friends for help. One of them was a badass girl I know whom I'm going to call Andy. She had been in special ops, one of those quiet professionals like Rob, but in the Army.

She had had a bad parachute accident. When I told her about my anxiety, she told me, *I got a guy. You need to try this treatment*. She gave me the name of a doctor near Washington who specialized in a treatment for PTSD and anxiety. I won't lie—I was skeptical. It seemed that everybody had a treatment that I *had* to try. On the other hand, I trusted my friends more than I trusted the VA, so I decided to give it a shot.

The doctor was a former Navy SEAL with a practice in Annapolis, Maryland. I flew up to D.C. and another friend drove me to his office. When the doctor came in, he was wearing street clothes with a backpack. There was no one else in the office, because he had closed the practice for the day; he had cleared his whole schedule to look after me personally.

He laid me on the table and explained that he was going to give me an ultrasound, and then inject pain medication into my neck, followed by another injection of an anesthetic called a stellate ganglion block. It suppresses the flight-or-flight instinct, along with the anxiety that comes with the heightened state of vigilance from PTSD.

At this point, my anxiety was so constant and so overpowering that if someone told me they were going to cut my head off to make me feel better, I would have done it. As he injected me in the neck, I remember thinking, *If this doesn't work, I don't know what I'm gonna do*. Bring it.

It was instant relief. As I lay there on the table, the anxiety just melted away. I started crying, which startled the doctor. "Are you all right?" he asked. I didn't say anything, because I didn't want to talk and I didn't want to move and I didn't want it to end.

I thought that this was going to be the solution for me, that it would solve everything. In October 2018 I even went on *60 Minutes* to talk about what a success story it was for me. The problem was that the injections helped prevent the anxiety attacks, but they weren't permanent. Sooner or later, the anxiety came back, and I'd have to stop whatever I was doing to go back to the doctor for another injection. My attacks were so severe that I couldn't bear to lapse back for a minute into that panicked place that I fell into in Wasilla.

In late 2019, another dude I knew told me about a new kind of treatment for anxiety and PTSD. But there was a catch—I couldn't get it in the United States, because it wasn't legal here. I had to go to a clinic in Mexico. Go figure.

Some people call this treatment "the toad." It's a psychedelic called 5-MeO-DMT, and it comes from the dried venom of—you guessed it, Sherlock—a toad. It's usually used in conjunction with another drug called ibogaine.

Not a fucking chance, I said. *I don't believe in that shit. It's all a bunch of snake oil.*

He swore to me that it worked.

I decided to go. Not to get better, but to call bullshit on it. *I'm going to blow this all up.* That was my only objective.

After I flew to San Diego, the clinic sent a van to pick us up and bring us across the border to Mexico. The highway ran along the Pacific coast of endless Baja California beaches looking out across the ocean to the hazy horizon. I didn't look much at the vista, I just watched the run-down buildings go by as we left Tijuana and drove south. After about an hour, we arrived in a town called Ensenada.

We pulled into a subdivision of huge houses and stopped in front of a three-story stucco house. We all went in, turned over our cell phones, and chilled out a while. It was a relaxing and stress-free environment—no TV and barely any sound. A half-dozen staff worked at the clinic, mostly women. I called them my hippies, because they were all relaxed and new age and shit. It was kind of a funny contrast—the long-haired, mellow staff, and then me and a bunch of jacked, tattooed special ops veterans as clients.

At about 8 P.M., the clinic staff came around with a pill and water to wash it down, and then we all went up to the third floor, where the treatment center was. There were mattresses on the floor, so that we couldn't fall out of bed and get hurt. The nurses put in an IV port, and taped EKGs on our chests to monitor our hearts, and we all lay down. And after about forty-five minutes, the ibogaine kicked in.

There's no real way to capture what this was like. The best way I can describe it is like watching a movie of my own life, except all the good parts had been left on the cutting room floor. Every so often I'd retch as if I was throwing up, but we hadn't eaten anything so there was nothing to throw up. I saw visions of all the bad shit in my life that I'd been pushing down and that caused me anxiety and worry. I saw anyone who had hurt me throughout my life. I had a vision of myself standing in front of a room filled with every person in my life whom I had disappointed, and I could just feel the scorn they were heaping on me. The visions just kept rolling over me, one after the next. The worse they got, the sicker I felt, and the harder I retched. I was retching so hard the nurse who was with me put her hand on my back to comfort me. I felt as though I didn't care anymore—I could die and I wouldn't care. Nothing mattered. Then I saw this big ball of light, and I ran to it. When I reached the light, I saw my daughters playing, bathed in white sunshine.

The experience lasted for about sixteen hours. It was midday Saturday by the time the drug wore off. I had been awake the whole time. I was physically, mentally, and spiritually drained. When I reflected on the visions, I didn't recall seeing anything from combat. Nothing from Ganjgal, nothing from Iraq. Just my own childhood, my mother, the people I knew who triggered anxiety, all the garbage that was making me sick. Afterward, my nurse told me that she had never seen so much pain come out of a person in her care.

You would think that what she said would've made me feel better, but I was pissed. I was afraid that this experience was only going to make me feel worse. My biggest fear had been that looking into my psyche would open a Pandora's box of my worst fears and anxieties. *This hasn't helped me,* I told my hippy nurse.

Just wait till tomorrow, she said.

After a light meal and a night of heavy sleep, I was ready for the second phase. One by one the nurses took us back to the third floor. With a nurse on each side of me, they had me inhale a test amount of 5-MeO-DMT. The toad. And then they had me inhale three more times and lay back on the pillow. As I did, I felt my thoughts let go, and I slid feetfirst into a pillowy world of white.

There are no words in the English language that can describe this. It wasn't a physical sensation—it was internal—as if my whole consciousness had poured out of a broken receptacle and into a cloud of the most beautiful white I'd ever seen. I've never seen a white as pure as that.

All the guilt and pain and anxiety I'd felt for so long just fell away and left a singular sensation of peace. It was the ultimate reset.

And then it was over. After maybe twenty minutes, I sat back up, feeling better than I had in years, maybe in my entire life. We spent another day resting and thinking about what we had just gone through. The staff gathered us together for follow-up sessions on mindfulness and staying stress-free, a bunch of hippy shit like keeping journals and meditating. On Tuesday morning, we got back in the white van and drove north. I got on a plane to Austin and went straight to pick up my girls.

A few days after I got home, my friend Brandon came to pick me up so we could go work out together. He flew to my place in his helicopter, and after he put down on the helipad outside my house, I ran over and jumped into the passenger seat. As he powered up the rotors and took off, we started talking about Bristol. She had done something or posted something crazy on social media. I don't remember exactly what it was, but it was the kind of thing that would have gotten me all spooled up. This time, I shrugged.

"I'm not going to let it ruin my day," I told Brandon. He looked at me like I had grown a tail. Brandon, surprised by the change in me, asked about what had happened in Mexico. He had been skeptical of the whole thing, figured it for a bullshit treatment that had a placebo effect at best. As we skimmed over the Texas lake country, I described it to him like this: that I spoke with the devil one day, and then I spoke with God the next day, and afterward, I hadn't had one ounce of anxiety. I was calmer, and I was present in life. I was a better father. I told him that I was sleeping better than I had in my entire life. And I was going to be a better friend as well. "I've never had this much peace," I said.

Rob and I both had to look outside the VA for some help, something that would help us untangle the knots left over from our service. We had to try something unconventional, something that neither of us would have been comfortable with if we hadn't reached a breaking point. I guess I can thank the VA for one thing—if it hadn't been for the operator in Anchorage who told me to check myself into a psych ward, I might never have tried any of these things. I might still be entangled in bureaucracy and bad management. I might still be chasing guys in little cars who don't know how to lay off their horns. I might still be chasing myself, trying to find the better person who I knew was there, but never could seem to catch.

12

BUILD YOUR CIRCLE

ROB

Keep the Circle Tight

On a late afternoon in November 2012, I walked out of my gate in the Billings, Montana, airport, and scanned the waiting faces for my dad. He was there with my nephew Kolten, and he greeted me with a big grin and a bear hug. I collected my bags and piled into Dad's pickup truck, which was loaded with hunting gear, before getting on the highway and driving east with the setting sun behind us.

I had been looking forward to this hunting weekend for weeks. A friend in Washington, D.C., had a cabin out in eastern Montana along the Powder River, a wild, unspoiled area close to the Wyoming and South Dakota lines. I had hunted throughout western Montana with my dad my whole life, but had never set foot on the Powder River. It's legendary in Montana for having some of the biggest mule and whitetail deer in the state. When I invited one of my friends to come along, he said, "Oh my God, we're going to the Serengeti."

I had corralled nine of us for the trip. There was my dad, of course, and Kolten, who's a fanatical outdoorsman. I had also invited Fitzy, a friend from Boston, and his son, Sean. Then there were three child-hood friends of mine from Butte: Josh, whom we called "Swift"; Eric, whom we called "Smooth"; and Ed. Finally, there was my brother Tommy O, who wasn't exactly the outdoor type. He's a DJ in Butte, and even though he gets up every day before dawn for his drive-time show, he's not an early riser by choice. He also isn't in the best shape, and his idea of communing with nature is breaking out a blunt and smoking up. He drove by himself from Butte with his dog Daisy, who constantly barked at deer on the roadside. He tried to get a radio station while he drove, but all he got was static.

From Billings, my dad drove us east to a town called Broadus, which was a couple of homes, a garage, a grocery store, and more bars than the town probably needed. Then we headed south through ranch land and rolling prairie. For the last twenty-six miles, we met up with a local guy who kept us from getting lost by leading us along a bumpy dirt road, our headlights flashing over cottonwoods and jagged hills. There's no dark in the world like the wide-open Montana sky at night, except for maybe over the Hindu Kush. We felt like we had driven off the face of the earth. Until, that is, we turned into the driveway of the cabin.

Outdoorsmen get used to the rustic parts of hunting; in fact, we like it. Cooking over a campfire, rubbing your hands together to keep warm in a blind with wind whistling through the boards, then returning to sleep on creaky bunks in a cabin with a hole in a board for a crapper. If you're lucky enough to have a kitchen, there are probably drawers full of rusty forks, mouse turds in the pots, and curtains with moth holes. If you're really lucky, maybe there will be a dead possum in the wall, or a squirrel that will come down the chimney while you're trying to light it.

That was not the situation we found when we finally approached the house. As we pulled up the driveway, floodlights lit the pavement and the immaculate landscaping, which the sprinklers were still irrigating at night. A satellite TV dish pointed skyward on the second floor of the house. This was not exactly a rustic log cabin where we'd be huddling over battery-powered lamps and making peanut butter sandwiches on a linoleum counter. Not even fucking close.

We got our bags and walked through the door to find a fully stocked bar, a man cave on the first level, plasma TVs in every bedroom, and Wi-Fi that was steadier than what I had at home. It was a five-star cabin, with little bowls of chocolates next to the bed and housekeeping service, for Christ's sake. The only thing it didn't have was cell phone service (after all, we were still in the middle of nowhere). As I picked my bedroom and looked at my pillowy king-sized bed, I wondered if we were actually going to do any hunting this weekend.

———————

AFTER I RETIRED FROM THE NAVY, I went back to Montana as often as I could. I had no real home to speak of. I was single, I had settled my daughters anonymously in a distant corner of the country, and I was traveling constantly—a morning breakfast speech in one city, a lunch speech in another, a dinner gala in a third. Any kid who enlists and goes to war gets homesick, and that was true of me as well. I tried to get back to Butte at least once a month. I could lay my head down anywhere in the world, but I wanted to be back in the comfortable environment that I had grown up in, where I could be myself. New friends don't always have your best interests in mind, but old ones do.

That fall in 2012, I looked forward to getting back to Montana more than I ever had in the sixteen years since I had headed to boot camp. Part of that was the simple desire to be home. But another reason was that after years of hunting people, I wanted to hunt animals. It was my love of hunting and my skills as a rifleman that had sent me into the military. Now that I was out, I wanted to use those skills again, but for the reasons that had drawn me to the outdoors in the first place. Not for war. Not because of terrorism. But because of these majestic animals, and the smell of crisp autumn air, and the dance that the dawn light made on the mountaintops. And maybe the taste of a cold beer after a hunt.

Since we had arrived at the lodge in the middle of the night, our plan was to get a little sleep then get up before dawn to hunt. We'd be in place at sunup, when we would be most likely to find game. We executed the first part of the mission like champs, stowing all our equipment and choosing our bedrooms. Actually, going to sleep for an early rise didn't go so well; we ended up kicking back a couple of drinks, telling stories, and laughing before heading to bed.

The alarms started going off around 4 A.M. One by one, everyone staggered out of their bedrooms to suck down coffee in the kitchen and gear up. We had two options for the day: cross the dirt road we drove up and hike the ridges above looking for mule deer and elk, or go out the front door toward the river and try for whitetails in the woods.

We decided to hit the hills. In our camouflage and hunting orange, we walked with our rifles two by two up the ridge, peeling off in groups to each of our spots. I went with Fitzy and Sean to a near hill, where we got settled and waited for the sun to come up, anticipating that to be the ideal time to catch muleys coming up from the river to bed down in the mountains.

Kolten and my dad went up one ridge, and Swift and Ed drove even farther so they could get out and walk after elk. Both had already filled their game quota that year, so they were just along for the ride.

I had been on the ridge for about an hour when my radio crackled with a call from Swift: *Emergency! Ed just shot himself and we need to get back.*

I responded calmly, "Say again, Swift. Ed SHOT himself?"

"No. Ed just SHIT himself. We need to get back now."

"How bad is it?" I asked.

"It's in his boots!" Swift replied.

A footnote here for strong emphasis: the drive from Butte to Broadus is six hours with another hour and a half on dirt roads to the cabin. Along the way here, Ed and Swift had stopped for gas on a reservation a bit east of Billings, Montana. Ed was hungry, and against Swift's advice, he fished a Reuben sandwich from under the heat lamp in the deli. He scarfed it down with a Mountain Dew, while they drove several hours more to the cabin.

Ed's Reuben had apparently been under the heat lamps for a while and was past its expiration date. I'm guessing the Mountain Dew didn't help. What I do know is that somewhere off in the darkness, as the two of them were sitting in a truck, Ed sharted in what had to have been Montana's worst case of Montezuma's revenge. Game over.

While Ed headed back to the lodge to change his shorts and everything else, Smooth had paired up with my brother, Tommy, and was leading him on an epic journey. The rest of us were dug in, waiting for deer to come to us, but Smooth and Tommy kept walking up into the hills together, which entailed Smooth walking ahead and waiting for Tommy to catch up. After about thirty minutes, Smooth said he was going ahead to scout. "I'll stay within eyesight," he said, and disappeared.

Looking back on it, the two of them were not a good fit. Smooth was a badass Army vet who served in South Korea and loved the outdoors. He could hike for days and was probably the best hunter I knew. He was the first one to put in for special permits. If *Field & Stream* magazine came with a centerfold, he'd get a hard-on. He probably rubbed deer urine on his clothes and practiced mating calls. Neither pain nor weather bothered him. Smooth was there to hunt.

Tommy, on the other hand, liked to smoke weed, take a lot of breaks, and retire early for a leisurely spot on his home couch. For him, brushing snow off his windshield without a glove is an act of courage and sacrifice.

While Tommy watched Smooth up ahead, jumping ravines and scaling a rock-covered embankment like a gazelle, he made his way up the hillside slowly, wondering whether a fall would kill him or just break all his bones. Eventually he reached the top of the ridge and looked out. From high atop the plateau, the flatlands seemed to roll on forever. It was a beautiful sight, and it was what he came for.

He reached inside his coat pocket for a little taste of something he had brought with him. It was a sticky package that he had picked up for thirty bucks from a guy wearing a Def Leppard jacket in a 1982 Buick Regal. Premium Montana ragweed.

Just as he lit the bowl and turned from the vista to exhale, Smooth appeared out of nowhere, like an annoyed genie. "What in the fuck do you think you're doing?" he asked.

"Having a smoke, for Christ's sake," Tommy answered. "You up for a little?"

"Shit, no," Smooth said. "What about the deer?"

Tommy shrugged. "I didn't bring enough for the deer," he said, and lit up.

The deer didn't get any weed, and after hiking seven miles over the hills, Tommy and Smooth didn't get any deer. Nor did any of the rest of us. None of us cared. We were enjoying ourselves so much that getting a deer felt secondary. After we got back to the camp, we had a whiskey-fueled night of laughs and went to bed early.

The next morning, I woke up first around 3 A.M., put on my gear, and started coffee brewing. We decided that we would go for white-tails that day, since they were likely to be right in front of the house and wouldn't require hiking up any mountains.

I went to wake up Tommy O, who was still recovering from his Amazing Race with Smooth.

"Fuck off, Rob," I heard after I knocked on the door. He wanted nothing to do with hunting today. Tommy was sleeping in.

The rest of the crew gathered and discussed how the bend in the river in front of the house was the perfect crossing to catch big white-tail bucks. Smooth and I set up two teams and a plan with military-level precision: Fitzy and Sean would stake out one designated spot in the field, and Dad and Kolten would sit by a bend in the river. Smooth and I would walk down the road, turn right, and walk through the brush toward the two teams. In combat, this is called an "L-shaped" ambush, and we were going to use it to bag deer. The key to success is to not move and wait for the deer to come to you.

Smooth was deadly serious about getting a deer that day—he was in camo head to foot, including his undershirt and boonie hat. We set up our teams, then Smooth and I went out wide to the edge of the owner's land. Then we walked toward our ambush sites, knowing that the deer would hear and smell us and run. Which they did. Smooth and I also knew that once the deer were fired upon, the smarter, bigger bucks would run back to us. Which they also did.

As we expected, we flushed out the deer, and we started hearing shots. Sean got a nice one, exactly where we said he would. As Smooth and I walked through the trees, deer ran everywhere. I was a hundred yards to the left of Smooth when a very nice whitetail buck ran up. I took the shot and got him.

That's when the buck appeared. He was a monster stag that materialized right in front of Smooth. He had an excellent shot. I held my breath as Smooth carefully aimed his rifle. Then he lowered it again.

"God dammit!" he yelled.

I was confused. "Smooth—what the fuck?" I yelled back at him.

"I looked through my scope and all I saw was two things: that huge buck and your fucking dad!" he shouted.

My dad can't stay in one place for any length of time, even though that's the one thing we asked of him. He felt so bad. "Next time, just shoot," he mumbled to Smooth.

The day had begun perfectly. I had my buck, Sean had his. Even though he didn't get his big buck, Smooth took one of the ATVs to go back and get celebratory beers while we dressed the animals, lit a fire, and got ready to enjoy venison for breakfast. There was just one person who wasn't there to enjoy it, as far as I was concerned, and it was Tommy.

I shouldn't have worried. After a few minutes, Smooth came roaring up on the ATV again, all excited.

"Tommy O got his buck, too!" he said.

I couldn't believe what he was saying. The last I had heard from Tommy was his lazy ass under the covers in his bedroom, yelling at me to go away. "That's not possible," I said. "Tommy didn't wake up. He slept all morning."

I was only half-right. While we were out in the woods, stalking and sweating, Tommy had been dead asleep right in his bed where I left him. When the shooting started down by the river, the deer started stampeding away from us, which meant *back toward the lodge*. Ed and Swift had stayed in, since they couldn't hunt, and they spotted all the deer running toward the house. They ran to Tommy's room and banged on his door to get up. He told them to fuck off. A few minutes later, they came and banged on the door a second time, begging him to get up, and he still wouldn't. Finally, they came back a third time and practically knocked the door down, yelling, "Dude! Get up now! Or else." Tommy finally got his ass out of the bed, went upstairs through the kitchen to the second-floor porch. Still in his Chicago Bears sweatpants that he had worn to bed, he stepped onto the porch and looked straight into the eyes of an enormous, four-by-four point buck staring right at him. So he ran inside, grabbed his rifle from inside the house, ran back out, took aim, and killed the buck with one shot from the porch.

When Smooth got there, he couldn't believe it. "Why did you shoot him from the balcony?" he asked Tommy.

"He was coming right for us!" Tommy said, like he had just shot a marauding bear or chased the British out of Concord. It was the first deer he'd ever shot, and he had no idea what was supposed to happen next. "What do we do now?" he asked.

"Now you put on your orange jacket and your pants and boots," Smooth said. Tommy needed to at least pretend that he had genuinely been hunting when he shot the buck, not just hanging around the house in his pajamas. "Grab a knife, too!"

It was still early with the sun low as we met up alongside the river. Under a cloudless blue sky that wrapped from the mountains to the horizon, we cracked celebratory beers and took photos of our trophies in the brush. Tommy had pulled baggy jeans over his sweatpants and put on an orange hat and hunting vest, to look the part. Unlike what I had left behind in Virginia Beach, I had a feeling of brotherhood again, of unity, as we toasted each other with the winding Powder River to our backs.

I used to daydream about Montana when I was still in the Teams. I'd be on missions where I'd hike three hours in the Iraqi desert in January toward a target, or walk along goat trails through the mountains of eastern Afghanistan. My mind would wander, and I'd think about getting a pizza at the Vu-Villa, or stopping in at the Freeway Tavern or Pork Chop John's for a chop sandwich, or a garbage omelet at the M&M. Instead of going over the mission that night, I'd remember the smell of sage or pines in the morning air when I would hike into Beaverhead-Deerlodge National Forest tracking elk or bighorn sheep.

After I left the Teams and retired from the Navy, I expected to have the best friends I could possibly have wanted for the rest of my life, an iron circle of brothers forged in fire. Turned out that wasn't quite the case when things fell apart after the bin Laden raid. Some of them are still brothers to me, but the fellowship isn't there as I expected. I had to leave the Navy to realize how important my friends and family were, how those relationships survived years of separation and distance. I realized that my memories of Montana were so ingrained because of those friends and family who had shared the indelible experiences that carried a lifetime of meaning. Those were the people who mattered to me. Those were the people who completed my circle.

As our hunting trip wound down, we spent one more night at the lodge, and the next morning packed up all our gear and loaded it into our trucks. I drove with Dad back to Butte, where I spent another week seeing more friends and stopping at my familiar haunts that I remembered so well that I could walk to them blindfolded. I always say that when something's over, it's over, whether it's high school, a relationship, or a military career. You move on. I would probably never set foot in the ■■■ Squadron team room again. But I'll never move on from the most important parts of my life, or the places that give them meaning. Montana was where my circle began and that's where I expect it may end one day. On the banks of the Powder River, I was keeping that circle tight.

DAKOTA
Find Your Circle

In 2017, I was working out one day at the gym with my friend Tim Kennedy when I made a joke about how fat I had gotten. It was a dumb, offhand comment—the kind of thing I'd say when I was feeling out of shape and down on myself and needed somebody to pick me up.

I could always talk to Tim, because he'd been in the shit, like me. He had been in Special Forces and became an MMA middleweight fighter. Sparring with him is no joke.

Arguing with him is no joke, either. Tim's a straightforward, no-bullshit, intense guy. He is not going to say anything to me that he doesn't believe, and that he hasn't thought out, and that isn't in my best interest. He wants to hear about a problem once and give me his two cents on the solution. Then, if I'm not talking about how I'm going to do it, he doesn't want to hear any more about it. He's done.

We were working up a good sweat when I complained to him about how I was getting fat. If misery loves company, Tim Kennedy is the wrong guy to have around. He paused whatever rep he was doing and looked me in the eye. "Hey, check it out," he said. And then he laid into me. "The world looks up to you and knows you as a warrior. So you better look like one, you better act like one, you better present yourself like you're one, because that's what they expect when they hear your name."

Then he went back to working out.

I'll tell you something: I never forgot that. I felt like he had kicked me in the head when I was down. I mean, it hurt. But it was what I needed to hear. It was what made me like Tim from the moment we met. That's what I like about all the guys who are my circle. They're transparent, honest to the point of being infuriating. But I've always had a circle of people around me who will give it to me straight, and who won't dance around what needs to be said. That was why my dad and pepaw had such an impact on me. That was why I was a good fit for the Marines. That was why I fell apart when I left the Marines. And that's what I got back in Austin.

My friends don't give a fuck about the Medal of Honor or what went down in Ganjgal. They care about what I'm doing today—that's what they'll judge me by. Don't get me wrong; they have the utmost respect for what I've accomplished. But if I suck today, they're going to tell me right to my face: *You suck. There, I said it.*

———————•——————•———————

WHEN I GOT BACK FROM MEXICO and my treatment with the hippies of Ensenada, one of the first things I did was drop the dead weight from my life. By dead weight, I mean the people who leeched off me, who created stress and anxiety instead of helping me get rid of it. Ever since I received the medal in 2011, people were always looking for something from me. Sometimes it was money. Sometimes they wanted to boast about knowing me. Sometimes they wanted me to retweet something, to raise their own profiles and boost their egos. More often than not, I'd say yes because I wanted to please people. One thing that has always been true of me is that I hated to disappoint. But then after I helped someone out, I'd never hear from them again.

That's done now. Mexico helped me break out of the cycle of guilt and anxiety that came out of my PTSD, but it also helped reestablish my priorities. The best way I can describe it was like hitting a reset button on a frozen computer—all the crazy conflicts and overloaded circuits shut down and came back on the way they were supposed to. All the things that pushed my buttons, that got me spun up and angry, it all just melted away. And the people who caused those things to happen, they melted away, too. Maybe a better way to describe it is that I scraped them off me, like barnacles off a rock. When they were gone, I knew who my true friends were.

I had a new set of standards for my friends now, and it was simple: to surround myself with people who were better than me, who I could aspire to be. I didn't care anymore what some shithead on TikTok or Instagram wanted from life, but I knew what I wanted. I wanted to be a better father. I wanted to be a good friend. I wanted to be a servant. I wanted to be a good family man. I wanted to be a successful entrepreneur. I wanted to be a good leader. I wanted to be a good human being.

On the flip side of that, there's people I don't hang out with. I don't hang out with cheaters. I don't hang out with alcoholics. I don't hang out with guys who prefer drinking over doing the right thing. I don't hang out with partiers. I don't hang out with guys who are broke. You know why? Because broke people attract broke people, and many are broke because they've made shitty decisions.

These days, I can count about a half-dozen friends in my life who meet my standards, and really mean something to me. Only three of them are around me on a day-to-day basis. Tim's one of them. The other two guys in my immediate circle are Shane and Brandon. The three of us train together a couple of days a week. We go for hikes, we shoot guns, we lift, we roll jujitsu. I know that none of them are going to say or do something malicious to hurt me. Day to day, these guys are there for me, and I for them. Rob's part of my circle, too, but he's more like my lifeline—the guy I call when I need to break the glass in an emergency.

Here's how I look at Tim, Brandon, and Shane: If I want to be a warrior, I need a sword, a shield, and armor. Without those things, I'm vulnerable. I'm exposed. But those guys are my arms and provisions when I'm around them. With them, I'm armed and protected. I can take on anything.

Tim's the blade. His edge is constantly honed to razor sharpness, he cuts right to the heart of the matter, and he's always ready to cut through whatever bullshit is in front of him. This guy, it's like he's been preparing for his life from the moment he was born and grew up in California. He started doing martial arts as a teenager and continued during college. And after September 11, he enlisted in the Army, and eventually became a Green Beret, a sniper, and an MMA fighter. He's also a damn nice guy and a great father, and loyal as hell.

When I moved to Austin, he and I just started hanging out. Since we're both military and well known, it was just a matter of time before we met. What I liked about Tim when I met him, and what I still like about him, was that he opens his heart to you. He will take his shirt off his back for you. No matter how busy he is, he'll take the time to teach you whatever you need to know. It was Tim who brought me to the jujitsu mat for the first time and showed me what front toward enemy means in grappling. He's a three-stripe black belt, and he'll give any knowledge he's got if you ask him. The one thing that Tim expects from you in return is to bring 110 percent of your fucking effort every single day. Tim's going to give you the best he's got. So you'd better do the same damn thing.

THAT'S WHY TIM SPOKE TO ME the way he did back in 2017, when he grabbed hold of me and made me stop feeling sorry for myself when things were at their lowest with Bristol. It was no big surprise that I was feeling bad. Nothing was clicking between Bristol and me; we couldn't agree or get along on any level. We were just fighting all the time. I was practically living out of my vehicle, and my whole world was tumbling down.

Tim couldn't fix my PTSD or make my anxiety attacks disappear, but he could make me see how I allowed myself to be dragged down by the things around me, and how I showed that to the world. The fact is that any of my guys would have done the same thing. If you surround yourself with a circle, a true circle, people who speak to you in the ways that you respond to, they hold you accountable. Like I said: Tim's the blade, he cuts right through the tangle, and he doesn't waste any time doing it.

Shane, he's the shield. He's a protector. He's laid-back and friendly, a little less blunt and aggressive than Tim. He's the quiet one you don't expect. The nice one who's underestimated. Do that at your own risk, though, because Shane is a beast and he will rip your damn head off if you're not careful.

I met him at the gym one day while working out with Tim. Shane was a jacked-up, tattooed monster with a big smile and a crazy mullet.

"Hey, what do you do?" I had asked him.

"Oh, you know, I used to play in a band," he said casually. I didn't think anything of it. I'd been working out with Shane a few days a week for, gosh, two to three weeks. And then one day when I was at home, I was messing around with iTunes. I had this country music song on my phone called "What if She's an Angel," and the song popped up and it's got a picture of a long-haired singer with perfect teeth who looked nothing like Shane. It said the musician's name was Tommy Shane Steiner. I started googling, and I looked at more pictures, and I realized that Tommy Shane Steiner was Shane from the gym. Except that this skinny-ass, blue-eyed, pretty-boy Music Row country singer had turned into the ripped beast that I had been lifting with at the gym for weeks.

I called him immediately. I confessed, "Dude, I'm such an idiot. I grew up listening to your song."

"Yeah, that's me," he said. "That was back in the day." He probably never would have mentioned that he had a number two song on the *Billboard* charts if I had never said it first. He's a humble guy.

It turned out that we had a lot in common other than the song, and one of them is a love of flying. Around August 2019, I was talking about how I was planning to learn to fly and buy a plane. Shane told me not to bother, because a plane's not that useful for getting around. It's only as convenient as the nearest airport, unless you plan to land on a freeway. But with a helicopter, you can drop in practically anywhere, and you don't need a landing strip and an air traffic controller. Texas being pretty laid-back about aviation and everything else, flying a helicopter is about as easy as it gets, once you get a license.

I was almost convinced, but not quite. My daughters were about two and four years old at that point, and I wasn't sure I wanted to strap them into booster seats in a helicopter when I needed to get them to their mother's house. "Yeah, but it's too dangerous for my kids," I said.

"Come fly with me," Shane said. I met him on a Sunday, and he took me up in his helicopter. We flew up over Lake Travis, where a dam on the Colorado River forms a huge reservoir northwest of Austin. I looked out the window, watching the curving shores of the lake and hills rising up from the shores as Shane took us up and down and across the water. It was the closest thing to pure freedom that I had ever felt.

And then he did something that convinced me that he was right about being a helicopter pilot. My biggest fear was that if the engine died, the helicopter would just drop out of the sky like a stone. As we flew, he told me over the headset that that wasn't true, and he would show me why. Even if the engine died or was disengaged, a condition called "autorotation" would keep the rotors turning, which would keep the helicopter stable as it descended to the ground, sort of like a plane can glide to a landing if its engines die. We were hovering at about fifteen hundred feet in the air when he cut the throttle. Suddenly the cockpit was almost silent. Even though he said it was safe and there was nothing be afraid of, there was a pit of fear in my stomach as the helicopter began to descend. But just as he said, the rotors kept spinning, and he brought that helicopter down as smooth as an owl landing in the forest. I barely felt a thing when we touched down. I looked at him in amazement.

"That's it?" I said.

"That's it," he said.

"I'll buy this off you right now," I said. By the next morning, I was in flying classes, and I had my pilot's license eighty-four days later.

Here's why I love telling that story. If Shane had been a real dick, he could have scared the shit out of me by cutting the power and letting that helicopter down without telling me, and allowing my fear to take over. Instead he just gave me that gentle smile of his and told me exactly what he was going to do. I couldn't have felt any safer or less scared as the ground gently came up to meet his chopper. Like I said, he's a shield. From danger, from anger, from fear, from doubt.

The third member of my circle, Brandon, has a special place. He's my armor. I feel like nothing can touch me when he's around, because he's always ready to help me in whatever way he can when I get in a pinch. I talk to Brandon pretty much every day, sometimes three or four times a day. He grew up in Austin, and he's done well as a businessman. We've got a lot in common: we were both adopted, and we both grew up knowing what *hard* was.

I met him in 2019, before I became a pilot. Our meeting was beyond random, and it makes me wonder sometimes what hand is guiding our lives. I do a lot of skydiving, and I wanted to do a helicopter jump. My friend Crispy—his real name is Omar Avila—said he knew a guy with a helicopter, and he gave me Brandon's number. So I called him up.

"Hey, I heard you have a helicopter. Could I come jump out of it?" I asked him. I had no idea if he was a good pilot, and Brandon didn't have a fucking clue who I was—I called out of the blue with my volume turned up to ten as usual, asking a complete stranger if I could jump out of his helicopter. He thought I was a little nuts, but Brandon's mind-set was, *Fuck, if you want to do it, let's do it.*

We couldn't get our schedules to match up, though, because I was off speaking all the time and Brandon was busy running his business. Finally I called him up and told him, "Fuck the helicopter jump.

Let's go get some lunch." He picked me up in his helicopter and we flew out to eat at a place called Salt Lick Barbeque in Driftwood. It's a pain in the ass to drive to, probably an hour and twenty minutes, but it only takes about fifteen minutes in the helicopter.

We flew out there for some brisket or ribs or whatever, and we set down next to the vineyard there. Every time you go anywhere in a helicopter, people whip out their cell phones and take video because they think Jay-Z is going to get out. When we flew in, everyone lined up against the fence with their phones out, recording us. Boy, were they disappointed when we appeared.

Over our plates of barbecue, we talked about our businesses and our lives. Regular stuff. But something strange happened as we talked. Even though we had just met, it was like we were old friends and had known each other our whole lives. We were cracking each other up, but we were also talking serious things, the kinds of things that you talk about with lifelong friends. The kind of people you welcome into your circle for life. By the time we got back in the helicopter, it was like we had known each other for thirty years.

Our families have gotten so close, and we spend so much time together that my girls call him Uncle Brandon. He's just an incredible guy, the first dude I'd pick up the phone to call to come get my kids if something happened to me. Like Shane, he's humble. He's the kind of guy who will do anything for you without asking. I'm not exaggerating—he will decide to do things for me and the others before we even know to ask for them.

Take Thanksgiving of 2019. By then I had my pilot's license, and I flew my helicopter over to Brandon's mom's ranch to do some work at her house. Afterward, I flew down to Marcus Luttrell's ranch. Marcus was the SEAL featured in *Lone Survivor,* and Rob was one of the SEALs sent in to rescue him.

Before I took off for Marcus's, Brandon told me to be careful of the weather. The temperature was supposed to drop, and when the dew point and temperature get close, you get fog. So Brandon told me to get my ass home because the temperature was falling. "You're gonna get stuck out there," he told me. Since I had just gotten my license, he was always on me to be a better pilot, because he didn't want me to be a statistic. "If shit gets bad, call me," Brandon said. "No big deal."

Marcus's ranch is an incredible place, just beautiful, with giraffes roaming across the fields. After the Thanksgiving meal, I started to fly back to Austin with another friend, John Resig, who founded the Chive with his brother and made a ton of money. While we were in the air, a rain shower came up and the temperature dropped. We were still about thirty minutes northeast of Austin, and the fog began to form right in front of me. I flew lower and lower, trying to keep the ground in sight, until the fog closed in and I couldn't see enough to keep going. *Shit.* Meanwhile, Brandon was waiting for the text from me that we always send, "DNC," for "down and clear." He wasn't getting it, and the fog was getting thicker and thicker.

Finally I called him from the air. He was in the middle of Thanksgiving dinner with his mom. "Uh, hey, man. I don't think I'm going to make it back," I told him.

"No shit," Brandon said. "I fucking told you that."

I looked out on the foggy blanket below me. "I don't know where to land," I said.

So Brandon guided me to a place called Apache Pass, where there was a little private landing strip. "Is this going to clear up anytime soon?" I asked Brandon.

"Nope," he said after consulting the weather maps. "I'll come pick you up."

"No, no, no, I'll get an Uber," I told him.

"Yeah, you go ahead and get an Uber," he said, and hung up.

I spent about ten, maybe fifteen minutes trying to get an Uber, and of course there's no fucking Uber in the middle of Apache Pass. So I called Brandon back, sheepishly.

"Let me guess: You can't get an Uber?" he answered.

"Yeah," I said.

"No fucking shit," he said. "That's why I'm already on my way. I'm forty minutes out."

He had left the dinner table to drive an hour to get me, and then an hour back to Austin. The caretaker for the landing strip had come out to meet us and invited us into his house, which—no shit—was filled with chickens. By the time Brandon got there, John and I were sitting on the couch with the shirtless caretaker and his chickens, drinking beer and watching the Cowboys lose to the Bills.

Brandon drove us back in his truck, giving me shit the whole way. "Hey, you know, it's cool, man. You screwed up my family Thanksgiving, and here I am picking up your sorry ass in the middle of a field in the middle of nowhere," he said. "Don't worry about it, it's only Thanksgiving."

He was planning to just drop us off at John's house. Instead John invited us in for one drink and broke out his best bourbon. Five drinks later, we decided we needed to get something to eat, so we went out to get food. We ended up drinking all night and closed the restaurant down in the morning. That's how we spent our Thanksgiving. Because even when I mess up, Brandon will always be on his way to come get me and protect me from myself. Like I said, he's my armor.

Being a warrior means a lot of things to a lot of people. In some ways, there are so many people throwing that term around today that it's become almost meaningless. The part about being a warrior that gets lost is that no one fights alone. You need your circle around whom you can trust to have your back, who can help you. That's why Ganjgal was such a trauma for me. I felt like my circle died in that valley. And that's why Tim and Shane and Brandon and Rob mean so much to me now. They're better than me, and so they're teaching me all the time. They're in the circle, and that's where I need them to stay.

———

NOT THAT LONG AGO, I was able to do the same for Brandon that Tim did for me. Around February 2020, I noticed that a lot of guys around him were running him ragged, hitting him up to go fly in his helicopter, inviting themselves to hunt at his ranch, forcing him to entertain them when he had work to do. *Will you do this, will you do that.* I could tell he was down and he was tired because all these people were using him.

"We're having a meeting at the ranch. Be there this weekend," I told Brandon. "Nobody else is coming. You're not letting anybody out here this weekend."

He was surprised but agreed. When we got out there, we sat down at the bar. "We need to talk," I said. "Everybody's mooching off you. They always want something and you're always bending over backward to help everybody else out. They're like leeches sucking you dry." Brandon was silent, listening. "Hey, man," I continued, "if they're not calling you just to ask you how you're doing, you don't need 'em. We need to fix this. If people are always just asking you for shit, that's not a friendship. When do they call you to just say, 'How you doing?'"

Brandon hadn't even considered it like that. I was sure he was going to get defensive and say I was wrong. Instead, he thought about what I said. "You're right, you're right," he told me. We talked for about two hours. He couldn't really see what we could, but as soon as I told him what we saw, it was like his eyes opened and he could see what I was talking about. And it was just like me after going to Mexico. He started dropping people from his life who weren't a positive influence for him, who didn't reciprocate.

After Brandon and I talked, we went out and worked the ranch. I always do that when I visit. We refill the livestock feed bins, we work the cattle, we clear brush. I help him, just like he helped me. Just like Tim and Shane have. It's part of our deal. The work never ends. Just like our circle of friends, I hope it never does.

BE A FIREFIGHTER OF LIFE

ROB

Make Your Own Luck

Music played and drinks flowed at a reception at the Eau Palm Beach Resort, where I had been invited to deliver a speech in April 2015. The resort near West Palm Beach, Florida, was a dreamscape of swaying palm trees and beach-side cabanas and manicured lawns, the kind of place featured in vacation ads in the dead of winter and that say *Plan a Trip, Chase Your Paradise.* I was speaking to the Northeast chapter of the National Electrical Contractors Association, a trade group that represent the outdoors electric construction industry. That group knew how to pick a prime meeting location.

After dinner, drink in hand, I chatted up the chapter manager, a guy named Michael Gilchrist. He had appeared in Life cereal commercials in the 1970s with his real-life younger brother, the "Little Mikey" who became an urban legend when he was rumored to have died when he ate Pop Rocks and Coke. The older Michael Gilchrist looks like a fifty-five-year-old version of his boyhood self in the ads, sitting at the breakfast table with his brothers, trying to trick Mikey into eating Life. I was enjoying a joke and laughing with him when he introduced me to a striking woman with long black hair. She was the assistant chapter manager and host of the event.

She was slim and gorgeous in her green pantsuit, with a wide smile and dancing eyes and a big laugh. The association meeting had been filled with beefy guys with mustaches, former electrical linemen, and power company executives in suits. This woman was like a swan who had landed in a rhino herd. She was so stunning that she completely threw me off my game.

The next morning, she brought me up to the stage for the speech. Like the previous night, she left me fumbling for words. When I started to speak, I was so smitten after talking with her that she was the only person in the organization that I remembered to thank; I forgot all the other people I was supposed to be grateful for. She had planned to leave the hall to go golfing but decided at the last minute to stick around to hear me talk. Afterward, I skipped golf, too, and hung around the beach bar with her. This time she wore a bikini with pink polka dots. I nearly fainted.

Her name was Jessica. She was outgoing, she was the funniest person I'd ever met, and, most important, she had *no* idea who I was. She admitted that she hadn't planned to stick around for my speech and that she had wanted someone else entirely to speak at the conference— Frank Abagnale Jr., whom Leonardo DiCaprio portrayed in the movie *Catch Me if You Can*. That is, until her boss Mike suggested that a con artist might not be the ideal speaker for a leadership course.

Before I left the conference, I made sure to get her number. I had been single since I had left the Navy, and I didn't really expect to see her again—she lived in New York, and I was still living in Dallas at the time. The chances of seeing her again seemed like a moon shot for me, but I sent her a text anyway a few weeks later, telling her that I was going to be in New York for work. Maybe we could connect, I wrote, and pressed send.

I was bending the truth a little about a work trip to New York. I really had no business there at all; I just wanted to see her. So I arranged to make a brief appearance for an event in June at the Yale Club and invited her to come. She arrived shortly after I had begun and winked at me over the heads in the crowd.

Afterward, I brought her to a bar in Chelsea. It was loud and crowded, so we moved to a quieter bar across the street. We had an amazing night, just like we had in Florida. And then we said good night. Out of respect, I didn't even kiss her before I hailed her a taxi.

She told me later on that she went back to her apartment and told her roommates, *I had a blast with that guy and I think I might be in love with him, and I'm never going to see him again.* There were tears. There were glasses of wine. They talked her down. And the next day, I texted her and told her that I wanted to see her again.

———•———

JESSICA CALLS ME the luckiest unlucky guy in the world. There must be something to that, because I could have died a hundred different ways on my missions, and I was never injured once. After my relationship with the Navy soured at the end of my career, I could have cratered, but I ended up on the speaking circuit and became buddies with Steve and Peter Doocy and other Fox personalities. And after my first wife and I separated and divorced, I could have stayed single and lonely my whole life, but only luck can account for how I ended up meeting an amazing woman like Jessica. Throughout my life, bad shit would happen, and then a stroke of luck would turn that misfortune into a golden egg.

To see Jessica again, I needed luck, but I needed a little something else, too: I needed more excuses to fly up to New York. The next time was for an appearance at Fox News headquarters. Like before, I didn't really need to go to New York for it; I could just as easily have done it from Dallas. But it gave me a reason to ask her out again, which I did.

I stayed a few blocks from Fox at the Waldorf-Astoria to put some shine on my story about returning to New York for work. I had invited my cousin Cory to join us for drinks, so it wasn't too obvious that I was interested in her. Poor Cory, though, because it wasn't long before I was dropping hints to him that he was a third wheel and needed to leave. He stayed for two drinks before he beat it.

I kept finding ways to see her, and we dated about two years. I eventually proposed to her in Florida, during another event for her company. We were in the hotel with her dad, Tom, who also worked for the association, and a bunch of her coworkers. Her mother, Mary, and Mike were there as well. I told Jessica I had left something upstairs and asked her to come with me. In my pocket, I had a ring that I had custom made, with the help of a diamond dealer I had met in the Cayman Islands. While everyone waited downstairs, we went up to our room together. She was startled when she walked in and saw a bottle of wine and glasses set out on the balcony table. After we sat, I moved her glass to the side, took her hand, and got down on one knee.

"What the hell are you doing?" she asked, baffled. Maybe she thought I was unlucky again and had lost a contact lens. She didn't even see it coming when I brought out the ring. When we returned downstairs, champagne corks popped all around us.

Sometimes I think you have to make your own luck, and that's definitely true of my relationship with Jessica. I didn't go looking for her, but when she appeared in my life, I wanted to make sure that I didn't let her slip away. And thank God I didn't. She's my rock. She's always there for me, and she's become best friends with my girls. She and Dakota have become buddies, too. We have fun all the time, wherever we are. Boredom and complacency can kill you on the battlefield, but it can also smother a relationship as well. Everything I did with Jess was an adventure, and full of laughter, and I knew I would never get bored with her.

Jessica was from Massachusetts, and her dad was adamant that we get married at a place called the Chatham Bars Inn, a resort on the elbow of Cape Cod. It's a beautiful spot that looks out over the Atlantic. We wanted a wedding that none of the guests would forget. I remember when Jessica's mom, Mary, said in her Boston accent, "We got two hundred steaks and two hundred lobstah tails, and fucking chicken fingahs for Mikey." Yes, just like that.

I flew my whole family out from Butte. Kid Rock was one of my groomsmen and his fiancée, Audrey, was a bridesmaid. I had met him through the Doocys, who had a house across the street from him in Jupiter, Florida. His real name is Bob Ritchie, but even though we're good friends, I have a hard time calling him Bob.

The hotel had booked Bob—ahem, Kid Rock—in a regular room. All the rooms are beautiful, but since he's a rock star and he likes nice things, I told the hotel staff that there was no way he'd be staying in one of their typical rooms. Instead we rented an entire house for them. That became the informal reception hall for the entire wedding weekend.

Following the rehearsal dinner, we went to a bar in Chatham called the Squire. It was a dark and crowded local hangout, and Jessica's dad, Mike, Kid Rock, and a bunch of SEALs all crowded in, bunched in different groups. I arrived late, right after a local guy spotted Bob and decided to pick a fight, probably thinking this was the moment that he would brag about for the rest of his life, the night he told off Kid Rock in a bar. I'm pretty sure he thought the story would end with Kid Rock slinking away, humiliated. Instead Bob looked back at me and the other SEALs and smirked, and suddenly the loud-mouth Masshole was surrounded by Navy SEALs. Bob looked at the bouncer, who was in his corner, and asked, "We good?" and he said, "Oh, we *good*."

It was a pretty ridiculous situation, and everyone knew exactly how it would end if it came to a fight, except maybe for the guy who got in Bob's face. That is, until Mike Gilchrist went all ninja and suddenly pulled two swords out of his pants. They weren't real. He had just won them with his sons at a pirate museum that day. I don't know how or *why* he was hiding them in there, but no shit, there they were. The fight didn't materialize, everyone laughed, and the crowd dispersed. Probably to the relief of the guy who started it off.

The next day, our wedding day, Jessica's dad texted me before the ceremony: "Whatever you do, don't forget the rings." When we arrived at the church, of course I had forgotten the rings. I asked my buddy Shorty to run back to the hotel to get them. Shorty had become a close friend since meeting him a few years prior in line for drinks at a New Orleans Saints game.

"Okay, where are they?" Shorty asked.

"I have no idea," I told him. "They're probably locked in my room somewhere."

Shorty tore back to the Chatham Bars Inn in his car, ready to break down the door if he needed to. Fortunately, my absent-minded bride-to-be had left the door wide open. He found the rings and hauled ass back to the church.

Understand that I had armed security around me and the church, and these guards were not my usual guys. I wasn't the only one who was jittery; these guys were jumpy, too, because crowds are hard to control. In the middle of the pre-ceremony craziness, Shorty screeched up in front of the church, hopped the curb, and left the car door open as he sprinted toward the church, fumbling in his pockets for the rings as he ran.

From a security point of view, this is not an ideal scenario. My boys almost drew down on Shorty with their sidearms, thinking ISIS might have sent him to take me out.

Somehow—fuck knows how—Shorty talked his way out of this without getting shot, sprinted into the church, ran down the aisle, and tossed me the rings. Then he ran out the back and around to the front door again, just in time to proceed down the aisle of the church as the music played and Jessica pulled up outside. Incredible timing. And, I would add, pure luck.

I had hired my friend Tim Montana to play at the reception after the ceremony. Jessica's father was a little nervous about this. Tim's band doesn't typically play weddings, and Tom wanted everything perfect for his daughter. "You got to trust me on this one," I told him. "You *really* want Tim Montana to play."

After the speeches—including one from my best man and brother Tommy O—Tim's band got up to play. And when they hit the first chord of the first song, everybody ran out there and started dancing. I mean, it was incredible. The music was badass. And then Jessica's mom, Mary—never a dull moment—convinced Bob—Kid Rock—to play as well.

Bob got up onstage and started freestyling, and that's when everything went crazy. You could hear the music all over the resort, and people began trying to crash the wedding from the beach, and suddenly my security were really earning their wages, keeping out nighttime beachgoers and hotel guests who wanted to see what was going on. Jessica's mom wandered into another bar, where someone asked her who was playing. And Mary, in her Boston accent, pretended not to know. "I don't know, I heard it's the Rolling Stones or somethin'," she said.

The after party moved to a dance hall that we rented out on the same property as Chatham Bars. Inside, Jessica set up a karaoke stage where she could impress the guests with her pipes. Unfortunately, the wedding was the same night as the McGregor-Mayweather middleweight title boxing match. Because Bob and I wanted to watch the fight, we set up an adjacent room and rented a satellite where, hopefully, only a few of the groomsmen could watch the match and nobody would notice. Jess, being the wiser of the two of us, knew this was a terrible idea because everyone would want to be where Kid Rock was rather than listening to an off-key version of "Livin' on a Prayer" in a dance hall. I told her it wouldn't be a problem, because the fight would last one round and then we'd all go in for karaoke. Of course, the bout lasted forever, finally ending with Mayweather's TKO win in round ten. I tried to make it up to her by doing my best impersonations of Bobby Darin's "Mack the Knife" and Sinatra's "Fly

Me to the Moon." Let's just say it was fortunate for me that we had already exchanged rings earlier in the night.

In the morning, I stumbled downstairs with Jessica, planning to head out immediately for the airport, and found Shorty and Pete Hegseth from Fox News, Bob and his fiancée, and a few others on the outdoor terrace. In the light of day, we all looked at each other, ordered drinks, lit up cigars, and started partying over again.

I don't know if we're allotted a certain amount of luck in our lives, or some people are just blessed to have more of it, but sometimes I feel as though I've had enough good fortune to spare. As we danced and drank and celebrated, with the Atlantic Ocean spread out in front of us and surrounded by friends and loving families, we were writing a hundred new stories that we'd tell for years into the future. Stories that we'd tell our kids one day, ones that we'd remember with joy as we grew older and grayer. I was dancing on the sand with my bride, surrounded by a circle of friends and a family that had doubled in size with two simple words, "I do."

It's hard to believe how much my life has changed, especially since going public in 2014. Everything could have gone sideways for me, and yet there I was with a gorgeous wife whom I loved deeply. I was speaking hundreds of times a year to people who wanted to hear every detail of what the team had done. Politicians and public figures courted me, looking for endorsements and support.

Most people are fortunate if they get to shake the hand of one president in their lives. I shook the hands of three presidents, one Democrat and two Republicans. Obama and Trump have both taken plenty of knocks, but I like them both. Obama was the one who made the decision to send us to Abbottabad. A failed mission could have turned him into the Jimmy Carter of our generation, but he made the hard call and trusted his military advisors, and it paid off. As much as it pisses off people on the right, I was proud to shake his hand at Fort Campbell.

President Trump has caught a lot of flak as well, but he made hard decisions, too, like approving the missile strike that killed Iranian major-general Qassem Soleimani and green-lighting the operation in which ISIS founder Abu Bakr al-Baghdadi blew himself up.

I've only hung up the phone on one of them, though. In 2016, President Trump called me early on a Saturday morning to ask for my endorsement for his first presidential campaign. I was still living in Dallas, one time zone earlier than New York, and I was dead asleep, alone in my guest room, after a wild party the night before, when the phone rang. I picked up the receiver and groaned "Hello?"

"Hey, O'Neill, this is Donald Trump calling because I want to run for president," I heard on the other end of the line.

"Fuck you," I said. "No, it's not." Then I slammed down the phone and turned over to go back to sleep, thinking it was a buddy pranking me.

The phone rang again. I picked up a second time. "Seriously," said the voice on the other line, "I'm thinking about running for president and I'd like for you to endorse me." I was a little more awake this time, and I told Donald J. Trump that I'd come up to New York to talk. The candidate had me on speakerphone in a room full of people when he called, so they all heard me tell the future president what I thought about his first "robo-call."

I brought my dad up to Trump Tower in New York. His work space was the messiest clean office I've ever seen, filled with stacks of magazines with his face on the cover. Trump gestured for me to come over close while he made a phone call. As I waited, he dialed up Patriots quarterback Tom Brady and put him on speakerphone, just like he did with me.

"Rob, I got Tom Brady on the phone. The guy's a killer. Speaking of killers, I've got Rob O'Neill here, he's the guy who killed bin Laden." He was so excited to be talking to both of us at the same time. Brady didn't tell him to fuck off, but the conversation only lasted probably thirty seconds before Brady got off the phone and Trump got to why he had invited me up.

I told him I couldn't officially endorse him because I was working with both Democrats and Republicans. He tried to get my father to convince me, telling him, "I'm asking you for your son's endorsement for me to run for the president of the United States." That didn't work, either, but our conversation was productive and respectful. We had more than a few laughs, though this is the first time I realized that when you are in the room with Donald Trump, he does most of the talking.

I didn't want to be "That Guy" to ask for a picture in the man's office so we departed. I was having second thoughts as we rode down in the elevator, but as we were leaving through the lobby, Trump popped out of another elevator and ran back to us. He wanted a photo, too. I was happy to oblige.

The next time I saw Trump was with Jessica, in 2018. Pete Hegseth from Fox asked me if we wanted to join him at the White House for dinner. When I told Jessica about the invitation, she was anxious, which is understandable. I don't care which side of the aisle you're on—meeting the president of the United States is nerve-racking. "Okay, so it's a big dinner though, right?" she asked, thinking it must be a gala or a state dinner.

"No," I said. "It's going to be the six of us: me, you, Pete, his wife Jen, the president, and Melania."

That made her even more nervous. "Okay, well, I'm not going be sitting near him, am I?"

She would be sitting right next to him, I told her.

"Oh, my God," she groaned. "What am I going to say?"

"The good news is, you don't have to worry about that because he's not going to stop talking," I said laughing.

The night of the dinner, we arrived in the dining room after a brief delay at security. The president walked right up to us, looked first at Jessica then at me, and winked. He said to me with a very surprised look, "She's beautiful." *Nicely done.* It was a jab, a friendly joke as if to say he didn't think I had it in me. For some reason, Melania was unable to join, so the dinner suddenly got even more intimate.

The five of us had a great dinner, with Hope Hicks lurking in the background to make sure the president didn't blurt out any classified information or state secrets. Every so often, the president would say something like, "And this is semi-off-the-record," and she would interject, "That's *one hundred percent* off the record." After the entrées, we had his usual three scoops of ice cream. And then he asked us if we wanted to see the Lincoln Bedroom.

Of course we wanted to see the Lincoln Bedroom. We walked upstairs to the second floor of the residence, and there was Abraham Lincoln's bed. Off to the right was Lincoln's desk. And toward the back of the room, next to a window facing the South Lawn, there was another desk, and under a piece of glass lay one of five original copies of the Gettysburg Address with Lincoln's signature.

I almost shivered looking at one of the most important documents in our nation's history. I turned around and looked at everybody. President Trump was leaning against the wall. "You know Rob, not everybody gets to see this," he said. "Unless, of course, you donated to the Clinton Foundation."

"You just can't stop!" I laughed, and he did, too.

He called it a night, but before he headed to the master bedroom, he yelled to the Secret Service, "Hey, go show those guys where the Limeys started the fire in 1812." We said good night to Trump, then trooped downstairs to the basement to see where the British tried to torch the White House. Afterward, they let us go outside on the South Lawn, where Jess and I got a selfie, with the White House lit up behind us and the Washington Monument bright against the night sky in front.

As we stood there on the White House lawn, everything felt new and fresh. We were as giddy as the day when Shorty ran down the aisle to deliver our rings. Luck can only take you so far, but I feel blessed that it's taken me as far as it has. There are days when I look at Jessica, and I feel as though I've lived someone else's life. If hadn't joined the Navy, I might have ended up parading around Butte for the rest of my life in a faded varsity letter jacket. If I hadn't made it through BUD/S, if I had panicked instead of stayed calm, I might have ended up a surface warfare sailor in the Navy, instead of on a SEAL team. If I had gone left, instead of right, on any one of the hundreds of missions in Iraq or Afghanistan. If I had been point man or the number three man going up the stairs in Abbottabad. If bin Laden had been wearing a suicide vest. So many ifs. I could go crazy thinking about all the places where things went right when they could have gone wrong. None of them did. It was nothing less than a miracle that I was still breathing after all the missions. But no shit, there I was, standing between two monuments to freedom that represent the country that I fought for, and one of which would have been reduced to a smoldering ruin if Osama bin Laden had been successful on September 11, 2001. After we took the picture, we went home with another story to tell.

I HAVEN'T MENTIONED the real reason that Jess calls me the luckiest unlucky man in America. It's not because I married her, or because I still have my hair at forty-four, or because I made it out of the SEAL teams without injury. It's because I killed Osama bin Laden. Here's the catch, though. She doesn't consider me lucky at all to have been the man who killed the world's most wanted man; just the opposite. Jess believes that I was unlucky that night in Abbottabad in 2011, and I think she's right. It's been a burden to carry that responsibility with me, and I often wish that I wasn't that person. It would have been so much easier if I had been the third or fourth person going up the stairs in Abbottabad, or the first. If I had peeled off to clean out a second-floor room in the compound, someone else would have gone up to the third floor and put the bullets into the head of al-Qaeda's leader. If that had happened, there might never have been the wedge between me and my teammates. I might never have been a pariah among operators in the Special Forces. I wouldn't have had a target on my head for the rest of my life. Sure, it made me famous, but it also came at a cost.

Sometimes, though, things happen for reasons that can't be accounted for or explained. Sometimes those reasons don't reveal themselves for a long time. Being the shooter and eventually going public about it put me in a bizarre and unique position in the fall of 2020. While my politics are no secret, I never expected that I would be pushed into the political limelight in the way I was right before the presidential election. And it happened because of one of the two presidents I had met. Take a guess: it wasn't Obama.

Jess and I were on vacation in Phoenix, sitting poolside at our hotel. I had my baseball cap in my lap and a drink in my hand when my phone started blowing up, a little bit like when I was outed as the shooter in 2014. This was different, though—my phone was blowing up because President Trump had just retweeted a batshit-crazy tweet from an account connected to QAnon, the demented conspiracy theory that Trump was leading a secret global war against pedophiles. The tweet claimed that my guys ███████████████ had killed bin Laden's body double rather than the actual terror mastermind, and that Obama had ordered the downing of Extortion 17, the Chinook that the Taliban shot down in 2011 with fifteen ████ Squadron SEALs aboard, to cover up the fact that bin Laden wasn't dead and still roamed the earth.

It doesn't matter that I held bin Laden's ruined skull together on the floor of his bedroom so that we could take pictures, or that we collected duplicate DNA samples for confirmation, or that I wasn't on Extortion 17 when the Taliban shot it down. Somewhere in the rotten basement of the Internet, QAnon's freaky pedophilia conspiracy theory had merged with this other conspiracy that bin Laden wasn't dead. Now I was in the middle of a fucked-up political smear that the president of the United States—the man who had asked for my endorsement, welcomed me into the White House, and joked around with my wife and me—was now spreading.

As I sat there by the pool, guys from my team were sending me texts asking what to do. They were genuinely freaked out. I even had the father of one of my friends who died on Extortion 17 contacting me to ask what was going on. I tweeted some snarky responses to the batshittery ("Shit. I just found out that I killed Osama bin Johnson. Drinks are on me, I guess . . ."). Truthfully, I thought the whole thing was a pathetic joke at first. But it quickly became clear that this was different than the other bullshit that the president tweeted out. The president was giving wings to an asinine conspiracy theory that my teammates and I hadn't killed the most wanted man in the world, and that Obama had murdered soldiers to cover it up. The idea would have been laughable if it weren't so dangerous, and yet here was the president promoting it through social media. It was obvious that I needed to do something more than just swat it down on Twitter. To have the president amplify a dangerous fiction that undermines the military, undercuts our national security, and smears the legacies of dead heroes murdered by the Taliban was beyond the pale. And while there were plenty of high-level intelligence people who could go on TV to counter the president, not one of them had fired the bullet that killed bin Laden. Sometimes luck—call it good, call it bad—comes with obligation.

Within a week, I went on CNN twice to refute what the president was saying and, yes, rebuke him for using his office to spread complete bullshit. What the president did was embarrassing and shameful, and, as I said on television, it was an insult to everyone who put their lives on the line for that mission. As in 2014 when I went public, I took a lot of flak for speaking out against the president. Even going on CNN— enemy territory to the right-wingers—was blasphemy enough for me to be excommunicated by former supporters who loved me when I criticized Democrats. On the other hand, I got a lot of thanks for what I said on CNN from former teammates, from friends, from families of operators. Even someone at Naval Special Warfare Center, where I was probably persona non grata, texted to say thank you. I appreciated that, though I rolled my eyes at the sudden love I was getting.

So there I was, back in the spotlight. Lucky me. I couldn't predict the future, and I didn't know what the consequences of my speaking out against the president would be, though I was pretty certain it would be some time before I'd get invited back to the White House. There are still people who don't believe me when I say I'm neither a Democrat nor a Republican, but an American. I don't expect anyone to take my word for it. I would argue that the evidence is in the picture of Jess and me posing on the South Lawn of the White House. What mattered that night was not that Trump had invited us, but that majestic building, regardless of its occupant, stood through war and strife and conflict. And yes, it still stood after September 11, when it might have been turned into a flaming pile of rubble if not for the determination and courage of the passengers of Flight 93 who made sure that the plane didn't reach its target. And contrary to what the president had suggested, my team was successful that night for reasons that, I'm sad to say, too few in Washington know anything about: Preparation. Courage. Honor. Patriotism. Brotherhood. And those things have nothing to do with luck.

DAKOTA
Live by the Rule of Two

On my twenty-eighth birthday, I held a dying woman in my arms. It was 2016 and I was back in Kentucky and driving with a friend when I approached a stoplight for an intersection that connects to a road called the bypass. The bypass skirts Columbia to divert traffic away from downtown. It relieved traffic when it opened, but it also created a lot of accidents.

As we reached the light, I saw a smashed-up Toyota pickup in the middle of the intersection. The pickup had collided with another vehicle and was so recent that the two vehicles had barely stopped moving when we pulled up, and the occupants of the second vehicle hadn't yet gotten out.

The collision totaled the Toyota, and there wasn't any doubt in my mind that there would be injuries, and serious ones. I pulled over, grabbed the med kit I always keep in the backseat of the truck, and ran to the accident. Some of the passengers had been thrown out of the truck. One of them was a woman, and she was pinned under one of the truck tires. Incredibly, she was still alive.

Something happens to me in situations like that. It's impossible to explain. It's like a switch flips in my head, and I click into standard operating procedure, as if on a battlefield. I assess the situation, I look for casualties, I decide on priorities. Everything narrows into a tunnel vision, and I bear down on the crisis in front of me. Everything else falls away. The more chaotic it is, the calmer I get. A lot of people panic, but I embrace the pressure.

The only thing that I could see was this lady pinned under the tire. Shards of broken glass sliced my fingers as I cradled her head with my hands to keep her from moving. She was conscious but going into shock. As I sat there in the middle of the road, holding this dying woman's head, the tunnel vision widened for a moment, and I looked up.

In the short time since I stopped, at least seven other cars had pulled over. People had gotten out of their cars. And standing there, they held their cell phones in front of their faces, taking videos, recording me and this woman dying on a bed of broken glass.

I LIVE BY WHAT I CALL "the rule of two things." I wake up every day and I do something to make myself a little better. And then I do something to try to make the world around me a little bit better. If I do those two things every single day, the rest will figure itself out. It's that simple. People make life so complicated. It's not. But just because it's simple doesn't mean it's easy.

When a car goes off a bridge into a lake, some people dive in to pull the passengers out. Others just watch from behind the safety of guardrails. When there's a fire, some people run into the smoke. Others just stand there. And when a car rolls over on the highway, some people pull over to look for survivors, while other people just pull out their cell phones.

I don't think of myself as a hero for running to help people in a crisis. I don't do it to be able to pound my chest about it. I do it because that's how I deal with healing my own pain. I've done so many different kinds of treatments, so many therapies to help control the damage that was done to my psyche in Afghanistan. Some have worked and some haven't. But the remedy that most people consider the hardest—putting myself in harm's way to help someone else— comes to me easily. Why that is, I don't have a clue. It's just hardwired into me. All I know is that every day between rising in the morning and going to bed at night, I need to do one thing to help a fellow human being. If stopping at the roadside to help someone achieves that, then that's what I will do.

I couldn't save that woman under the wheel of the truck. After an ambulance rolled up a couple of minutes later, I yelled to the EMTs: "Hey, we need to get some help to pick the back of this truck up. You guys just worry about stabilizing her and moving her out."

"No, we got to wait for the fire department to get here," he said.

"Fuck that, we ain't waiting for no fire department to get here to pull it off," I said. I yelled over to the rubberneckers across the street that I needed help. A couple of them came over and picked up the truck just enough for the EMTs to pull her out. A medevac chopper was coming in overhead, and everything seemed to be under control. I jumped back in the truck and headed off. When I called later to find out what had happened, I learned that the woman had died.

I can't be certain that my being there could have helped to save her, but I do know this: if I had done nothing, she *definitely* would have died. I've said this before, but my biggest fear is that someday, someone will need me to do something, and I won't be able to do it. I won't have the skill for it, I'll be in the wrong place, I won't have the strength or the will, and I'll end up a disappointment or worse. And so I give 100 percent to everything I do. My friends will tell you; there's nothing between 1 and 10 on my dial; I'm just always at volume and terminal velocity, all the time. Sometimes I wonder if maybe God is preparing me for something in the future, but I don't know what it is yet. I don't mean that in some kind of self-important way; I just mean that maybe there's a plan that I don't understand. Maybe everything in my life so far—the Marines, Iraq, Ganjgal—all of it was a prelude to a purpose that's still coming, a path that I can't see. A purpose that I have no way of knowing.

Part of the reason I wonder if I'm being tested or prepared is that roadside accidents happen everywhere I go. Take the time when I was living in Wasilla with Bristol, while we were still trying to make it all work. I flew back to Alaska after a speaking gig in Minneapolis, and I was wearing a suit. To get to Wasilla, I had to fly into Anchorage, which is a long flight and usually lands around midnight or 1 A.M. After that, there's an hour drive to Wasilla on what's called the Glenn Highway.

On the night that I flew in, there had been a snowstorm that dropped about eighteen inches in just a short time. Just another night of light precipitation in Alaska. After I got on the Glenn Highway, I watched cars skidding on the pavement all around me. It was just a matter of time before I passed a car that had slid off the road. I crept past that one, but it wasn't long before I came to a second one. *Fuck it,* I thought. *I can't do this.* So I pulled over, put on my hazards, and ran to the car in my suit. After I checked on the occupants, I got back in my truck. It only took a few minutes for me to reach another car that had skidded off the road. I pulled over for that one, too. And the next one. And the next.

It took me two and a half, maybe three hours to reach home because I stopped to check every car on the way to make sure that nobody was trapped inside.

When I moved to Texas around March 2017, I saw that my town, Spicewood, had a volunteer fire department. I started helping them out on calls by doing whatever I could to support them, and it just sparked my interest. It was a natural thing for me to do, given how regularly I ended up on the roadside, helping stranded drivers or accident victims. I loved being able to help people and make a difference in their lives. My daughters loved it, too. I bought boots for them that they would pull on when they heard my emergency tones go off, and they put together their own emergency kits. Sometimes when I responded to a call, they came along and sat in the truck cheering me on, strapped into their car seats in the back.

One time, an accident happened right in front of me. I even remember the date: September 5, 2018. I was driving behind a car that was going through an intersection, and a truck or a van just plowed right into the car. T-boned it. The truck went right into the driver's side door, and I think the driver's head bounced right off the grill.

I left my truck parked in the middle of the road with the hazards on, grabbed my med bag from the back, and ran up to the car. The woman who had been driving was unconscious, but I could tell she was about to wake up. I could also see that her skull was fractured. I was trying to stabilize her head and make sure she could breathe.

There was only one other person there who had stopped to help, a woman. As I tried to help the driver, the woman and I looked at each other. Then she said, "It's all right, I'm a veteran, too." Her voice was completely calm, almost mystical. The vet knew from looking at me, from how I acted, that I was a veteran, too, that I was accustomed to dealing with crises. And then I looked down inside the car, and I could tell from the things that spilled out of the driver's purse onto the floor of the car that she was a military spouse.

After the EMTs arrived and started extricating her, I told them, *Thank you so much for what you do,* and I started to drive off. As I continued down the road, I began to crash from the waves of adrenaline that had hit me and started to feel sick. I might have gotten half a mile down the road when I had to pull over. I opened the door of the truck and started throwing up.

There's been research into why some people leap into action while others just watch without doing shit. The psychologist Philip Zimbardo, who's famous for the Stanford Prison Experiment, where regular students became authoritarian monsters, has begun studying heroism. He calls heroes deviants because they jump out of the pack to do something risky to help someone else. To do nothing is instinctual, because staying safe is self-preservation, but jumping into the fire requires thinking about the greater good, about helping someone else. Does that make it insane?

I just always seem to be around when accidents happen. Or maybe accidents happen all the time, but I'm just the guy who stops. I've lost track of the number of times in my life I've pulled over to help with serious accidents—maybe ten or a dozen. Rob calls himself the luckiest unlucky man. Sometimes I wonder if I create bad luck. Maybe the accidents happen around me because I'm there. So much bad shit has followed me around over the years that a lot of people have called me the black cloud, the kiss of death. Maybe I attract misfortune. Maybe I'm a shit magnet.

In April 2020, I went on a call that changed everything for me. Spicewood Fire and Rescue contracts with an ambulance service called Marble Falls Area EMS. I went with them on a CPR call. We pulled up in front of a big house with a pool in the back. A parked car blocked the gate, so we couldn't drive in. We unloaded all of our equipment and sprinted up the driveway.

A guy had overdosed on the porch. I was CPR-certified and had been on plenty of calls but didn't have the advanced training of an EMT. I'll never forget how they handled the scene. I felt like I was watching surgeons in an operating room. Everyone communicated flawlessly, moving quickly around the motionless man on the porch, everything synchronized and perfectly timed, as if they had been practicing for this exact scenario, except that they were out in the field on a call that was completely unique.

I want to be one of them, I thought to myself.

Within a week, I had applied for a two-week EMT course in Tempe, Arizona. The course was a boot camp for certification, compressing what can often take months of training into just two weeks. There were sixteen students: four women and twelve men. Most of the students were younger than me, in their twenties and some even in their teens. They came from all over the country, from all different backgrounds and ethnicities, but they all shared a goal of serving their communities.

At the start of the course, the instructor went around the class and asked each of us to say why we were there. None of them had a clue who I was, at least at first. When the instructor got to me, I said that I felt a duty to do what I can for my community. With that comes responsibility to get training and to be as good as you can.

As the instructor went around the circle, he reached a much older student who had silver hair that poked out from under his cap. He was kind of standoffish. He said something about how he was only there because his company required it, and he thought he was signing up for a glorified CPR class. *The joke's on me, right?* he said. *Man, they really tricked me.* It kind of rubbed me the wrong way, like he didn't really want to be there at all.

Every day was a crash study of human physiology, first aid, and medical procedures, even baby delivery. We worked from 8 A.M. until late at night—studying, practicing, training—and there was little time for socializing. As we reached the end of the course, we began to prepare for the certification exam.

One afternoon, I was sitting and studying in a classroom with the older, silver-haired student. We started talking, and he leveled with me. What he had said that first day was bullshit, he said. The real reason he was there was that his wife was slowly dying of cancer, and he wanted to be able to care for her as best as he possibly could. I didn't know how to respond—*what do you say to that?* When he told me that, everything that I had assumed about that man vanished. Suddenly he was just like me, trying to prepare for the uncertainty ahead that he and the most important person in his life would face.

A few weeks later, I did another course in Dallas, this one for firefighter certification. That was a ton of work as well, training for how to do all the things that we assume emergency responders know how to do. It was natural that after I did EMT I would also get trained as a firefighter—they go hand in hand.

With both of those certifications under my belt, I started working full-time for Travis County Fire and Rescue, about fifty miles from my house in Spicewood. I heard from a friend that they had an opening, and it turned out that I had met the chief a few years earlier. From the moment I walked in the door of Station 1101 for my first 7 A.M. shift, I was in awe. Those EMTs and firefighters were badass. Every time we got a call, they responded as if it were the most important call they had ever had. On my first day, we responded to a couple of car wrecks, and then about ten or eleven calls the day after. When we weren't on a call, we trained and drilled constantly so that we were completely prepared for any emergency that fate or chance threw at us.

It's better than any job I've ever had in the Marine Corps. As much as I don't like to admit it, the Marine Corps doesn't exist to improve lives—it's to train warfighters, to provide our national security, and to defend against enemies. It's to support your circle and make sure you get out alive, but it's *not* to help people. In Station 1101, however, everybody's pushing each other to improve every day. But it's not just for their own sakes; they're making a difference. They're truly changing lives.

That doesn't mean I haven't had doubts. I've wavered in my conviction that this is what I should be doing, wondering to myself if I'm doing it to simply fill an emotional sinkhole in my life. I was racked with uncertainty when I came home after one call in early June 2020, just before the EMT certification. It was a CPR call, and it was a hard one. An older man who had gone into cardiac arrest at home while his wife was there. The guy had died right in front of her. Fucking horrible.

On the way home, I completely forget that my daughters would be there. When I walked in the door, they jumped all over me yelling "Daddy, daddy, how was the call?" And as they tried to climb on me, I felt like I was covered in death. This was months into the COVID-19 pandemic, so who knows what I might have been exposed to in the house. My whole existence felt toxic, as though the man's death had siphoned off a piece of my own life. Instead of gathering the girls up in my arms, I recoiled and pushed them away and warned, "Don't touch me, don't touch me." I didn't need to look at them to see the hurt and confusion on their faces.

I went into my bathroom and turned on the shower. After I got under the rushing water, I just started to bawl. For a moment, I felt as though what I had seen that day had summoned back the demons in me. With the water streaming down over my head and my shoulders shaking, I just kept saying to myself, over and over, *I don't fucking need this. I don't fucking need it. I'm done.* I don't know how long I was in the shower, but it didn't wash the feeling away. I almost didn't go to EMT school after that. I almost walked away. *Almost.*

But then there are other calls, ones that end well, that leave me feeling as though it all makes sense, as though I'm there for a reason. In August 2020, my pager went off for a call right near Spicewood. There's a private swimming park there called Krause Springs, a hugely popular, 115-acre camping and recreation site, with swimming holes shaded with huge cypress trees. When we got there, about a half dozen of us scrambled down a path to a rock embankment, where we found a guy who had dived into a swimming hole and had hit his head on the bottom.

When we reached him with our equipment, the diver was out of the water and on the rocks. He was there with his son, and though he was conscious, the dive might have broken his neck. We got him into a C-collar and onto a backboard, and hoisted him up and out of the swimming hole as the other bathers looked on. I was by his side the whole time, talking him through it, trying to distract him.

As I was getting up to leave, the guy called out to me, *How do I find you to thank you?*

You don't have to worry about that, I told him.

No, no, I want to, I want to find a way to thank you and get in touch with you, he insisted.

Well, you can just ask these people, I said. *They'll let you know who I am.*

Afterward, I went back to my daughters, and this time I hugged them when they came to the door and asked me how the call had gone. I wanted to tell them that the call couldn't have been more perfect. The reason was that I was able to help someone, and who I was had nothing to do with it. It had nothing to do with my past, or the medal that the president hung around my neck. The guy we helped based what he thought about me on my performance and on my training. I didn't do it for a picture to post on Instagram or Twitter, or try to be an influencer by imparting some bullshit wisdom. I don't have a clue what plan it was that brought me there, all the way from the projects in Lexington to Big Mike to the Marines and then out again. I don't know whether Kreitzer screaming "Nine lines! Nine lines!" at me at K-Bay turned me into an EMT, or whether it was seeing my team shot dead in a ditch in Ganjgal. All I know is that I did something to help that day, something that I didn't have to do, but wanted to. I put my hands on another human being who was in pain and helped him live another day. I also know that after I went to sleep that night, I would wake up in the morning and follow my rule again. Who knows where I would end up—along another roadside, on the porch of another stranger's house, in an airport or a swimming hole. And every day afterward. I wouldn't have it any other way.

Acknowledgments

ROBERT O'NEILL

This book is the result of actual experiences, incredible friends and family, and proof that life is a series of adventures that do not stop when you graduate, move, or retire. It goes on. Life happens around you as you are planning for something else, and you get out of it what you put in. Most of the stuff you worry about never happens anyway, and it is easier to smile than it is to frown. Never give up your hill. Never give up your sense of humor. You're never out of the fight.

Obviously, this wasn't possible without Dakota, the humblest warrior I have ever met. Thank you for your time and patience while putting up with me!

To my wife, Jessica: My rock. You know what you did. It's a lot. I love you more every day and I'm so grateful for this life we've built together. The best is yet to come . . .

To my kids: You have all been so composed while dealing with so much. Thank you for enduring everything since day one. Your futures are bright and limitless. I love you more than I can even say.

Mother: Once again, thank you for being there for me when I call and for always taking my side . . . unless Jessica calls first!

Father: Thank you for joining me on most of these adventures and always handling shit. As for the jump shot, you still got it!

Kris: Thank you for always keeping your composure and saving me from one or more "complications." So glad you joined the team!

Tommy O: Thank you for all the laughs at even the darkest of times and for hunting with me . . . once. I'm going to set the family Pac Man record, eventually.

Kelley: Thank you for always letting me know what's important—family first. And if life gives you lemons, blow 'em out your ass!

Tommy and Mary: Thank you for making such an amazing wedding happen and for always providing a safe place to land. Your love and support mean the world.

To Mike Gilchrist: Thank you for hiring me in 2015 and changing the course of my life by introducing me to my wife. We appreciate your friendship and how I can count on you to bring swords to any fight!

The boys in Butte—Slick, Swift, Smooth, ED, Barney, Magic Man: The stories keep writing themselves and will for years. Thank you for having my back.

To Bob and Audrey: Thank you for great advice from the beginning, the amazing wedding gifts, and impromptu reception performance that made my security earn their paychecks!

Tim Montana: Thank you for making the wedding reception one to remember.

To the entire team who made this happen: Howard Yoon, Matthew Daddona, Carrie Thornton, Matt Jones, and the fantastic team at Dey Street Books. It's been a pleasure working with you and I cannot thank you enough.

Finally, to Theo Emery: During such a weird, new time, we were able to make the most of a quarantine by spending a lot of it on the phone and computer. It was great to collaborate with you while you shared your humor and I shared some sailor language! Excellent job. Thank you for all of your hard work!

DAKOTA MEYER

Sailor Grace and Atlee Bay: Thank you for being my "why" and for showing me what unconditional love is.

Rob: Thanks for allowing me to share the stage with you and share my story in the same book as yours. It's truly an honor.

Jessica: Thank you for putting up with us on this roller-coaster ride. You don't have to tell me . . . I already know.

Dad: Thanks for everything. I wouldn't be the man or the father I am today without the example you have set for me.

Mandy: There are no words that could do justice in explaining how much you are appreciated. Thank you for being the anchor to my and the girls' life.

Brandon Harrell: Man, I appreciate you. Thanks for not only being an uncle to my girls but a brother to me.

Dr. Martin: Thank you for giving me my life back and continuing to bring good to people's lives.

Gov. Perry: Thank you for your friendship as well as your mentorship.

Steven: Sorry will never be enough but I hope you know I appreciate you, man.

Jeff Brincat: Man, talk about friendship. Thank you for everything.

Uncle Billy: Thanks for always helping me solve the world's problems.

Mike Keltner: Brother, thanks for always being a friend.

Mike Staton: Thanks for giving me something to look up to.

Coach Hodges: Thank you for always believing in me and holding me to my potential.

Sam: Thank you for your friendship as well as your mentorship.

Jocko Willink: Man, no words will ever be enough. You're the epitome of what great is.

Nick Bare: Brother, you're the real deal. I appreciate our friendship. Break the switch.

Sergeant Major Kent: Thank you for your mentorship as well as your friendship.

Liz: I don't even know where to start. Just . . . thank you.

Paul: Thank you for everything, including sleeping on a pile of coats in my basement at my wedding that I didn't get married at.

Dr. Mulvaney: Thank you for always making time and changing my life.

Tim and Shane: Thanks for allowing me to tag along and for always pushing me to be better.

Ed, Karen, Bob, Erin, John, Emi, Paul, and the entire Toyota team: Thank you, all, for never giving up and for your guidance. I wouldn't be where I am today without you all.

Don and Cheryl: Thank you for always being there for me over the last ten years.

Ragsdale: Brother, thanks for being a great friend and showing me the ropes.

Lark, Eric, Brett, Andrew, and Don: Thank you, guys, for always challenging me to be better. It's an honor to serve alongside you.

To the team that made this crazy idea become reality: Howard Yoon, Matthew Daddona, Carrie Thornton, Matt Jones, and the amazingly patient team at Dey Street Books. Thank you, all.

Theo: Man, I don't even know what to say. Sorry!!!! Hahaha. This would have never gotten across the finish line without you. Thank You.

To all the people who believed in me, even when I wasn't worthy of it. Thank you.

Johnson, Kenefick, Johnson, and Layton I hope I'm worthy. FTWGA.

Notes

2: TAKING AIM

32 *fastest land animals:* https://yellowstone.net/wildlife/pronghorn.

32 *after cheetahs:* https://www.nationalgeographic.com/animals
/mammals/p/pronghorn.

3: FIND YOUR HEROES

55 *50 million years ago:* https://pubs.usgs.gov/pp/0074/report.pdf.

56 *beacon for the school:* http://co.silverbow.mt.us/712/Big-Butte
-Open-Space.

5: DRILLING DOWN

87 *afraid of the open water:* https://www.psychologytoday.com/us
/blog/some-nerve/201412/how-overcome-fear-water.

6: OPEN YOUR EYES

107 *who bin Laden was:* https://www.cnn.com/2013/11/05/us/1993
-world-trade-center-bombing-fast-facts/index.html.

108 *So much for that mission:* "Threats and Responses; Ankara:
Turkey Limits Military Help to U.S. on Iraq," *New York Times,*
March 20, 2003, p. A-15.

108 *neighboring Sierra Leone:* Department of State Background
Note: Liberia, https://2001-2009.state.gov/r/pa/ei/bgn/6618.htm.

110 *to buy the land:* https://history.state.gov/milestones/1830-1860
/liberia.

118 *later at the hospital:* https://www.taskforcetrinity.com
/archives/6898#Daniel_Kreitzer.

7: IN THE SHIT

131 *ten people had died:* http://www.nbcnews.com/id/18033283
/ns/world_news-mideast_n_africa/t/suicide-truck-bomb-collapses
-baghdad-bridge.

10: HOMECOMING

185 *but I wasn't:* https://www.esquire.com/news-politics/a26351/man
-who-shot-osama-bin-laden-0313.

11: RECUPERATION

205 *patients' lives at risk:* https://www.va.gov/oig/pubs
/VAOIG-17-02644-130.pdf.

206 *"GO ELSEWHERE":* https://medium.com/@davidbrown_70853
/the-jason-redman-story-ff29ddefe14e.

210 *those sanctioned trials:* https://www.npr.org/sections/health
-shots/2019/08/14/746614170/mdma-aka-ecstasy-shows-promise-as-a
-ptsd-treatment.

213 *mild electrical shocks:* Alpha-Stim.

213 *after my panic attack:* P. G. Shekelle, I. Cook, I. M. Miake-
Lye, S. Mak, M. S. Booth, R. Shanman, and J. M. Beroes, "The
Effectiveness and Risks of Cranial Electrical Stimulation for the
Treatment of Pain, Depression, Anxiety, PTSD, and Insomnia:
A Systematic Review," VA ESP Project #05-226, 2018.

214 *killing themselves every day:* https://www.va.gov/opa/pressrel
/pressrelease.cfm?id=2801.

215 *PTSD and anxiety:* https://drseanmulvaney.com.

215 *vigilance from PTSD:* https://www.va.gov/
HEALTHPARTNERSHIPS/docs/CCISGBFactSheet.pdf.

216 *Sherlock—a toad:* https://www.forbes.com/sites/
davidcarpenter/2020/02/02/5-meo-dmt-the-20-minute-psychoactive
-toad-experience-thats-transforming-lives/#2e7de75b38a1.

216 *drug called ibogaine:* https://www.ncbi.nlm.nih.gov/pmc/articles
    /PMC5545647.

13: BE A FIREFIGHTER OF LIFE

241 *Pop Rocks and Coke:* https://neneca.org/chapter-personnel.
251 *with Lincoln's signature:* https://www.galeriemagazine.com
    /lincoln-bedroom-white-house.
260 *make it insane:* https://stanfordmag.org/contents/the-psychology
    -of-heroism.

About the Authors

—•—

ROBERT O'NEILL is one of the country's most highly decorated Navy SEAL combat veterans, involved in our nation's most strategic military campaigns, including the mission to kill Osama bin Laden. By the time he was honorably discharged after almost seventeen years of service, O'Neill held combat leadership roles in more than four hundred missions across four different theaters

of war. Among his fifty-two decorations are two Silver Stars, four Bronze Stars with Valor, a Joint Service Commendation Medal with Valor, and three Presidential Unit citations. O'Neill is the author of *The Operator,* his *New York Times* bestselling account of his years as a SEAL and the hunt for bin Laden. Today he is a public speaker, security consultant, philanthropist, and TV personality. Through his charity, the Special Operators Transition Foundation, O'Neill works to raise awareness and financial support for special operations military personnel making the difficult transition from the battlefield to the boardroom. He is from Butte, Montana.

DAKOTA MEYER is a United States Marine and veteran of the war in Afghanistan who became the first living United States Marine in forty-one years to receive the Medal of Honor, for his actions during the Battle of Ganjgal on September 8, 2009. His book about the events of that day, *Into the Fire,* was a *New York Times* bestseller. Today Meyer serves in the Individual Ready Reserve of the U.S. Marine Corps Reserve, is an advocate for American veterans, the creator of the podcast *Front Toward Enemy with Dakota Meyer,* and the entrepreneur behind Own The Dash and Flipside Canvas. Born and raised in Columbia, Kentucky, Meyer is a father of two beautiful daughters and lives in Austin, Texas.